Street Vending in the Neoliberal City

Street Vending in the Neoliberal City

A Global Perspective on the Practices and Policies of a Marginalized Economy

Edited by
Kristina Graaff and Noa Ha

berghahn
NEW YORK • OXFORD
www.berghahnbooks.com

Published by
Berghahn Books
www.berghahnbooks.com

© 2015 Kristina Graaff and Noa Ha

All rights reserved. Except for the quotation of short passages
for the purposes of criticism and review, no part of this book
may be reproduced in any form or by any means, electronic or
mechanical, including photocopying, recording, or any information
storage and retrieval system now known or to be invented,
without written permission of the publisher.

Library of Congress Cataloging-in-Publication Data

Street vending in the neoliberal city : a global perspective on the practices and
  policies of a marginalized economy / edited by Kristina Graaff and Noa Ha.
      pages cm
   Includes bibliographical references and index.
   ISBN 978-1-78238-834-0 (hardback : acid-free paper) —
   ISBN 978-1-78238-835-7 (ebook)
   1. Street vendors—Social conditions—Case studies. 2. Street vendors—
Economic conditions—Case studies. 3. Peddling—Social aspects—Case studies.
4. Peddling—Economic aspects—Case studies. 5. Informal sector (Economics)—
Case studies. 6. Urban economics—Case studies. I. Graaff, Kristina. II. Ha, Noa.
   HF5458.S774 2015
   381'.18—dc23
                                                                      2015003124

British Library Cataloguing in Publication Data

A catalogue record for this book is available from the British Library

Printed on acid-free paper

ISBN 978-1-78238-834-0 (hardback)
ISBN 978-1-78238-835-7 (ebook)

Contents

List of Illustrations   vii

Introduction. Street Vending in the Neoliberal City:
A Global Perspective on the Practices and Policies of a
Marginalized Economy   1
Kristina Graaff and Noa Ha

Part I. Responding to Urban and Global Neoliberal Policies

Chapter 1. Flexible Families: Latina/o Food Vending in
Brooklyn, New York   19
Kathleen Dunn

Chapter 2. Street Vending and the Politics of Space in
New York City   43
Ryan Thomas Devlin

Chapter 3. Creative Resistance: The Case of Mexico City's
Street Artisans and Vendors   59
Veronica Crossa

Part II. Street Vending and Ethnicity

Chapter 4. Metropolitan Informality and Racialization:
Street Vending in Berlin's Historical Center   81
Noa Ha

Chapter 5. Selling Memory and Nostalgia in the Barrio:
Mexican and Central American Women (Re)Create Street
Vending Spaces in Los Angeles   101
Lorena Muñoz

Chapter 6. Ethnic Contestations over African American Fiction:
The Street Vending of Street Literature in New York City   117
Kristina Graaff

Part III. The Spatial Mobility of Urban Street Vending

Chapter 7. The Urbanism of Los Angeles Street Vending   139
Kenny Cupers

Chapter 8. Selling in Insecurity, Living with Violence: Eviction
Drives against Street Food Vendors in Dhaka and the Informal
Politics of Exploitation   164
Benjamin Etzold

Chapter 9. The Street Vendors Act and Pedestrianism in India:
A Reading of the Archival Politics of the Calcutta Hawker
Sangram Committee   191
Ritajyoti Bandyopadhyay

Part IV. Historical Accounts of Street Vending

Chapter 10. Street Vending, Political Activism, and Community
Building in African American History: The Case of Harlem   219
Mark Naison

Chapter 11. The Roots of Street Commerce Regulation in the
Urban Slave Society of Rio de Janeiro, Brazil   233
Patricia Acerbi

Index   250

Figures

Illustrations

Figure 7.1. Typical food vending cart in East Los Angeles.	154
Figure 7.2. Female food vendor near an elementary school in the MacArthur Park neighborhood.	155
Figure 7.3. *Paletero* or Popsicle vendor around MacArthur Park.	155
Figure 7.4. A cluster of female food vendors in Koreatown, selling homemade foods such as tamales, tacos, yucca, *pastels* (meat pies), and *atol de elote* (hot corn drink).	156
Figure 7.5. A women selling from her car.	156
Figure 7.6. A street food vending location before operation at the corner of Beaudry and Second Street, downtown Los Angeles.	157
Figure 7.7. The same corner at night, when vendors have transformed the desolate parking lot into an open-air restaurant.	157
Figure 7.8. Map of the institutions involved with the practice of street vending in Los Angeles.	158
Figure 7.9. Food vendor at the subway station at Santa Monica Avenue and Western Avenue.	159
Figure 8.1. A policeman taking some tea and snacks from a permanent (unconsolidated) street food shop.	175
Figure 8.2. A group of policemen have called a mobile tea vendor to sell them some hot *cha*.	176

Figure 8.3. A popular street food vending site on Dhaka's University Campus before a police truck has stopped there. Two police officers are telling the vendors to leave the site. 179

Figure 8.4. Half an hour later, most street vendors have cleared the footpath and stored their food items and equipment behind the fence. Two policemen are patrolling. 180

Figure 8.5. Once the police truck and the officers have left, the vendors quickly return their equipment to the footpath and continue operating their street food shops as usual. 181

Tables

Table 8.1. Types of Street Food Vending and Livelihood Characteristics of the Vendors 170

Table 8.2. Types of Street Food Vending and Exposure and Sensitivity to Police Evictions 178

INTRODUCTION

Street Vending in the Neoliberal City
A Global Perspective on the Practices and Policies of a Marginalized Economy

Kristina Graaff and Noa Ha

On 17 December 2010, the Tunisian street vendor Mohamed Bouazizi burned himself to death in protest of the police's enduring, humiliating treatment of street vendors. He had been his family's main provider since he was ten years old. Selling fruits and vegetables on the streets of Sidi Bouzid, a rural town in central Tunisia, he was assaulted and harassed almost daily by local police officers who confiscated his goods and fined him for not possessing a permit (Ryan 2011). His self-immolation triggered the Tunisian Revolution, which not only led to the fall of then President Zine al-Abidine Ben Ali after a rule of twenty-three years, but also caused further revolts in numerous other Arabic-speaking nations, including Egypt, Libya and Syria. Nonviolent protest movements centrally located in public space also took place in Spanish, Greek, and eventually North American cities.

This account visualizes several central aspects of this anthology. It highlights street vending as a precarized economy, reveals public space as a contested territory, and points out local practices' inextricable ties to developments on a global scale. Aiming at an analysis of street vending from a multifaceted, global, transnational perspective, the volume comprises essays by international scholars from a variety of disciplines, including geography, history, cultural studies, and urban planning. Their contributions examine street vending activities and urban policies in cities as diverse as Berlin, Dhaka, New York City, Los Angeles, Calcutta, Rio de Janeiro, and Mexico City. With this selection of cities, we frame street vending as a global urban practice found in both the northern and the southern hemispheres. This approach attempts to repudiate the assumption that street vending is usually found in the Global South, especially in its so-called "megacities," and to reveal how street vending also represents an essential, constantly growing economic practice in urban centers of the Global North (Roy 2003). Focusing on vendors' positionalities, the contributions investigate their daily experiences as expert knowledge that has the potential to inform us about developments in our respective other hemispheres.

Defining Street Vending

In everyday language, the practice of street vending goes by many different local names. Depending on the respective region, anglophone countries use terms like street peddlers, street hawkers, informal traders, or street vendors, whereas Latin American countries deploy notions like *Ambulantes* and *Comerciantes*. In the academic context, street vending is the most commonly used term. Also serving as a basis for this book is a definition from India's *National Policy For Urban Street Vendors* of 2009, which frames street vending as a mobile, space-bound, predominantly urban practice:

> A street vendor is broadly defined as a person who offers goods for sale to the public without having a permanent built up structure but with a temporary static structure or mobile stall (or headload). Street vendors may be stationary by occupying space on the pavements or other public/private areas, or may be mobile in the sense that they move from place to place carrying their wares on push carts or in cycles or baskets on their heads, or may sell their wares in moving trains, bus, etc. [T]he term urban vendor is inclusive for both traders and service providers, stationary as well as mobile vendors, and incorporates all other local/region specific terms used to describe them, such as hawker, pheriwalla, rehripatri walla, footpath dukandars, sidewalk traders, etc. (Bhowmik 2010: xv).

Though an accumulation of numerous street vendors can lead to a market-like situation, it should not be confounded with formalized markets organized by a market operator and held on a regular basis at fixed times and locations, such as farmers' markets, Christmas, or flea markets. In this anthology, "street vending" thus refers to the selling of products by individuals or by groups of vendors, sometimes in a market-like situation.¹

Street Vending as an Informalized Economy

The chapters in this anthology examine street vending as not only a global and urban phenomenon, but also a type of informalized labor. Much research has been conducted on the informal economy (De Soto 1989; Portes, Castells, and Benton 1989; Guha-Khasnobis 2006), a terminology first coined in the 1970s (Hart 1970, 1973; ILO 1972). Understandings of the term, however, vary widely depending on which activities are counted as "informal." Often, informality is simply equated with illegal practices, but this equivalence is inapplicable to the street vending of legal goods examined in this book. It is equally difficult to fit street vending into the common definition of informality as "a process of income-generation … [that] is unregulated by the institutions of society, in a legal and social environment in which similar activities are regulated" (Portes et al. 1989: 12). Indeed, street vendors are not subjected to the same regulations as vendors of indoor businesses, but local municipalities in many nation-states nevertheless seek to gain control over their practices by either limiting outdoor vending or banning it outright. Since these state regulations minimize the vendors' income, daily vending practices commonly revolve around the circumvention or bending of formal laws. As it must negotiate an informal work setting with governmental attempts at formalization, street vending can be best described as an *informalized* practice, not just an informal one. This emphasizes the processual nature of street vending as a practice situated between avoiding and complying with governmental interference.

As the above definition of informality illustrated, studies on informality are often based on a rigid divide between formal and informal, regulated and unregulated labor. This is problematic not only because it neglects the state's involvement in the informal sectors, but also because often the divide also suggests a hierarchical view of the informal as an outcome of "faulty" developments in the regular labor market or as an indicator of a "backward" economy that will eventually become obsolete once "underdeveloped" nations adapt to the economic standards of "more developed" ones. This volume opposes such modernist and Eurocentric viewpoints by conceptualizing formal and informal(ized) labor as mutually related. As the case studies show, many street vendors participate in both the formal and the informal economy. The extent to which street vending itself is perceived as an income-generating practice is also closely tied to developments in the formal economy. Informal(ized) forms of labor can thus become more attractive with the increasing precarization of the formal employment sector, a common development in neoliberal economic regimes such as that in the United States.[2] The formal and informal sectors therefore have to be considered interdependent forms of production, whereas their interplay has to be acknowledged as inherent to (neoliberal) capitalism.

Street Vending and the Neoliberal Urban Economy

Street vendors are found in rural environments, but they are concentrated in urban areas (Bromley 2000). It is crucial to examine informal(ized) practices in urban settings not just because street vending is most common in cities, but because these settings best demonstrate how global economic developments play out on a local level. This connection is particularly visible in what Saskia Sassen (1991) refers to as "global cities." Among them are New York, Los Angeles, Berlin, and Mexico City, which are discussed in this volume. From these strategic spaces in regimes of advanced capitalism, the trading of goods is managed, the transnational flow of capital is organized, and international economic relationships beyond national borders are sustained (Sassen 1991). The growth of these new urban economies went hand in hand with an increase in service-oriented jobs and the decline of the blue-collar economy, resulting in a "spatio-economic polarization that goes well beyond the older forms of inequality that have always marked cities" (Sassen 2006b: 43). In a climate of growing income inequality, where low-income populations and their (indoor) businesses are displaced from neighborhoods that now cater to the needs of "new high-income urban elites" (44), informal(ized) practices like street vending gain new importance. They allow income generation under precarized conditions and simultaneously provide goods that meet the needs of low-income populations.

While street vending in global cities encapsulates the intertwining of formal and informal economies, it also illustrates how global economic trends affect daily vending practices more specifically. As the case studies on Berlin, Los Angeles, and Mexico City in this book reveal, vendors are deeply affected by the growing commodification, touristification, and (semi-)privatization of urban space that result from global competition between different cities. By advertising their location-specific advantages, cities compete for business investment in their particular regions. In the framework of international competition, public space turns into a commodity that cities use to promote themselves (Low and Smith 2005; Harvey 2006). Policy makers usually justify the overall refashioning of public space into a claimed location of leisure and shopping as a way of implementing "safety, order and security" (Smith 1996; Belina and Helms 2003). In order to realize and maintain this usage and appearance of public space, many local governments engage in public-private partnerships and extensively implement mechanisms of surveillance, policing, and control (Eick, Sambale, and Töpfer 2007; Graham 2011). These mechanisms of exclusion not only govern and push out local dwellers but also have tremendous impact on vendors for whom public space represents an indispensable resource of income.

Investigating the Positionalities of Street Vendors

Considering that street vendors all over the globe are exposed to governmental attempts to restrict or ban their business—including police raids, fines for vending violations, and confiscation of goods—it is important to ask *who* in particular is affected by these forms of enforcement. A central aim of the anthology is therefore to investigate the vendors' positionalities and how the intersecting categories of ethnicity, gender, and class shape daily vending practices (Crenshaw 1991). Location-specific differences and the lack of comprehensive data tracing how the three categories structure the street vending business mean that the contributions in this volume can only offer indications of general tendencies in how street vending plays out in the Global North and South. However, the anthology hints at a feminization of informal(ized) labor in both hemispheres and illustrates how in most cities, street vending is a highly precarized practice carried out predominantly by disadvantaged minority populations.

Most of the volume's case studies depict street vending as a precarious practice carried out by marginalized groups, including migrants and immigrants, people of color, and women—an observation confirmed by existing research (Spalter-Roth 1988; Austin 1994; Stroux 2006; Swanson 2007; Muñoz 2008; Estrada 2013). Some exceptions are found in the Global North, as in New York City, where increasing numbers of white middle-class vendors offer high-end fare from food trucks. The majority of vendors in the United States, however, are immigrants, on the West Coast predominantly from Latin America, and on the East Coast primarily from francophone West African countries, especially Senegal. By engaging in a practice governed by erratic state regulation, vendors are already in a vulnerable position. Taking into account that law enforcement in the United States especially targets Blacks[3] and people of color (Alexander 2010), for example by inundating them with stop-and-frisk practices at street level—the vendors' income platform—vendors of color are subjected to multiple forms of marginalization. Especially for those who cannot provide proof of their legal status in the United States, having to sell in a space as "out in the open" as the streets entails constant fear of potential incarceration and deportation. In cities of the Global South, vendors are often also rural-urban migrants; however immigrants too engage in the informal(ized) income practice.

As research on street vending in the Global South confirms, women make up 30 to 90 percent of street vendors in this hemisphere (Tinker 1997; Brown 2006; Brown, Lyons, and Dankoco 2010). In countries where Islam is the predominant religion, such as Bangladesh, fewer women visibly participate in the street vending business. However, they often take an important role in the preparation of products, especially food. Women's role in the domain of street vending is likewise significant in cities of the Global North. There, female migrants and women of color in particular contribute in versatile ways to family-run businesses. A closer look at their practices reveals that women often venture into street vending because it allows them to better reconcile reproductive and productive labor in their daily life—a fact that emphasizes how, regardless of such improvement, women continue to carry the double burden of family duties and income generation. As the volume's contributions illustrate, the vendor's gender is related to the type of product sold. Women engage more often in the vending of food in cities of both the South and the North. The profitability of vending spaces also affects the vendors' gender distribution: women usually work in less profitable areas (Bhowmik 2010: 12ff.).

How Vendors Navigate Space: Street Vending as a Daily, Politicized Practice

Street vending is a marginalizing practice, but that does not mean vendors have no leeway in navigating the various challenges they face. As the focus on their daily practices reveals, they engage in a variety of activities to carve out space that allows them generate income despite the many state-initiated obstacles (Morales 2000; Kettles 2004; Ha 2009). How they create supportive networks, navigate restrictions and (re)configure urban space is thus a core interest of this anthology. With this emphasis on the vendors' positionalities, street vending is examined not simply as a mechanism to cope with spatio-economic injustices but also as a space-producing activity. Although vendors are not usually equipped with conventional sources of power, they use location-specific tactics to circumvent restrictions and maintain their businesses (Duneier 2000; Stoller 2002). Many conceptual frameworks can be used to highlight this actor-oriented perspective. Applying de Certeau's distinction between strategies and tactics to the practice of street vending, it is especially the vendors' mobility that combines spatial and temporal tactics to allow them to momentarily circumvent the state's restrictive strategies, such as those that limit their access to public space. Equally useful to exemplify the vendors' scope of action is Bayat's "quiet encroachment," which he defines as "the silent, protracted but pervasive advancement of the ordinary people on the propertied and powerful in order to survive and improve their lives" (Bayat 2004: 90). It implies transgression and expansion of spatial and legal limits through atomized action, both individual and collective, and is neither as comprehensive as a social movement nor as reductionist as a coping strategy often conducted at the expense of other marginalized populations (90–91). Selling without a permit, avoiding payment of a vending tax, or offering goods out of the trunk of a car in areas where vending is prohibited can be viewed as forms of such quiet encroachment.[4] Though vendors more often engage in discreet noncompliance than in outspoken protest, their "seemingly mundane practices" (86) nevertheless represent political acts in that they claim access to opportunities and public space that state-sanctioned constraints would deny them. By using urban space to survive and better their living conditions, vendors demonstrate how the city, in particular the street, is a "concrete space for politics" where the "formation of new claims by informal political actors materializes and assumes concrete forms" (Sassen 2006b: 49).

Book Divisions and Essay Overview

Distinctly more research has been conducted on street vending in the Global South (Cross 1998; Bromley 2000; Donovan 2008; Bhowmik 2010), so this collection aims to stimulate questions about the applicability of concepts developed in a Southern framework to a Northern street vending context. While the essays investigate local vending specificities, such as how sellers navigate institutional control in different settings, they also reveal commonalities between the spatial practices in diverse cities around the world. Although street vending activities vary depending on site-specific regulations, the contributions illustrate how the urban practice can also reveal global ties and developments—in other words, the way "the global materializes by necessity in specific places" (Sassen 2006a: 84).

The division of the book into four parts reflects the specificities of street vending as a mobile urban practice affected by globalized neoliberal policies and processes of racialization, while also having deep historical roots. The first part, entitled "Responding to Urban and Global Neoliberal Policies," consists of essays that examine street vending practices in New York City and Mexico City in relation to neoliberal policies at the global and local levels. The second part, "Street Vending and Ethnicity," examines street vending as a racialized economy. It contains essays on Berlin, Los Angeles, and New York City that center on the positionalities of vendors of color, ethnic contestations over vending resources, and the use of common cultural experiences to market vending goods. The subsequent part, "The Spatial Mobility of Urban Street Vending," which contains case studies on vendors in Los Angeles, Dhaka, and Calcutta, examines how they produce and transform space through their mobile vending practices and avoid harsh governmental regulations through their spatial flexibility and archival politics. The final part of this volume, "Historical Continuities of Street Vending," illustrates the extensive past of outdoor selling with particular emphasis on the long-standing processes of racialization tied to this urban economy. Essays in this section discuss street vending in Rio de Janeiro in the nineteenth and twentieth centuries, as well as the relationship between street activism and street vending in Harlem since the early 1900s.

The first essay, "Flexible Families: Latina/o Food Vending in Brooklyn, New York," by sociologist Kathleen Dunn, examines the group vending practices of ten Latina families in the Brooklyn neighborhood of Red Hook. As she shows, the "flexible family" stands for a variety of practices and ideas. It describes female family members' movement between formal and informalized labor as they also carry out the work of social reproduction; represents a material and discursive resource for responding to the state's attempt to regulate their activities; and functions as a trope for solidarity among the entire group of vendors. Using the concept of the flexible family to describe a form of flexible, collective work organization, Dunn analyzes how families' selling practices respond to neoliberal policies of economic deregulation and the ideology of economic individualism. Though they must necessarily adapt to flexible production regimes, the family vendors oppose vending as a solitary entrepreneurial practice and instead show how informality can give rise to collective action.

In "Street Vending and the Politics of Space in New York City," regional planner Ryan Devlin scrutinizes the possibilities and limits of political engagement for noncitizen vendors in New York City. Focusing on the city's largest advocacy group, the Street Vendor Project, his text depicts a variety of alternative practices beyond the ballot box that vendors use to counter the negative portrayals of street vending perpetuated within the neoliberal discourse spread by Business Improvement Districts and their supporters within city government. As Devlin illustrates, street vendors take a conflicting position in claiming their right to public vending space: on one level, they seek to counter ideologies of New York as a tourist- and consumption-oriented city without street vending; but at the same time, they defend their access to public space by embracing free-market principles of individualism, entrepreneurialism, and self-reliance, whereby they reinforce the very hegemonies and inequalities they attempt to challenge.

The following essay by geographer Veronica Crossa also examines street vending in relation to neoliberal urban development policies. In "Creative Resistance: The Case of Mexico City's Street Artisans and Vendors," Crossa examines how, in Mexico City's tourist-oriented Coyoacán neighborhood, a "sense of place," that is, "personal connections to a particular location created through social practices," shaped the resistance strategies of vendors who were threatened with removal. Framed by a theoretical discussion on practices of resistance to urban neoliberalism in Latin America, Crossa exemplifies the particular responses of vendor groups at Plazas Limpias in Coyoacán by distinguishing between bounded resistance practices (using sit-ins and petitions based on local support from people who visited the plaza) and creative resistance practices (using paintings, music, and performance to draw on the symbolic characteristics of the place). As the text illustrates, these various resistance practices strive to fight the loss of not just an economic space but also a location inextricably linked to personal life and the vendors' cultural identities.

The anthology's second part, "Street Vending and Ethnicity," opens with an essay by urban studies scholar Noa Ha. In "Metropolitan Informality and Racialization: Street Vending in Berlin's Historical Center," she analyzes routines of racialization as they play out in the regulation of street vendors in the historical center of Germany's capital, a highly contested site of national representation in post-unified Germany. Conceptualizing street vending from a postcolonial perspective as a form of "metropolitan informality," her article aims to expose the mechanisms which lead to a racialized economy of street vending. By contrasting the working conditions of street vendors of color with those of white vendors, Ha's text reveals how both the racist dimensions of labor regulation and the racialization of labor itself fit into a hegemonic narrative of the European city, which is imaged as a primarily white, male, and bourgeois space.

Continuing with the perspective of Latina/o street vendors, cultural geographer Lorena Muñoz scrutinizes the daily practices of street vending in Los Angeles. Her essay "Selling Memory and Nostalgia in the Barrio: Mexican and Central American Women (Re)Create Street Vending Spaces in Los Angeles" explores how female immigrant food vendors (re)produce street vending landscapes from "back home" through specific selling practices, product ingredients, and a particular display and marketing of the food offered. Her text examines how both the vendors' and consumers' memories and nostalgic imaginations aid in the transformation of space, create a sense of place, and shape entrepreneurial vending practices. As Muñoz illustrates, street vending informed by memory and nostalgia is not only a conscious marketing mechanism; it is also a response to the host country's denial of citizenship. Street vending landscapes thus have the potential to provide noncitizen vendors with an alternative form of citizenship, a "Latino cultural citizenship."

The essay "Ethnic Contestations over African American Fiction: The Street Vending of Street Literature in New York City," by American studies scholar Kristina Graaff, examines vending practices in contemporary Harlem. It scrutinizes the frictions between West African and African American vendors in the selling of a popular literary genre known as street literature or urban fiction. Written mainly by African American authors, the novels emerged in the late 1990s and established themselves as a genre by being sold in informal ways on the streets of Harlem, Brooklyn, and North Philadelphia. Choosing two street literature vendors as case studies—an immigrant from the Ivory Coast who is part of the group dominating the street sale of street literature, and an African American vendor from New York City—Graaff's article works out the differing conditions of entrepreneurialism that the two groups have historically faced and draws upon economic, historical, and cultural explanations for the current mutual distrust between the two groups and their contestations over the street literature vending ground.

The following section of the volume "The Spatial Mobility of Urban Street Vending," opens with an essay by urban historian Kenny Cupers that attends to the sprawling, suburbanized urban area of Los Angeles. Based on a combination of ethnographic fieldwork and historical analysis, "The Urbanism of Los Angeles Street Vending" examines the spatial strategies of street vendors in this West Coast, car-based city. Taking up approaches developed by Lefèbvre and de Certeau, the essay conceptualizes the mobile strategies of primarily immigrant vendors as a form of "everyday urbanism" that adapts and responds to the changing temporal rhythms of the city and, at the same time, actively shapes and transforms Los Angeles.

The next essay, by geographer Benjamin Etzold—"Selling in Insecurity, Living with Violence: Eviction Drives against Street Food Vendors in Dhaka, and the Informal Politics of Exploitation"—addresses (semi-)mobile vending practices in Bangladesh, where street vending is officially illegal. Drawing upon Johan Galtung's conceptualizations of violence, it explores three different types of violence—physical, structural, and cultural—that food vendors in Dhaka experience. Etzold illustrates the various tactics that vendors use to avoid these forms of violence, exemplifying in particular how vendors use their mobility to circumvent evictions and confiscation of their goods, either by moving back and forth between hotspots of governmental regulation and temporarily safer grounds, or by hiding their wares. The essay also elaborates on how the vendors' mobility intertwines with informal arrangements between street vendors and policemen, linesmen, and other local power brokers who have a share in the capital's expansive street vending business.

Ritajyoti Bandyopadhyay's essay "The Street Vendors Act and Pedestrianism: A Reading of the Archival Politics of the Calcutta Hawker Sangram Committee" addresses street vending in India since the practice was officially institutionalized by the Street Vendors Protection of Livelihood and Regulation of Street Vending law. Focusing on the significance of the pedestrian, Bandyopadhyay, a historian, discusses different legal interpretations of the uses of public space. As he shows, street vendor organizations strategically deploy and archive these legal documents to claim their right to public space and thereby create new forms of formalization.

In the last section of this collection, "Historical Continuities of Street Vending," historian Mark Naison revisits the tradition of street speaking, street organizing, and street commerce in the New York City neighborhood of Harlem from World War I to today. In his essay "Street Vending, Political Activism, and Community Building in African American History: The Case of Harlem," Naison illustrates how street politics and street economies were inextricably intertwined until the 1970s. Speakers such as the socialist Hubert Harrison or Marcus Garvey, founder of the Universal Negro Improvement Association, used Harlem's street corners not only to spread their political messages but also to benefit from public speaking as an income-producing activity. Promoting militant action by selling Communist Party or Nation of Islam movement papers outdoors was also an important street vending activity. Naison's article is a call for activists to reinvent and restore this tradition of street speaking and vending for political education in today's disadvantaged urban neighborhoods.

In the final essay of this anthology, historian Patricia Acerbi traces the historical origins of street vending regulation in Rio de Janeiro. In her essay "The Roots of Street Commerce Regulation in the Urban Slave Society of Rio de Janeiro, Brazil," Acerbi examines the historical conditions of street vending in Rio de Janeiro's urban slave society from 1808 until its abolition in 1888 and, subsequently, in its post-slave society. In particular, she focuses on the so-called urban *ganho* system (urban slave system), consisting of municipal and police administrations that put enslaved, freed, and free street vendors under the same regulatory work regime. Analyzing street vending under the ganho system as a "liminal space between slavery and freedom," Acerbi explores diasporic vending practices as well as the interactions between the three different vendor groups.

With *Urban Street Vending in the Neoliberal City: A Global Perspective on the Practices and Policies of a Marginalized Economy*, we aim to demonstrate the ongoing importance of the practice in the Southern hemisphere and the growing relevance of informalized labor in the North. The book seeks to bridge the gap between structural and actor-oriented approaches. By scrutinizing street vending as an informal(ized) practice from the daily perspectives of the vendors, structural limits imposed by state interventions intertwine with the vendors' mobilizing abilities. Since street vending is a versatile practice that touches upon a great variety of issues ranging from sense of place and mobility to neoliberal precarization, racial discrimination, and nostalgia, a multi-disciplinary perspective is particularly well suited to approaching it, as this volume suggests.

Kristina Graaff received her PhD in American Studies from Humboldt University of Berlin, Germany, where she is currently an assistant professor of (African) American literature and culture. She has been a fellow at the Transatlantic Graduate Research Program Berlin-New York and a visiting scholar at Fordham University's African American Studies Department, the Bronx African American History Project, and the University of Washington's Honors Program. Her areas of research include Black popular culture and its relationship to the U.S. justice system, critical race theory, law in literature, and the interplay between literary and entrepreneurial practices.

Noa Ha holds a PhD in Architecture from Technical University Berlin and is currently a postdoctoral researcher at the Center for Metropolitan Studies, Technical University Berlin. Her research interrogates the production of space from a feminist, de-colonial, and, critical race theory perspective and was funded by the Rosa-Luxemburg-Foundation and the Technical University Berlin. Currently she is conducting a study on the spatial production of Asian diasporas in European cities.

Notes

1. In fact, a wide range of intermediate forms of street vending practices take place between the two "poles" of vendors selling individually and groups of vendors selling in market-like situations.

2. There are no statistics that separately quantify the development of street vending in the United States. There are also no reliable data on the share of informal(ized) economies in the U.S. gross domestic product. Informal(ized) income activities are estimated to contribute from 6 to almost 42 percent of the nation's market value (Portes 1994). The breadth of this range is due to imprecise categorization of the informal sector as well as differences in quantitative measurements and evaluation of the data (Altvater and Mahnkopf 2002: 104).
3. Following Nana Adusei-Poku, the editors of this anthology decided to capitalize the word 'Black' because it "addresses first and foremost political and historical dimensions of the concept of Blackness, and relates only indirectly to skin complexion." We therefore do not capitalize the term 'white' because "this would obscure the use of the term 'Black' as an act of political empowerment and as a socio-political construct." (Adusei-Poku 2014, 7).
4. While conceptualized for cities of postcolonial societies, Bayat's quiet encroachment, applied to street vending, can put the analyses of informal practices in the Global North and South in dialogue.

Bibliography

Adusei-Poku, Nana. 2014. *A stake in the unknown*. Rotterdam: Hogeschool Rotterdam Uitgeverij.
Alexander, Michelle. 2010. *The New Jim Crow: Mass Incarceration in the Age of Colorblindness*. New York and Jackson, TN: The New Press.
Altvater, Elmar, and Birgit Mahnkopf. 2002. *Globalisierung der Unsicherheit: Arbeit im Schatten, schmutziges Geld und informelle Politik*. Münster: Westfälisches Dampfboot.
Austin, Regina. 1994. "'An Honest Living': Street Vendors, Municipal Regulation, and the Black Public Sphere." *The Yale Law Journal* 103 (8) (June): 2119–2131.
Bayat, Asef. 2004. "Globalization and the Politics of the Informals in the Global South." In *Urban Informality*, ed. Ananya Roy and Nezar AlSayyad. Lanham, MD: Lexington Books.
Belina, Bernd, and Gesa Helms. 2003. "Zero Tolerance for the Industrial Past and Other Threats: Policing and Urban Entrepreneurialism in Britain and Germany." *Urban Studies* 40 (9): 1845–1867.
Bhowmik, Sharit K. 2010. *Street Vendors in the Global Urban Economy*. New Delhi: Routledge India.
Bromley, Ray. 2000. "Street Vending and Public Policy: A Global Review." *International Journal of Sociology and Social Policy* 20 (1/2): 1–28.
Brown, Alison. 2006. *Contested Space: Street Trading, Public Space, and Livelihoods in Developing Cities*. Rugby, UK: Practical Action.
Brown, Alison, Michal Lyons, and Ibrahima Dankoco. 2010. "Street Traders and the Emerging Spaces for Urban Voice and Citizenship in African Cities." *Urban Studies* 47 (3): 666–683.
Crenshaw, Kimberlé. 1991. "Mapping the Margins: Intersectionality, Identity Politics, and Violence Against Women of Color." *Stanford Law Review* 43 (6): 1241–1299.

Cross, John C. 1998. *Informal Politics: Street Vendors and the State in Mexico City.* Stanford, CA: Stanford University Press.
De Soto, Hernando. 1989. *The Other Path.* New York: Harper & Row.
Donovan, Michael G. 2008. "Informal Cities and the Contestation of Public Space: The Case of Bogota's Street Vendors, 1988–2003." *Urban Studies* 45 (1): 29–51.
Duneier, Mitchell. 2000. *Sidewalk.* New York: Farrar, Straus and Giroux.
Eick, Volker, Jens Sambale, and Eric Töpfer, eds. 2007. "Kontrollierte Urbanität: Zur Neoliberalisierung Städtischer Sicherheitspolitik." Bielefeld: Transcript Publishing.
Estrada, Emir. 2013. "Changing Household Dynamics: Children's American Generational Resources in Street Vending Markets." *Childhood* 20 (1): 51–65.
Graham, Stephen. 2011. *Cities Under Siege: The New Military Urbanism.* London: Verso Books.
Guha-Khasnobis, Basudeb. 2006. *Linking the Formal and Informal Economy: Concepts and Policies.* Oxford and New York: Oxford University Press.
Ha, Noa K. 2009. *Informeller Straßenhandel in Berlin: Urbane Raumproduktion zwischen Störung und Attraktion.* Berlin: wvb Wissenschaftlicher Verlag.
Hart, Keith. 1970. "Small-Scale Entrepreneurs in Ghana and Development Planning." *Journal of Development Studies* 6 (4): 104–120.
———. 1973. "Informal Economy Opportunities and Urban Employment in Ghana." *Journal of Modern Africa Studies* 11 (1): 61–89.
Harvey, David. 2006. *Spaces of Global Capitalism: Towards a Theory of Uneven Geographical Development.* London: Verso Books.
ILO (International Labour Office). 1972. *Employment, Incomes and Equality: A Strategy for Increasing Productive Employment in Kenya.* Geneva. International Labour Office.
Kettles, Gregg W. 2004. "Regulating Vending in the Sidewalk Commons." *Temple Law Review* 77 (1): 1–46.
Low, Setha, and Neil Smith. 2005. *The Politics of Public Space.* New York: Routledge.
Morales, Alfonso. 2000. "Peddling Policy: Street Vending in Historical and Contemporary Contest." *International Journal of Sociology and Social Policy* 20 (3–4): 76–98.
Muñoz, Lorena. 2008. "Tamales… Elotes… Champurrado…': The Production of Latino Vending Landscapes in Los Angeles." PhD dissertation, University of Southern California, Los Angeles.
Portes, Alejandro. 1994. "The Informal Economy and Its Paradoxes." In *The Handbook of Economic Sociology,* ed. Neil J. Smelser and Richard Swedberg. New York and Princeton, NJ: Princeton University Press.
Portes, Alejandro, Manuel Castells, and Lauren A. Benton, eds. 1989. *The Informal Economy: Studies in Advanced and Less Developed Countries.* Baltimore: John Hopkins University Press.
Roy, Ananya. 2003. "Paradigms Of Propertied Citizenship: Transnational Techniques of Analysis." *Urban Affairs Review* 38: 463–491.
Ryan, Yasmine. 2011. "The Tragic Life of a Street Vendor." *Al Jazeera.* http://www.aljazeera.com/indepth/features/2011/01/201111684242518839.html.

Sassen, Saskia. 1991. *The Global City: New York, London, Tokyo*. Princeton, NJ: Princeton University Press.
———. 2006a. "Cities and Communities in the Global Economy." *The Global Cities Reader*, ed. Neil Brenner and Roger Keil. New York: Routledge.
———. 2006b. "Why Cities Matter." In *Cities: Architecture and Society*, exhibition catalogue of the 10. Architecture Biennale Venice. Venice: Marsilio.
Smith, Neil. 1996. *The New Urban Frontier: Gentrification and the Revanchist City*. London and New York: Routledge.
Spalter-Roth, Roberta M. 1988. "Vending on the Streets: City Policy, Gentrification, and Public Patriarchy." In *Women and the Politics of Empowerment*, ed. Bookman, Ann and Sandra Morgen. Philadelphia: Temple University Press: 272-294.
Stoller, Paul. 2002. *Money Has No Smell: The Africanization of New York City*. Chicago: University of Chicago Press.
Stroux, Salinia. 2006. "Afghan, Iranian and Iraqi Vendors in Thessalonica, Greece: Street Vending as Survival Entrepreneurship." *Ethno* 8 (1): 37–61.
Swanson, Kate. 2007. "Revanchist Urbanism Heads South: The Regulation of Indigenous Beggars and Street Vendors in Ecuador." *Antipode* 39 (4): 708–728.
Tinker, Irene. 1997. *Street Foods: Urban Food and Employment in Developing Countries*. Oxford: Oxford University Press.

PART I

Responding to Urban and Global Neoliberal Policies

CHAPTER 1

Flexible Families
Latina/o Food Vending in Brooklyn, New York

Kathleen Dunn

Contrary to the predictions of early observers, the urban informal sector continues to swell in cities of the Global North and South alike. Moreover, this sector is by all estimates disproportionately comprised of low-income women who live and work in precarious urban spaces. While many feminist scholars of globalization have documented how gender operates as a primary axis of economic restructuring, fewer urban scholars have analyzed how gender shapes globalization's impact on the organization of urban space. This chapter details how gender shapes the practice of urban street vending among the Red Hook Food Vendors (RHFV), a group of ten Latina/o families who work at a public park, the Red Hook recreational fields, in Brooklyn, New York. I discuss the case of the RHFV to illustrate how the street-level negotiation of gender and labor in the informal sector can accommodate and contest regimes of production and governance at the global and urban scales respectively, drawing upon practices and resources available to what I term the "flexible family."

Flexible families work to absorb the costs of global restructuring, and their solidarity can be deployed as a resource to overcome state sanctions against the poor and working class at the urban level. Family, promoted within dominant gender ideologies as a haven from the alienation of capitalist relations, nonetheless operates in dialectical correspondence with modes of production, as Haraway (1991) suggests. Neoliberal globalization, including what Harvey (1991) terms its "regime of flexible accumulation," increases social costs for poor and working-class families through degraded wage labor earnings and benefits, which in turn stimulates the global expansion of the urban informal economy. Flexible families respond to these dynamics of dispossession by combining work across the formal and informal sectors as a collective survival and mobility strategy, and by cohering as a family to combat state-led attempts at eviction from the spaces needed for these activities.

The swelling of the urban informal economy has precisely paralleled the expansion of what Davis (1992) termed the militarization of public space. Because they work in urban public space, street vendors are regularly subject to state sanctions, including intensified police surveillance and harassment, eviction, confiscation of vendors' goods, and arrest. The growth of street vendor labor organizations across the cities of the Global South, and increasingly in the North as well, testifies to vendors' need to unite in collective action to survive policies that aim to "cleanse" public space of economically and racially marginalized inhabitants of urban spaces (Cross 1998; Crossa 2009; Çelik 2011; Dunn 2013, 2014). In these conditions, drawing upon familial bonds is one way of mounting a moral objection to the injustice of market-driven growth logics, and also facilitates a marshaling of material resources, including the pooling of the time, money, and effort needed to organize against dispossession.

Flexible families may consist of immediate relatives connected by blood and/or law, but often extend to co-ethnic group members (Hill-Collins 1998) or other bases of solidarity, eschewing potentially competitive relations between group members. Given that family as an ideological construct is positioned in *opposition* to the vicissitudes of capitalist relations, it should not be particularly surprising that its bonds and forms may in fact be diversified and strengthened by the splintering effects that neoliberalism creates, in both its economic and spatial practices. Indeed, the construction of familial bonds as a basis of resistance to neoliberal globalization and urbanization reveals how modes of economic and spatial production structure the scale of the household (Marston 2000).

Within this scale of organization, family can nonetheless remain a social context in which women's work is over-productive and under-recognized. The promulgation and regulation of gender norms around work and space can rely upon traditional cultural practices while also opening up to new ones that families need to survive and prosper within changing urban economies. The flexible family absorbs the costs of neoliberalism largely with the overtime labor of women family members. For immigrant families in the United States, second-generation women in particular play a pivotal role in sustaining family livelihoods. Yet the outsize contributions of women's time and labor tends to be naturalized, and thus often rendered invisible, within cultural explanations of the family solidarity requisite to surviving both insufficient formal labor market opportunities and the precarity of the urban informal sector.

The practice of food vending by Latina/o families in Red Hook was pioneered by first-generation Latina spectators of the Latino soccer leagues operating at the park in order to supplement and sustain family livelihoods. The women who founded the RHFV were able to begin food vending fairly easily, though precariously, due to a lack of municipal oversight in the outer-borough, spatially isolated neighborhood. By the time the first members of the RHFV began vending in Red Hook in the mid 1970s, the neighborhood's transformation from a white ethnic enclave shaped primarily by a robust shipping industry to a deindustrialized waterfront populated overwhelmingly by African Americans without pathways to employment on the docks was well underway (Kasinitz 2000). The soccer leagues and subsequently the vendors began to access Red Hook's ample public space for leisure and work, though in conditions that the RHFV perceived nonetheless to be dangerous at times. As vendors carrying their earnings in cash, their work involved no small amount of risk to both their physical and financial well-being: robbery was common, and police were not reliably responsive. Thus the RHFV viewed themselves as an extended pan-Latin family, a group of ethnic outsiders in a neighborhood challenged by street crime associated with large-scale disinvestment in the waterfront neighborhood. Looking after one another, rather than working against each other as competing businesses, was crucial to the group's survival at the park.

As these women's earnings increased, their vending operations became organized as family businesses. Today, the work of the RHFV is carried out by married couples, their children (predominantly the daughters), and often nieces or daughters-in-law as well. Though men are present among the RHFV, intergenerational transmission largely passes the family business to second-generation women who staff family vending operations while also maintaining jobs in the formal economy. For the RHFV, women's overtime labor has been central to each business's success, commodifying women's knowledge and expertise with Latina/o culinary traditions first for co-ethnic customers, and subsequently for a wider clientele seeking "authentic" street food experiences within the Latina/o community in New York (Zukin 2011).

As Red Hook gentrified and municipal oversight of the group increased, the RHFV's familial bonds also became a resource to survive a wholesale but unsuccessful eviction attempt in 2007, a complex and costly transition to compliance with city vending codes, and a successful bid for a vending permit from the city's Parks Department—an agency that exemplifies what Harvey (1989) termed the entrepreneurial model of urban governance through its revenue-generating strategy of auctioning food vending rights off to the highest bidder. Organizing specifically as a *family* of vending businesses enabled the RHFV to share sacrifices, pool resources, and act as a united front with the city government in order to defend their space at the ball fields. These findings add to the growing body of research documenting that precariously employed women in urban economies are increasingly taking a lead in both labor- and community-organizing (Goldberg 2014; Chen 2001; Das Gupta 2006; Milkman and Terriquez 2012; Perry 2013).

Indeed, for vendors like the RHFV, the street is not only a space where neoliberalism *happens to* the economically and racially marginalized, where states and markets mete out punishment to the poor and working class. Rather, the street is also a much-needed resource for its inhabitants, a crucial site of employment and industry, and increasingly a space in which bonds of solidarity are constructed and campaigns against dispossession are waged—and, in the case of the RHFV, won. The RHFV illustrate how family in particular can be shaped in response and resistance to the global restructuring of urban space.

Globalization, Gender, and the Informal Sector

Globalization has not proven to be a gender-neutral process, particularly as it relates to the world of work. Gendered divisions of labor, along with the role of citizenship in delineating labor opportunities and rights, have placed (im)migrant women at the forefront of the flexibilization of labor (Brush 1999; Chang 2000; Eisenstein 2010; Fernandez-Kelly and Sassen 1995; Ehrenreich and Hochschild 2004; Beneria 2003; Aguilar and Lacsamana 2004; Vosko 2010). Flexibilization refers to the increasing insecurity of employment conditions, including the rise of contract, temporary, and part-time work endemic to neoliberalism's assault on the New Deal–era social contract with organized labor (Vosko 2010; Neilson and Rossiter 2008). In the shift toward what Harvey (1991) identified as neoliberalism's mode of flexible accumulation, governments have excused themselves ever further from the provision of social protections (Beneria 2003; Brenner and Theodore 2005; Harvey 2005; Sassen 1998; Tickell and Peck 2003), thereby increasing the costs of social reproduction, the unwaged work of reproducing the labor force.

These reconfigurations have had deeply gendered effects. Nagar et al. (2002) point out that "as neoliberal states withdraw from the provision of social services, this work [of social reproduction] is most often assumed by women in the feminized spheres of household and community" (261). The shouldering of these costs also coincides with women taking on more responsibility in the arena of waged labor as well. As feminism was embraced and indeed deployed as a method of bringing women into labor markets on the global scale (see Eisenstein 2010), women increasingly began participating in the workforce precisely as work became more insecure—a process that can be summarized as flexibilization through feminization.

Nowhere are these stark realities more obvious than in the sector referred to as "the informal economy," that is, those economic activities that lie beyond the direct regulation of the state (Portes, Castells, and Benton 1989). As documented by a number of United Nations International Labour Organization studies, dramatic expansion of the informal economy is another of globalization's trademark effects (Chant and Pedwell 2008; ILO 2002a, 2002b, 2007). Indeed, the rise of the informal economy has distinctly formal origins, specifically through the proliferation of neoliberal labor policies that have strongly influenced growing participation in the informal sector (Olmedo and Murray 2002; Vosko 2010). The informal economy may in fact be considered the epitome of the flexibilization of labor, for work within this sector goes not simply unregulated but also unprotected, denied enforcement of any labor standards and without any concomitant entitlements.

Though women have long predominated in the realms of work that occur off the books, relatively few Western scholars of the informal economy have pointed out their disproportionate representation within this sector (for exceptions see ILO 2002a, 2002b; Chen 2001; Gallin 2001). In the case of street vendors, a 2002 ILO study found that women represent from 30 to 90 percent of the street vending work force in the developing world, depending on the national context (ILO 2002a). As women's participation in informal work becomes increasingly visible in city streets across the globe, the question of how urban spaces structure gendered experiences of labor and informality deserves far greater attention. Indeed, the relationship between space, gender, and labor has long been, and continues to be, fundamental to analytical conceptions of informal work.

The Spatiality of Gender and Labor

As Mitchell (2003) suggests, social relations—of class, race, gender, and sexuality, to name a few—are mediated through the production of space. Neoliberal urbanization, notably the increasing inequality of social relations between both groups and spaces, has yielded a revanchist urbanism (Smith 1996) in which the corporate- and state-led spatial practices are increasingly hostile to the growing precariat (Standing 2011), a large proportion of whom inhabit marginal urban spaces (Davis 2006).

Though such inequities are normally charted along the axes of class and race, gendering practices are no less consequential to the restructuring of urban spaces and industries. Many feminist geographers have investigated how the production of space under neoliberal urbanization has impacted women, children, families, and gender and sexual minorities where they live and work (Ruddick 1996; Bondi 1990; McDowell 1983; Massey 1994; Katz 2006). Of central importance to understanding the gendering of space and labor is the divide between public and private space.

The development of the public/private binary engendered by industrialization channeled women—and crucially, their work—into the "haven" of the home, a space purportedly sheltered from the social relations of production. The structural privatization of social reproduction, not viewed as work within this gender ideology and subsequently not governed by a wage, reveals how both the valuation and regulation of work has long been shaped by a gendering spatiality. Gendering ideologies and consequent practices of work and space are thus mutually constitutive. What has come to be known as "the informal sector"—work that lies beyond the direct regulation of the state—has thus historically been women's domain. In this light, an often overlooked yet historically significant development in the informal economy since the 1970s is that it has become more visible (operating outside the private space of the home) and now includes a growing number of men.

Thus, as neoliberal globalization has reconfigured the gendered spaces of work on a global scale, what Harvey (1989) identified as the entrepreneurial mode of governance on an urban scale has shifted state actors away from the redistribution of public goods and services and toward policies intended to maximize competition and profit. Because the turn away from redistributive social services disproportionately impacts women in the spheres of household and community, urban entrepreneurial governance has quite direct gendering outcomes for the social organization of urban livelihoods and spatial practices, including the practices of public space.

Several urban scholars have noted that entrepreneurial governance has enclosed and even militarized urban public spaces, often through heightened surveillance, policing, and eviction of the poor and working-class (Swanson 2007; Crossa 2009; Davis 2006; Low and Smith 2006; Mitchell 2003). Ironically, entrepreneurial governance therefore entails suppressing the entrepreneurialism of the urban precariat who rely on public space to earn a living. As ILO data show for street vendors in both OECD and developing countries (ILO 2002a; Chant and Pedwell 2008), policies and practices directed against vendors disproportionately impact women, as they constitute the majority of the street vending workforce in many countries. Consideration of the working conditions of urban public space can reveal how the street, like other realms of production and labor, is a space structured not only by class and race relations but also, and just as centrally, by gender relations.

The Street as Stratified Workplace

Urban planners such as Hayden (1981) have illustrated how policies governing land use reinforce gender norms that assume a heteronormative, male-breadwinner household structure as the basis of social life, from the design of urban public transportation infrastructure to the mass suburbanization of the United States in the postwar period. Gender ideologies intersect with race, class, and sexuality, among other statuses, to produce quite different public spaces for differently coded bodies, an outcome that the targeting of young men of color harassed through "stop-and-frisk" policing brings into sharp relief.

It is therefore unsurprising that the mutually constitutive gender ideologies of space and work produce unequal conditions for the men and women who labor in city streets. The growing body of research on street vendors, taxi drivers, and workers in other often informalized occupations who rely upon the use of public space for their livelihoods indicates that public space, despite its degradation by the dynamics of neoliberalism, is in fact a pivotal space of labor and industry, though one that is mostly commonly occupied by marginalized groups,[1] including migrants, indigenous peoples, racial(ized) minorities, and women (Gallin 2001; Swanson 2007; Crossa 2009; Çelik 2011; Devlin 2010; Dunn 2013, 2014; Mathews 2008; Gaus 2014). In documenting the workplace politics of public space, gender emerges alongside race, class, and nativity as a key structuring force of occupational segmentation and stratification.

Research on public space must therefore be expanded to consider the patterns and dynamics that shape the working conditions of those who labor and work to build up businesses in city streets. As this research reveals, gender is a salient structure that impacts entry into street vending, choice of location and thus level of possible income, experiences of crime and policing, and methods of organization to combat state-led attempts to block marginalized groups' access to city streets as a workplace.

26 • Kathleen Dunn

Methodology

This chapter draws on a subset of data collected from 2008 to 2012 during the course of an extended case method research project (Burawoy 1998) on criminalization and gentrification in New York's street vending industry (see Dunn 2013). Interviews[2] and observations with seven of the ten families vending at the Red Hook Recreational Fields were carried out primarily in the summer of 2008, with follow-up interviews done in 2009 and 2010. Approximately twenty family members between the seven families were interviewed for the research. Of these twenty family members, sixteen were women and four were men. Women headed five of the seven family vending operations, and women staffed all of the businesses, save for two men (also family members).

Formal interviews were semi-structured and lasted between thirty and ninety minutes. They were held during the vendors' regular business hours, when they had time to stop and talk with me—usually at the start or end of the workday. Informal interviews also occurred during the course of fieldwork. Observations were conducted both at the park and at an alternate location where three of the vendors sell their food, the Brooklyn Flea Market. Respondents' names have been kept confidential, except for the RHFV representative Cesar Fuentes, who agreed to have his name used in publication.

The Red Hook Food Vendors: A Thirty-Year Tradition

Red Hook, Brooklyn, is an isolated waterfront neighborhood cut off from surrounding areas by the six-lane Gowanus Expressway. The neighborhood is filled with a mix of light to heavy manufacturing buildings, a small number of commercial businesses, and limited residential housing stock. Though it has undergone significant gentrification since the mid 1990s, the majority of Red Hook's 13,000 residents live in the Red Hook Houses, one of the largest public housing complexes in New York City. From the 1970s to the 1990s, Red Hook experienced both the effects of deindustrialization and a dramatic growth in crime connected to the drug trade in the Houses (Kasinitz 2000). This left the nearby ball fields, a huge expanse of six soccer and baseball fields developed under the Robert Moses era, largely underused. Latina/o food vendors have operated at the Red Hook Recreational Fields since the mid 1970s, when a number of different Latino soccer leagues began to use the park for weekend games and tournaments. The food vendors began their work along the sidelines of these soccer games, precisely during the time of serious disinvestment in neighborhood infrastructure.

The vendors currently operating at the park are a diverse group in terms of both national origin and their length of participation in vending in Red Hook. One family has been vending there for over thirty years, whereas the most recent addition to the group has been in Red Hook for just four years. Most of the families however have been operating there for at least ten years. Families' countries of origin include El Salvador, Mexico, the Dominican Republic, Guatemala, Chile, Argentina, and Colombia.[3] Vendors note that interactions between these different nationalities were initially characterized not by conflict or competition, but curiosity over the different kinds of food and cooking practices each group brought to the park. Today the group has coalesced as a distinctly pan-Latin family of vendors, where differences of nationality are viewed as advantageous to attracting a broad clientele.

With scores of eager customers lining up to buy Latina/o street food staples such as tacos, pupusas, and huaraches, the RHFV work long, physically demanding days. As a seasonal operation from May to October, vendors tend to work ten- to twelve-hour shifts on Saturdays and Sundays. The average shift pays from $100 to $175 per day. Some of the larger vending stands hire nonfamily workers to help out, but most stands are run exclusively with family labor.

Vending in Red Hook began informally and was undertaken primarily by first-generation Latinas, often to supplement income earned from primary jobs in the formal sector. For several women, however, street vending became their primary source of income. A second-generation daughter describes how her mother came to sell food in the park:

> She says they were coming as a family trip, on a picnic, and her uncle had a lot of friends here. And people would come over to her and ask her about her food. She brought steaks and arepas, you know? For the picnic. And so many people started asking her, "Do you sell it?" So she said yes, and she started bringing more and selling it. And more or less, she started making more here than at her job. She used to work in a factory. But she made more here than she did at the factory, and she had her kids with her. ... Plus here it was just on the weekends.

The informality of food vending at the park yielded more income than gendered employment options within the formal economy while simultaneously allowing mothers to spend more time with their children. The decision to leave the factory for street vending can thus be understood as a gendered response to problematic formal labor market options for immigrant mothers, reflecting a "forced entrepreneurialism" (Portes and Hoffman 2003). It is important to note the familial context of these gendered responses, a context in which family flexibility still requires women to perform both productive and reproductive labor.

In keeping with ILO (2002a) data documenting women's over-representation among street vendors, the beginnings of the RHFV show that women chose, and were encouraged by family members, to establish food vending operations in Red Hook. A male second-generation vendor describes how his mother was "recruited" to sell food at the park:

> I've got about 17 years of being in this park. So I was coming here, and I met [another food vendor], and we are very good friends. So I started coming and after awhile they started telling me, you know, why don't you bring your mom over? So I brought my mother and they told her, you know, do something. And then she started. She started with tacos, fried tacos.

Food vending represented a feasible yet distinctly gendered employment opportunity for first-generation Latina women. The ball fields of Red Hook, a space of leisure for male soccer players, became a space of work for women on the sidelines.

The question of how and why women began to sell food in Red Hook, more so than men, is in part answered by the informality that neighborhood's spatial isolation afforded the would-be vendors. The Red Hook soccer fields do not enjoy much foot traffic from random passers-by, as to get there one must cross a six-lane highway and walk several blocks past a major public housing project with few supporting bus routes. Red Hook's spatial isolation became racialized from the 1970s on, when urban disinvestment, which accompanied both the deindustrialization of the waterfront and the devastating impacts of the city's 1975 fiscal crisis, dramatically altered the landscape of the neighborhood. Previously notorious for white ethnic gang affiliations, during the 1980s and 1990s Red Hook became known as a space of crime and violence, presumed to be carried out by nonwhites from the Red Hook Houses (Kasinitz 2000). The police presence in Red Hook was therefore focused heavily on surveillance of African Americans around the Houses, deflecting attention from the small but growing informal food vending carried out by Latina women at the nearby ball fields.

In fact, most women vendors in New York work in the city's outer boroughs, while men dominate vending in the more lucrative Manhattan (Dunn 2013, 2014). One explanation for this stratification is that women street vendors in New York tend to work close to where they live, maximizing the flexibility of their schedule in order to care for their children, and they tend to live in low-income communities far from central business districts (Dunn 2013, 2014). The women of the RHFV are therefore somewhat exceptional in traveling to a neighborhood far from where they live to work within a rigid time frame—weekends in summer. Yet their choice of Red Hook as a destination is certainly in keeping with a gendered strategy of women vendors selecting vending locations in less densely trafficked, and thus less lucrative, locations.

In addition, women vendors are more likely than men to operate without all of the needed municipal authorizations, thereby putting themselves at greater risk of arrest (Dunn 2013, 2014). A crucial reason for this resides in the soaring price of the de facto rents created by New York's food vending permit system. Save for a biannual lottery that doles out a very small number, permits are no longer directly available from the city government due to a long-standing cap on food permits and merchandise licenses. Since the 1980s, when the caps were instituted, an underground rental market for the permits has materialized, with prices incrementally increasing over the years. More recently, however, as the "gourmet" food truck trend has taken hold in New York and other cities across the United States, New York's food vending permit prices have escalated rapidly, now topping $20,000 as opposed to the $200 they would cost if obtained directly from the government. The cost of purchasing or renting a mobile food vending unit creates further stratification, as units in compliance with city codes begin at $5,000 for smaller carts and can reach over $200,000 for the larger food trucks (Dunn 2013). These inflated costs represent significant barriers to women who seek to vend in full compliance with city codes, given that women persistently have less access to financial resources and services than men (Mirchandani 1999; Beneria 2003; Eisenstein 2010). Taken together, these patterns resonate with research documenting women's ongoing disproportionate concentration in the most precarious segments of the informal sector, in cities of the Global North and South alike (Sassen 1991; Gallin 2001; Chen 2001: ILO 2002a; Aguilar and Lacsamana 2004; Ehrenreich and Hochschild 2004).

Women Working Overtime

What began as "women's work" on the sidelines slowly evolved into family businesses as the soccer leagues grew in size and more customers spurred growing demand for food vending at the park. Although husbands and sons are present within the RHFV workforce, women continue to predominate. What explains this abiding prevalence of women among the RHFV? The vendors' own accounts tend to privilege cultural explanations of their participation in the family business. Cooking practices are passed down, by and large, among female family members. In discussing how she learned to make pupusas, a second-generation female vendor described it as such:

> No, my mother didn't know [how to make pupusas], but my aunt did. And then my cousin, my aunt taught my cousin, her daughter. So I just started taking the money, I was the cashier. And she was the one making them, and my mother was flipping them and serving them to the people. That's how we started. And then little by little, you know, I was like, I wanna learn too!

The perception that cooking is "women's work" is expressed by a male first-generation vendor, one of the few men selling food front-of-house. Speaking of his female employees, most of whom are nieces and cousins:

> I taught these girls how to make them but I don't make them, because in Central America you would never see a man making pupusas. It's a woman's job.

For most first- and second-generation Latina vendors, however, carrying on this cultural tradition of "women's work" entails working two jobs. Women's combining of earnings from both formal and informal labor is thus a key way in which flexible families survive downgraded economic opportunities under neoliberalism. Several first-generation mothers continue to maintain primary jobs characterized by difficult hours and low wages. As two second-generation children describe it:

> We all have full-time jobs, except for my father. Before, actually my mother—all of us had full-time jobs. My mother, she had full-time a job. She would go there at 3 A.M. because she worked for a restaurant, she would do the laundry, the table clothes. And then she would fold them and do everything and then by 8 A.M., she would have finished. And then she would come here. It was very hard for my mom then.

> My mother's always kept her apartment-cleaning job. As a matter of fact, for over thirty years, she's helped support me and the family she left behind.

In both of these examples, first-generation mothers are both holding down low-wage jobs within the formal economy and with food vending work with their families on weekends. The familial context that shapes these economic roles and responsibilities requires women to work off hours and double shifts to provide for families near and far, a finding that resonates with the research documenting transnational families (Francisco 2012; Levitt 2001). Work within the informal economy is, for many, more lucrative and family-friendly than formal-sector work, but neither provides a high enough wage to sustain vendors' livelihoods. Thus most vendors in the families of the RHFV combine wages from each sector to make ends meet, a strategy also evidenced by Sandoval's (2007) research on street vending families in Brazil.

The vast majority of second-generation vendors interviewed were either daughters or nieces of the founders. These women took on their work at the ball fields as a side job to help their parents, often while they were in school or pursuing careers in the formal economy. The reproduction of these family businesses now relies mainly upon second-generation female labor. As one second-generation daughter points out:

> It's a family business. Well, *I work more than all of them* [my emphasis] but it's a family business!... Because before, [my mother] just worked here, her and my father, by themselves. Now, she needs our help so we come help her.

By "we" she is referring to herself and her sister; they also have a brother, who does not participate in the vending business but works in the formal economy. In describing whom she and her sister are coming to help, this vendor emphasizes her mother, underlining the primacy of her mother's role in establishing and running the business.

Even though most second-generation women maintain jobs in fields such as nursing and health care, education, and the financial industry, their participation in the family business reveals a deeply gendered responsibility of care. In describing how her family coped when her mother became ill, another second-generation daughter comments:

> Actually, my father and then my [female] cousin, we continued with the business. And then my sister-in-law came in, you know. It's a family business, we all had our responsibilities, and everyone would chip in. So *he would do some, and she would do the rest* [my emphasis]. She does a lot of cooking, you know, she prepares the rice and beans. And I do whatever I can! But we all have full-time jobs. ... I do like 30 something hours, cause I'm a nurse, so I only work two days and then the other days that's it! So this is a little extra for me, you know. I wish I could retire!

The costs of surviving neoliberal urbanism *as a family* are borne predominately by women, a finding that resonates with the literature detailing globalization's gendered effects. Likewise, Sandoval's research among vendors in Brazil has illustrated the way in which the working-class family serves as a mediator between work in the formal and informal realms, pointing out that workers may retain formal-sector employment individually while also engaging in informal work with their families (2007: 87).

Yet what Sandoval's study omits is an analysis of how the family also organizes a distinctly gendered division of labor, specifically how women's continuing responsibility for reproducing the family itself intersects with increased participation in waged work, whether formal or informal—an omission that pervades much of the U.S. literature on family entrepreneurship among recent immigrants (Sanders and Nee 1996; Portes and Rumbaut 2006; Foner 1997; Light and Bonacich 1991; Kibria 1994).

Stepping in when one family member falls ill, for example, largely falls to other women family members. The labor of care, which usually necessitates both waged and unwaged overtime labor by women, is the invisibilized work that sustains family entrepreneurship.

The Street and the State: Contesting Urban Governance

The RHFV also draw heavily upon the notion of the family to construct group solidarity, first expressed in terms of their survival in a neighborhood ravaged by the effects of deindustrialization and disinvestment. All the vendors reported that crime and insecurity were the norm in the early days of their operations at the park. As one second-generation daughter described it: "Back then it was ... it was bad. I mean bad. ... A lot of drugs, a lot of crime." The vendors formed a collective sense of solidarity as co-ethnic workers who were outsiders in what they perceived as a dangerous public space. Interestingly, in interviews conducted among both the RHFV and other women vendors in New York City (see Dunn 2013), women vendors spoke more freely and more often of experiences of robbery and fear of both street crime and harassment by police officers than did men within the interview sample.

The notion of family was prevalent among accounts of intra-group relations. As an aunt and niece described it: "If people need help, brother or sister, then you help. We'll help them." The language of family here refers to the "family" of the RHFV, comprised of intergenerational families working together as an extended co-ethnic family. The construction of the RHFV as a family of Latina/o vendors resonates with Hill-Collins' (1998) analysis of the utility (and flexibility) of family as both an ideology and a powerful form of social organization, particularly for racial and ethnic minorities seeking to mobilize solidarity.

The vendors' familial bonds were strengthened in 2000, when they encountered their first serious threat from municipal officials. According to Cesar Fuentes, the RHFV spokesperson, the vendors at that time had been operating under a Temporary Use Authorization (TUA) permit provided to the Ligua Guatemala, a league of soccer teams operating inside the ball fields. Now the Parks Department was threatening to suspend these permits due to garbage proliferating and alcoholic beverages being sold at the park. These problems were associated, rightly or wrongly, with the vendors, who had to answer to the Parks Department.

The vendors responded to this crackdown by organizing more formally to secure and maintain their right to work at the ball fields. As a male first-generation vendor described it:

It was then we formed a group, we went to the [Parks] Department to deal with the conditions of the park. The group decided that Cesar Fuentes, who's our current representative, would represent the group, to present a different form of work where the people would have more security, so they would have sanitary services. We ourselves would represent all of the people of the park. And we would have confidence and a more stable permit situation.

Interestingly, the mobilization to meet the permitting requirements of the city government was led by one of the few second-generation sons among the RHFV, despite the predominance of women among the group. In 2006, Mr. Fuentes created the RHFV Association, incorporating the group as a 501(c)(6) nonprofit trade association. The strategy of forming a collective association is quite common to street vendors facing punitive state sanctions from municipal governments (Cross 1998; Gallin 2001; Çelik 2011; Dunn 2013, 2014).

This proved a prescient act, as the group encountered further significant challenges in 2007 when mounting media attention drawn by a broader, non-Latina/o clientele attracted increased municipal oversight of the group's activities. Many of the RHFV felt that this round of government intervention was not spurred by the diversification of their growing clientele, but by the impending arrival of an Ikea big box store on the docks that once housed shipping and port industries (see Zukin 2011). Whatever the reason, this time the city suspended the vendors' TUAs entirely and accused the group of not complying with health codes.

To defend their space at the ball fields, RHFV members had to work together to pool the resources needed to survive this attempt at eviction. If they wanted to remain in operation at the park, they were obliged to purchase costly mobile food vending units (trucks or carts) and leave behind the tables and tarps that had contributed to the Latin *marqueta* ambiance that they and many of their customers enjoyed. In addition, they had to have these units inspected and approved by the Department of Health and Mental Hygiene, all their businesses had to get tax IDs and go "on the books," and each individual vendor had to obtain a food vending license. Most crucially, the group had to submit a proposal to win a six-year permit to operate at the park from the Parks Department.

The New York City Department of Parks is perhaps the city's most successfully entrepreneurial agency. Indeed, in 2009 alone the Parks Department's concessions division generated $110 million for city coffers,[4] a considerable sum that reflects the high cost of entry to food vending on publicly held land under the department's jurisdiction. Food vending permits for Manhattan's Central Park are the most costly; they can top $1 million for a 4-year contract.[5] For a park vending spot in Red Hook, the

RHFV estimated that a bid of $10,000 a year might suffice for the permit that the Parks Department advertised in its request for proposals.

In navigating the bureaucracy of municipal regulation, the RHFV's familial bonds brought both advantages and costs. They approached the regulation process as a collectivity of families wherein all vendors across the individual family businesses stuck together. This meant ending and beginning the season as a group. As a second-generation female vendor points out, the 2007 season ended three months early:

> We tried to stay working, we begged them to let us keep working. And there wasn't a reason for what happened, and our families depend on the business. So we finished the season on the condition that next season would be different. So then the Department of Health came to inspect us weekly, every Saturday and every Sunday, they would come to inspect us. Of course, supposedly the process was about showing us how to work…BUT, constantly they came where we were. At least we learned the rules of the Health Department.

There was also a serious delay in everyone getting up to code for the start of summer season 2008. As a first-generation female vendor points out:

> With the trucks now we need to do all these things. So we have to set things up so that we can go out there together. And there are people [fellow vendors] who still haven't bought the trucks, made the appointments, nothing, they haven't done anything. There are like two or three who are ready to work, but the others. … But since we are a group, we have to wait for them.

To "have to wait" for the group as a whole to come into compliance with the multiple requirements of legally vending at the park was a necessity that reveals the vendors' collective strategy for surviving the regulatory process, an example of how bearing the costs of urban governance could only be sustained by acting as a flexible family willing to make adjustments and even sacrifices for the good of the greater group.

Coming up with the money to buy the required mobile food vending units, whether they be trucks or carts, posed a significant problem for the vendors. Many relied on their families to raise the necessary funding, from one family raising the money from family members in their country of origin to another family taking out a home equity loan to purchase the truck. As a male first-generation vendor described it:

> Everything happened in the following way: when we were notified for sure that we had to get a truck—that we had to buy a truck or a pushcart—unfortunately the majority of people don't have the economic resources. I dreamt that we could get help, maybe with loans, but it's practically impossible. There are a lot of problems. … Nobody can lend you that kind of money. What happens is that we have our families, friends, we do what we can, but we don't know when we can pay them.

The cost of coming into compliance pushed three families out of vending. But for those who managed to survive, family capital and solidarity were two key ingredients for success.

Beyond their own material investments, the RHFV made sure to publicize the city's eviction attempt to their clientele in frequent press interviews and outreach via the Internet. In these communications, Mr. Fuentes stressed that the RHFV were "a family affair," deploying a "mom-and-pop" narrative that underscored the moral injustice of the city's sudden, swift move to close down their operations. Several local politicians seized upon the story to demonstrate their sympathy for hardworking immigrants, creating some political pressure on the Parks Department to accept a more reasonable figure for the permit bid. Ultimately, the city accepted the RHFV's proposal and issued them the six-year permit to continue vending at the park.

Almost all the vendors viewed their solidarity as one of the main reasons they were able to remain working at the park. As a first-generation female vendor describes it: "Now together we have more strength, there are more people, we are doing well now." Working cooperatively rather than in competition with each other, the RHFV scaled up individual family businesses first to a community of family businesses, then to a state-sanctioned 501(c)(6), finally becoming the official permit holders for food vending at the Red Hook Recreational Fields. The RHFV also undoubtedly benefited from the savvy leadership of Mr. Fuentes, who, through a combination of his own college education in politics and social movements and his extensive networking with a variety of allies, made use of associational tools—specifically establishing the group as a 501(c)(6)—to aid their transition from informal to formal food vendors. The formalization of their practices, however, has done little to assuage the precariousness of their vending businesses. They have now purchased the right to vend in the form of a food vending permit, but this "right" expires in six years with no guarantee of renewal. Indeed, under the Parks Department's Request For Proposal (RFP) process of awarding food vending permits to the highest bidder, the RHFV could easily be outbid.

Conclusion

The RHFV offer a street-level case study in how flexible families can accommodate the shifting economic opportunities of global restructuring while also contesting urban governance regimes' various attempts to rein in their cities' informal economies. The first-generation Latinas of the RHFV augmented their downgraded employment opportunities in the formal sector for more lucrative and autonomous—and thus more family-friendly—work, despite the risks and costs this work brought with it. Urban public space offered them an alternative to struggling in the low-wage labor market. Given the precarity that characterizes the income-generating opportunities available to these women in both the formal and informal sectors, it is small wonder that most chose the advantages of being their own boss and being able to maximize time spent with loved ones, regardless of the risks of working off the books in an isolated, crime-challenged neighborhood.

The women who founded the RHFV both chose and were encouraged by family members to take up informal vending as an alternative preferable to jobs in factories, restaurants, and housecleaning, despite everything from the physical and economic insecurity of their early days of vending to the later risk of being put out of business by municipal regulation as the neighborhood gentrified. Their entry into vending in Red Hook therefore speaks to how gendered family dynamics combine with gendered workplace inequities—including the spatial stratification of women vendors, who work in less lucrative and more precarious spaces of the city—resulting in a heavily feminized Latina/o vending community in Red Hook.

Children, husbands, and other family members joined their successful businesses, showing how the family can flexibly respond to absorb the costs of neoliberal economic landscapes, albeit through increased reliance on women performing both productive and reproductive labor. The role of second-generation women among the RHFV is of particular interest. As these businesses grew into more successful operations, second-generation women stepped in to both secure their parents' income and improve their own. Income-generating strategies among these immigrant families are therefore collective projects, though ones which also require women to engage in multiple and overlapping worlds of work. On the whole women have achieved intergenerational mobility, yet their central role in sustaining the family vending business reveals a gendered responsibility to help secure their families'—particularly their parents'—incomes as well, one that requires their overtime labor.

The flexible family proved an invaluable resource when the neighborhood's gentrification brought increased municipal surveillance of their activities. The RHFV were able to successfully deploy a "mom-and-pop" moral objection to the sudden "clean-up" efforts of multiple city agencies. This family discourse played well with the wide clientele the group had attracted by then, helping to mobilize sympathetic media accounts of the attempted displacement. However, neither the media accounts of the RHFV nor the vendors' own characterizations of their affairs make much mention of the fact that the group is comprised largely of women. The invisibility of gender dynamics among the RHFV reveals the extent to which such dynamics are naturalized within the family structure (Hill-Collins 1998), to say nothing of how and why "family" remains such a salient principle of social organization.

On the street, their solidarity as a collective of families—solidified first by their outsider status and then by the threat of state-led eviction—was key to their ability to survive the transition to compliance and remain in the park. The pooling of material resources and their decision to open and close seasons as a unified group reflect an intra-family solidarity that strengthened their ability to keep this practice and place alive after thirty years. However, three families could not scale up to the level of state-sanctioned food vending. Moreover, in the transition to becoming the official permit holders for food vending at the park, the RHFV who remained lost some of their cultural autonomy, having to relinquish the *marqueta* ambiance so valued by both the vendors and their customers as tables gave way to city-regulated carts and trucks with noisy generators. Yet the majority of the RHFV succeeded in defending their space by relying on intra- and inter-family material and logistical support, highlighting the high cost and complexity of New York's vending oversight regime for an industry almost entirely composed of first-generation immigrants (SVP 2006; Devlin 2010; Dunn 2013).

The Parks Department's RFP system for food vending permits is a shining example of what Harvey (1989) identified as entrepreneurial urban governance, wherein city agencies act not to redistribute public goods, such as public space, to those who need them, but rather treat such goods as commodities to generate revenue for the city. The state's primacy in intensifying the deleterious effects of neoliberal globalization for those in the lower stratum of changing urban economies helps to explain why so much of the labor and community organizing of these workers targets municipal governments, particularly as the dynamics of dispossession cut across issues of housing and employment. Pushed to the margins of neighborhoods and labor markets, the poor and working class must increasingly act collectively to successfully claim spaces for both employment and inhabitance (Çelik 2011; Dunn 2013, 2014). Given that women play a disproportionate role in defending the spheres of household and community, scholars should direct greater attention to how gendered practices shape the urban scale of both globalization and resistance to it.

The story of the RHFV illuminates the street-level manifestation of intersecting macroeconomic trends, and the collective work it takes to negotiate the combined forces of flexibilization and feminization. In this light, the flexible family can be read as not only an accommodation but also a rebuttal. Whereas neoliberal globalization has advanced an ideology of economic individualism, we see that coping with its effects can also give rise to collective action, an unintended but much-needed outcome. In the process, groups like the RHFV demonstrate how flexible the family can—if not *must*—be to overcome the challenges presented by both economic restructuring and entrepreneurial urban governance.

Kathleen Dunn is an assistant professor in the Department of Sociology at Loyola University Chicago. She holds a PhD from the Graduate Center at the City University of New York, and an MA in Urban and Environmental Policy and Planning from Tufts University. Her research centers on urban and new labor studies, with a focus on class, race, gender, and sexuality. She is currently completing a manuscript based on her multi-year study of criminalization and gentrification within New York City's street vending industry. She also serves as a section editor for the forthcoming *Wiley-Blackwell Encyclopedia of Urban and Regional Studies,* and sits on the steering committee of Loyola University Chicago's Women's Studies and Gender Studies Program. Professor Dunn teaches graduate and undergraduate students in urban theory, urban sociology, social inequality, and gender and sexuality.

Notes

1. Increasingly in U.S. cities, however, the street vending sector has seen a mass influx of middle-class, native-born vendors operating as "gourmet" food trucks, a segment that has ballooned so rapidly since the Great Recession that it is now charted by marketing and research firms and estimated to be a $1 billion industry.
2. Interviews conducted in 2008 were commissioned by Sharon Zukin for her book *Naked City: The Death and Life of Authentic Urban Places.*
3. For the purposes of confidentiality, national origin has been omitted in the description of the data.
4. http://www.nycgovparks.org/opportunities/concessions.
5. http://www.thenewyorkworld.com/2012/10/01/theres-a-new-top-dog-in-town.

Bibliography

Aguilar, Delia D., and Anne E. Lacsamana, eds. 2004. *Women and Globalization.* Amherst, NY: Humanity Books.
Beneria, Lourdes. 2003. *Gender, Development, Globalization: Economics As If All People Mattered.* London: Routledge.

Bondi, Liz. 1990. "Progress in Geography and Gender: Feminism and Difference." *Progress in Human Geography* 14: 438–445.
Brenner, Neil, and Nik Theodore. 2005. "Neoliberalism and the Urban Condition." *City* 9 (1): 101–107.
Brush, Lisa. 1999. "Gender, Work, Who Cares? Production, Reproduction, Deindustrialization, and Business as Usual." In *Revisioning Gender*, ed. Myra Marx Ferree, Judith Lorber, and Beth B. Hess. New York: Rowman Altamira.
Burawoy, Michael. 1998. "The Extended Case Method." *Sociological Theory* 16 (1): 4–33.
Chang, Grace. 2000. *Disposable Domestics: Immigrant Women Workers in the Global Economy*. Boston: South End Press.
Chant, Sylvia, and Carolyn Pedwell. 2008. *Women, Gender and the Informal Economy: An Assessment of ILO Research and Suggested Ways Forward*. Geneva: ILO.
Chen, Martha A. 2001. "Women in the Informal Economy: A Global Picture, The Global Movement." *SAIS Review* 21 (1): 71–82.
Çelik, Ercüment. 2011. "Rethinking Street Trades as a Promising Agent of Reempowering Labour Movement in Contemporary South Africa." *Global Labour University Conference, "The Politics of Labour and Development,"* Johannesburg, South Africa.
Cross, John C. 1998. "Co-optation, Competition, and Resistance: State and Street Vendors in Mexico City." *Latin American Perspectives* 25 (2): 41–61.
Crossa, Veronica. 2009. "Resisting the Entrepreneurial City: Street Vendors' Struggle in Mexico City's Historic Center." *International Journal of Urban and Regional Research* 33 (1): 43–63.
Das Gupta, Monisha. 2006. *Unruly Immigrants: Rights, Activism and Transnational South Asian Politics in the United States*. Chapel Hill, NC: Duke University Press.
Davis, Mike. 1992. *City of Quartz: Excavating the Future in Los Angeles*. London: Verso.
———. 2006. *Planet of Slums*. London: Verso.
Devlin, Ryan. 2010. "Informal Urbanism: Legal Ambiguity, Uncertainty, and the Management of Street Vending in New York City." PhD dissertation, University of California, Berkeley.
Dunn, Kathleen. 2013. "Hucksters and Trucksters: Criminalization and Gentrification in New York City's Street Vending Industry.'" PhD dissertation, City University of New York Graduate Center, New York.
———. 2014. "Street Vendors In and Against the Global City." In *New Labor in New York: Precarious Worker Organizing and the Future of Unionism*, ed. Ruth Milkman and Ed Ott. Ithaca, NY: Cornell University Press.
Ehrenreich, Barbara, and Arlie Hochschild, eds. 2004. *Global Woman: Nannies, Maids and Sex Workers in the New Economy*. New York: Holt.
Eisenstein, Hester. 2010. *Feminism Seduced: How Global Elites Use Women's Labor and Ideas to Exploit the World*. New York: Paradigm.
Fernandez-Kelly, Patricia, and Saskia Sassen. 1995. "Recasting Women in the Global Economy: Internationalization of the Changing Definitions of Gender." In *Women and the Latin American Development Process*, ed. C. E. Bose and Belen Acosta. Philadelphia: Temple University Press.

Francicso, Valerie. 2012. "Together but Apart: Filipino Transnational Families and Caring From Afar." PhD dissertation, City University of New York Graduate Center, New York.

Foner, Nancy. 1997. "The Immigrant Family: Cultural Legacies and Cultural Changes." *International Migration Review* 31 (4): 961–974.

Gallin, Dan. 2001. "Propositions on Trade Unions and Informal Employment in Times of Globalisation." *Antipode* 33 (3): 531–549.

Gaus, Mischa. 2014. "Not Waiting for Permission: The New York City Taxi Workers Alliance and Twenty-First Century Organizing." In *New Labor in New York: Precarious Worker Organizing and the Future of Unionism*, ed. Ruth Milkman and Ed Ott. Ithaca, NY: Cornell University Press.

Goldberg, Harmony. 2014. "Prepare to Win: Domestic Workers United's Strategic Transition Following Passage of the New York Domestic Workers' Bill of Rights." In *New Labor in New York: Precarious Worker Organizing and the Future of Unionism*, ed. Ruth Milkman and Ed Ott. Ithaca, NY: Cornell University Press.

Haraway, Donna. 1991. *Simians, Cyborgs, and Women: The Reinvention of Nature.* New York: Routledge.

Harvey, David. 1989. "From Managerialism to Entrepreneurialism: The Transformation in Urban Governance in Late Capitalism." *Human Geography* 71 (1): 3–17.

———. 1991. *The Condition of Postmodernity: An Enquiry into the Origins of Cultural Change.* Malden, MA: Blackwell.

———. 2005. *A Brief History of Neoliberalism.* London: Oxford.

Hayden, Dolores. 1981. "What Would a Non-Sexist City Look Like?" In *Women and the American City*, ed. Catherine R. Stimpson, Elsa Dixler, Martha J. Nelson, and Kathryn B. Yatrakis. Chicago: University of Chicago Press.

Hill-Collins, Patricia. 1998. "It's All in the Family: Intersections of Gender, Race, and Nation." *Hypatia* 13 (3): 62–82.

ILO (International Labour Organization 2002a. *Women and Men in the Informal Economy: A Statistical Picture.* Geneva: ILO.

———. 2002b. *Decent Work and the Informal Economy.* Report VI. Geneva: ILO.

———. 2007. *The Informal Economy.* Committee on Employment and Social Policy. Geneva: ILO.

Kasinitz, Philip. 2000. "Red Hook: The Paradoxes of Poverty and Place in Brooklyn." *Research in Urban Sociology* 5: 253–274.

Katz, Cindi. 2006. "Power, Space, and Terror: Social Reproduction and the Public Environment." In *The Politics of Public Space*, ed. Setha Low and Neil Smith. New York: Routledge.

Kibria, Nazli. 1994. "Household Structure and Family Ideologies: The Dynamics of Immigrant Economic Adaptation Among Vietnamese Refugees." *Social Problems* 41 (1): 81–96.

Levitt, Peggy. 2001. *The Transnational Villagers.* Berkeley: University of California Press.

Light, Ivan, and Edna Bonacich. 1991. *Immigrant Entrepreneurs: Koreans in Los Angeles 1965–1982.* Berkeley: University of California Press.

Low, Setha, and Neil Smith, eds. 2006. *The Politics of Public Space*. New York: Routledge.
Marston, Sallie A. 2000. "The Social Construction of Scale." *Progress in Human Geography* 24: 219–242.
Massey, Doreen. 1994. *Space, Place and Gender*. Minneapolis: University of Minnesota Press.
Mathews, Biju. 2008. *Taxi! Cabs and Capitalism in New York City*. New York: The New Press.
McDowell, Linda. 1983. "Towards an Understanding of the Gender Division of Urban Space." *Environment and Planning D: Society and Space* 1: 15–30.
Milkman, Ruth, and Veronica Terriquez. 2012. "'We are the ones who are out in front': Women's Leadership in the Immigrant Rights Movement." *Feminist Studies* 38 (3): 723–752.
Mirchandani, Kiran. 1999. "Feminist Insight on Gendered Work: New Directions in Research on Women and Entrepreneurship." *Gender, Work, and Organization* 4 (4): 224–235.
Mitchell, Don. 2003. *The Right to the City: Social Justice and the Fight for Public Space*. New York: Guilford Press.
Nagar, Richa, Victoria Lawson, Linda McDowell, and Susan Hanson. 2002. "Locating Globalization: (Re)readings of the Subjects and Spaces of Globalization." *Economic Geography* 78 (3): 257–284.
Neilson, Brett, and Ned Rossiter. 2008. "Precarity as a Political Concept, or, Fordism as Exception." *Theory, Culture and Society* 25 (7–8): 51–72.
Olmedo, Clara, and Martin Murray. 2002. "The Formalization of Informal/Precarious Labor in Contemporary Argentina." *International Sociology* 17 (3): 421–443.
Perry, Keihsa-Khan. 2013. *Black Women Against the Land Grab: The Fight for Racial Justice in Brazil*. Minneapolis: University of Minnesota Press.
Portes, Alejandro, Manuel Castells, and Lauren A. Benton, eds. 1989. *The Informal Economy: Studies in Advanced and Less Developed Countries*. Baltimore: Johns Hopkins Press.
Portes, Alejandro, and Kelly Hoffman. 2003. "Latin American Class Structures: Their Composition and Change during the Neoliberal Era." *Latin American Research Review* 38 (1): 41–82.
Portes, Alejandro, and Rubén Rumbaut. 2006. *Immigrant America: A Portrait*. Berkeley: University of California Press.
Ruddick, Susan. 1996. "Constructing Difference in Public Spaces: Race, Class and Gender as Interlocking Systems." *Urban Geography* 17 (2): 132–151.
Sanders, Jimy M., and Victor Nee. 1996. "Immigrant Self-Employment: The Family as Social Capital and the Value of Human Capital." *American Sociological Review* 61 (2): 231–249.
Sandoval, Salvador A. M. 2007. "Alternative Forms of Working-Class Organization and the Mobilization of Informal Sector Workers in Brazil in the Era of Neoliberalism." *International Labor and Working-Class History* 72 (Fall): 63–89.
Sassen, Saskia 1998. *Globalization and Its Discontents*. New York: The New Press.
———. 1991. *The Global City: New York, London, Tokyo*. Princeton, NJ: Princeton University Press.

Smith, Neil. 1996. *The New Urban Frontier: Gentrification and the Revanchist City.* London: Routledge.
Standing, Guy. 2011. *The Precariat: The New Dangerous Class.* London: Bloomsbury.
SVP (Street Vendor Project). 2006. *Peddling Uphill: A Report on the Conditions of Street Vending in New York City.* Available at http://streetvendor.org.
Swanson, Kate. 2007. "Revanchist Urbanism Heads South." *Antipode* 39 (4): 708–728.
Tickell, Adam, and Jamie Peck. 2003. "Making Global Rules: Globalization or Neoliberalisation?" In *Remaking the Global Economy: Economic-Geographical Perspectives,* ed. Jamie Peck and Henry Wai-chung Yeung. London: Sage.
Vosko, Leah F. 2010. *Managing the Margins: Gender, Citizenship, and the International Regulation of Precarious Employment.* New York: Oxford.
Zukin, Sharon. 2011. *Naked City: The Death and Life of Authentic Urban Places.* New York: Oxford University Press.

CHAPTER 2

Street Vending and the Politics of Space in New York City

Ryan Thomas Devlin

Street vending is a highly contentious issue in New York City, where a long tradition of the practice is deeply rooted in the cultural landscape (Bluestone 1991). At the same time, for as long as people have been selling goods on the street, real estate and business interests have vehemently opposed vending, arguing, among other things, that vendors represent unfair competition, produce congestion on sidewalks, and generally create disorder in the city's public spaces. During the late 1970s and throughout the 1980s, New York imposed a number of strict vending regulations, banning vendors from many of the city's central, high-value areas, such as Midtown and the Financial District, and severely limiting the number of vending licenses available (Devlin 2010). These moves were a response to political pressure placed on politicians by business and real estate interests, who viewed vendors as an impediment to a redevelopment agenda based in part on producing more ordered, strictly controlled public spaces (Vitale 2008).

One might assume street vendors are hopelessly overmatched in the political realm. And indeed, their main opponents are some of the wealthiest, best connected real estate and business interests in the city. Furthermore, the ranks of street vendors in New York are largely made up of immigrants who lack voting rights, meaning they are unable to use the ballot box to put pressure on local politicians. Unable to mobilize as a voting bloc and lacking the financial resources to influence local leaders' decision making, some street vendors turn to the realm of public discourse to advocate for their rights and defend their place in the city.

"Public discourse" can be conceptualized as a collection of conversations, myths, and commonly held beliefs—in this case about street vending, entrepreneurialism, and the proper use and image of public spaces. All of this is reflected in the mass media, from newspapers and magazines to television reports. However, as Beauregard states, "discourse is not merely an objective reporting of an incontestable reality, but a collection of contentious interpretations. The 'real world' provides material for discourse, but these understandings are then mediated socially through language" (2003: 21).

This concept of the contentious nature of public discourse and its ability to shape physical reality can be related to Don Mitchell's concept of landscapes. The term landscape here refers to an ideological representation of space that naturalizes socio-spatial relations to support and legitimize particular regimes of accumulation (Mitchell 1996). Mythmaking and discourse play an important role in producing landscapes. According to Mitchell, "representations of landscape become pure ideology, able to be reshaped by all manner of powerful interests, and available to be put to use to structure and control not just meaning, but also the lives of those who live in the landscape" (1996: 9). The power to produce a landscape—to represent spatial relations as natural, inevitable, and settled—is a potent one. But it requires control over discourse. In New York, despite the best efforts of powerful property interests organized through Business Improvement Districts (BIDs) and their allies within city government, the representation of New York's public space is far from a settled question. Though BIDs and many government officials seek to construct neoliberal landscapes of carefully choreographed consumption, tourism, and entertainment that maximize the value of property, street vendors continue to interfere with the script by relying on powerful myths and discourses of their own. As a group, street vendors lack the direct power of the ballot box or the financial capacity to effectively lobby local politicians. Absent this, discourse, mythmaking, and the construction of counter-representations of space are important strategies that certain vendors employ to contest the city's regulatory practices and exert influence over politicians.

As this essay will argue, the politics of space can play out on the street, in the halls of legislatures through direct political pressure such as lobbying or financial donations, and in the more ethereal space of public discourse. This essay will focus on how one vendor advocacy group—the Street Vendor Project—skillfully utilizes discourses of entrepreneurialism and self-help, as well as the historicized local mythology of New York as a city of immigrant advancement, to stave off further restrictions. It should be noted that although the city has a number of other vendor organizations, the Street Vendor Project was chosen because it is by far the largest and also tends to be the most well-organized and media-savvy, able to present a clear, unified message in the sphere of public discourse. As we will see, however, while these discursive strategies can be effective, they also have their limits. For instance, they are more defensive tactics than offensive weapons: capable of protecting vendors from further exclusion from public space, they are nonetheless not very useful in winning new or increased rights to space. Additionally, by basing claims to space on free-market principles and neoliberal concepts of self-help and entrepreneurialism, they risk reinforcing the very hegemonies and inequalities of the contemporary city that they are challenging.

This research is based on in-depth interviews and participant observation conducted during twenty-four noncontiguous months of fieldwork in New York from June 2005 to August 2008, with the bulk of data gathered during fifteen consecutive months spent in New York from May 2007 to August 2008. Fieldwork included in-depth interviews with street vendors, vendor leaders, and advocates, as well as those within the real estate industry and business sector. Fieldwork also included participant observation with the Street Vendor Project. I attended monthly meetings, rallies, and protests, as well as other events, such as fundraisers, in order to gain an in-depth understanding of the way the organization functioned and its political approach.

Street Vendors and the Politics of Space: A Discussion

Street vendors sit awkwardly within the dominant framework of spatial politics. The idea that space is an important site of politics and class struggle emerged from neo-Marxist scholarship of the mid twentieth century, particularly the work of Henri Lefèbvre ([1970] 2003). Lefèbvre argued that urban space, as a significant site of capitalist production, exchange, and consumption, is therefore also an important site of struggle over these processes. Lefèbvre understood the city as a contested terrain where conflict unfolded between property interests primarily concerned with the exchange value or profit potential of urban space, and urban residents for whom the value of space derived from lived experience, what Lefèbvre termed "use value." Lefèbvre viewed the city as something that is produced, an *oeuvre,* or work. Ideally, the city is produced by all of its residents in an egalitarian, participatory fashion. The problem with the city under capitalism, as Lefèbvre saw it, was that the means of producing the urban had been usurped from the majority of people and controlled by capitalist interests—the city was being produced *for* us, rather than *by* us. As Mitchell (2003) describes it, Lefèbvre transferred classic Marxist notions of the relations of production from the factory floor to urban space. The goal of struggles over and in urban space, then, was to regain control over the means of producing the urban—or, using Lefèbvre's term, to claim a "right to the city."

This conceptualization of spatial conflict operates from a rather binary understanding of use value and exchange value of urban space. The notion of use value is, somewhat romantically, conceived of as existing in opposition to, and outside of, capitalist relations of spatial production. It is something fundamentally apart from exchange value. Following this framework, many urban scholars influenced by Lefèbvre have sought out examples of urban residents articulating—either explicitly or implicitly—claims to use value that directly challenge the ideas of private property and urban space as a site of capital accumulation and exchange (see Smith 1996; Mele 2000; Blomley 2004; Mitchell 2003). In the European and North American context, these studies have often focused on groups such as the homeless, illegal squatters, or neighborhood activists, whose claims to use value are relatively straightforward and uncompromised.

Street vendors as spatial protagonists sit uncomfortably within the framework of use versus exchange value. The study of the politics of street vendors lies on an ideological razor's edge, for it defies simple "left/right," "progressive/conservative" binaries. Do vendors represent the dispossessed urban poor, whose actions and presence in urban space undermine and challenge dominant capitalist regimes of accumulation and spatial production? Or do they, as Hernando de Soto argued in *The Other Path* (1989) and *The Mystery of Capital* (2000), epitomize the values of entrepreneurialism and self-help as small-scale businesspeople whose entrepreneurial energy is stifled by cumbersome regulations and state bureaucracy? Both approaches, of course, romanticize vendors and their struggle, ignoring the complexities of street vendor subjectivity by flattening them into either champions of the free market or the vanguard of progressive urban change.

The political claims of street vendors are rarely ideologically pure or purely oppositional, and this is true of vendors at the Street Vendor Project. Although these vendors' struggle to define the proper meaning and use of urban space generally occurs in opposition to more powerful real estate interests, vendors' claims cannot be defined exclusively as claims to use value. For vendors, urban space is important as a site of exchange value as well, though they deal on a much more modest scale than do corporate real estate developers and other large-scale business interests. As this chapter will demonstrate, vendors organized through the Street Vendor Project do not usually offer an explicit critique of the city under capitalism. Rather, through their identity as self-sufficient entrepreneurs, they hold liberalism to account, demanding that New York—the mythic city of immigrant success through bootstrap entrepreneurialism—live up to its promises. In this way, they expose the contradictions of an ideology that demands self-reliance from its poorer citizens yet erects barriers, such as laws passed at the behest of private property interests to restrict vending, that prevent the poor from carrying out these ideals and maintain inequality. Additionally, an examination of this discourse demonstrates the ways in which ideological notions of liberalism are not fixed but rather unstable, contradictory, and subject to contestation and multiple interpretations. In effect, vendors are asserting their own vision of what New York should be, one that emphasizes fidelity to the promises of success for small-scale entrepreneurs, particularly immigrant entrepreneurs, as they attempt to embed their own practices and struggle into the cultural and historical landscape of New York.

A Brief Profile of Street Vendors in New York City

Before discussing the discursive strategies of the Street Vendor Project in detail, it will be useful to briefly describe who exactly street vendors in New York are. Five main categories of vendors do business in the city: food vendors, military veteran vendors, general merchandise vendors, First Amendment vendors, and unlicensed vendors. These categories are established by local law, New York State law, and court rulings. Different ethnicities tend to cluster within these categories. For instance, food vendors tend to be immigrants from Middle Eastern and South Asian nations such as Egypt, Afghanistan, and Bangladesh. Meanwhile, military veteran vendors, who enjoy special rights to vend in areas otherwise off limits to vendors thanks to a nineteenth-century New York State law, are mostly whites, African Americans, and Puerto Ricans.[1] Veterans often sell tourist-oriented goods such as T-shirts and trinkets, or accessories like handbags, jewelry, and scarves. Licensed, nonveteran general merchandise vendors usually sell the same items as military veterans but are subject to much stricter street restrictions. For instance, nonveteran general merchandise vendors are excluded by law from all of Midtown

Manhattan. General merchandise vendors are a mix of ethnicities, but West Africans, particularly men from Senegal, dominate the trade.[2] First Amendment vendors are vendors who sell goods considered free speech, such as written material and artwork. The nature of their goods exempts these vendors from many of the street restrictions faced by other vendors.[3] A good number of First Amendment vendors sell their own original artwork, most of them setting up in art-themed areas of the city, such as the gallery-heavy SoHo neighborhood or Central Park around the Metropolitan Museum of Art. In other parts of the city, the most common types of First Amendment vendor are sketch artists offering to draw a customer's caricature, or sellers of mass-produced photographs, usually of New York landmarks or various celebrities.[4] Like general merchandise vendors, First Amendment vendors are ethnically diverse but dominated by a few groups. Street artists in central areas of the city tend to be recent immigrants from China. Chinese are also prevalent in the photograph vending trade, joined by immigrants from the Himalayas, mostly Bhutanese, Nepalese, and Tibetans. Meanwhile, book vending tends to be dominated by white, and African American men (Duneier, 1999). Unlicensed vendors do business across the city but concentrate mostly in the outer boroughs and low-income neighborhoods in Manhattan, where enforcement tends to be lighter. However, quite a few unlicensed vendors operate in central neighborhoods as well. Unlicensed vending in the central business districts of Midtown and Lower Manhattan is dominated by West Africans, again, mostly from Senegal. Unlicensed vendors in the outer boroughs are usually of the dominant ethnicity in their particular neighborhood.

It is difficult to reliably estimate the income of street vendors as a group, for income varies widely depending on what items an individual vendor sells and the vendor's location, work hours, and business savvy. Some vendors, particularly those with food carts in high-traffic areas, can make a decent living off their trade. For instance, a food vendor I spoke with who ran a popular operation in Midtown, though he did not disclose his income, nevertheless said he earned enough to expand his business to multiple carts across the neighborhood and, as the sole earner, provide a modest but comfortable middle-class life for a family of four in Queens. In general, however, street vending is not particularly lucrative. Few vendors I spoke with saw vending as a viable long-term career, citing low, unpredictable returns as one of the major reasons. Most saw vending as either a last resort or a step toward possibly starting a storefront business.

All of this makes political organizing a challenge. Vendors who see their trade as a temporary activity can be disinclined to put effort into political organizing for long-term change. Also, the legal division of vendors into different categories, each with its own rights and restrictions, hinders broad-based organizing. Finally, whereas in most cities with large vending populations elsewhere on the globe the vendors come from the same ethnic group or at least share a common language, the vendor population in New York is tremendously diverse and must overcome ethnic and linguistic differences to organize. These factors, added to the fact that most vendors, as immigrants, lack voting rights, pose significant challenges.

Yet broad-based vendor organizing has seen some success, much of it attributed to the Street Vendor Project, which was formed in 2001 as a vendor-directed advocacy organization. As of 2014, it counted nearly 2,000 members. The organization has members from all ranks of street vendors, including unlicensed vendors, but it is dominated by licensed food and general merchandise vendors. Often times, vendors are attracted to the organization because of its promise of legal advice and representation: they pay a $100 membership fee to join the organization and have the director, who is a lawyer, fight unwarranted tickets and fines. The ultimate goal of the organization, though, is to encourage vendors to look beyond individual problems and think more collectively. To a large extent, the Street Vendor Project has accomplished this and boasts a strong core of politically active vendors.

The Street Vendor Project utilizes several different political strategies, but underlying most of them is an effort to legitimize street vending by discursively inscribing the practice into broader narratives of New York as a city of immigrant opportunity realized through entrepreneurialism and self-reliance. It is to an analysis of these discursive strategies that we now turn.

Discursive Politics: Contesting Spatial Exclusion, Claiming Urban Citizenship

In August 1988, Tompkins Square Park on the Lower East Side of Manhattan was both the object and location of violent riots over the right to public space. Pitting anti-gentrification activists, homeless park dwellers, and neighborhood squatters against the New York Police Department, the riots erupted after the city attempted to close the park to the public to initiate a dramatic redesign that would, it was hoped, end the park's days as a refuge for the area's homeless population and other social outcasts.[5] Fast forwarding almost twenty years, to 29 September 2007, the city's efforts to clean up the park have succeeded, and Tompkins Square has become a green centerpiece in this section of the Lower East Side now known as the East Village and largely gentrified. At least for this one day, the park's role as a site of struggle over public space was revived, though one could be forgiven for not noticing.

On this pleasant early fall evening, a much more subtle chapter in the broader struggle over spatial rights in New York was unfolding in the park. Sitting on the park's asphalt basketball courts were five food vendor carts with lines snaking from them, twenty, thirty, forty people deep. Meanwhile, hundreds of people, having successfully negotiated the lines, enjoyed the street fare at long communal tables. This was the Third Annual Vendy Awards, an increasingly popular fundraising event put on by the Street Vendor Project. In the months leading up to the event, New Yorkers nominated their favorite food vendors, and the five most popular were chosen to square off at the "Vendys." At the event, each vendor's food was rated by a panel of judges (made up of food critics, chefs, and local celebrities), and at the end of the evening, the top food vendor in New York was crowned. This particular year, the Vendy Award went to Thiru "The Dosa Man" Kumar, a Sri Lankan vendor with a popular operation near New York University. Kumar's competitors were a Mexican taco truck, a Bangladeshi vendor serving halal meat over rice, a vendor from Trinidad selling Caribbean cuisine, and a Palestinian vendor known as the "King of Falafel."

At first glance, little about the Vendy Awards is overtly political. On the face of things, the event is simply a celebration of New York street food. But few things are apolitical in a city where the right to sell goods on the sidewalk is fiercely contested. The Vendy Awards are more than just a culinary event or fundraising strategy; they are also a way for street vendors to influence discourse surrounding the practice. For decades, business and real estate interests, and their allies within city government, have attempted to delegitimize street vending, calling it outdated, unsanitary, disorderly, and unfair to competitors. In the words of one city official during the initial fight to ban food vendors from Midtown, "it is simply not appropriate to set up a restaurant on the sidewalk. That's the breaks" ("A Bad Year" 1984). But production of legitimacy or illegitimacy is a process of constant inscription and reinscription. The Vendy Awards counter negative portrayals of street vendors by demonstrating the popularity they enjoy with the public, normalizing their presence on the city's sidewalks and its food scene, and emphasizing vendors' roles as classic small-scale immigrant entrepreneurs participating in a narrative that has been repeated time and again over the course of New York's history.

These counter-narratives were subtly woven into the otherwise lighthearted event. Throughout the evening, while diners enjoyed tacos, dosas, and oxtail, they were informed of the struggle of vendors in a number of ways. Vendors who were members of the Street Vendor Project attended the event and engaged diners in discussions about the obstacles they faced in their trade. A listening station allowed attendees to hear prerecorded interviews with street vendors that detailed the struggles they face on the street, from police harassment to the frustratingly complex vending code to harsh restrictions that severely limit legal vending locations. The stories at this station were told not just by food vendors but by general merchandise and unlicensed vendors as well. At the presentation of the winner's trophy, the director of the Street Vendor Project, Sean Basinski, was sure to mention the broader goals of the organization: to stand up not just for exceptional food vendors, but for all vendors. The awards were at once a celebration of New York street food and an assertion that all forms of street vending were legitimate spatial practices deeply engrained in the cultural landscape of New York.

With arguments hinging on notions of free-market populism and New York's mythic history of both street vending and immigrant advancement, the Street Vendor Project offers the clearest, most coherent outlet for vendor discourse. In press releases and public hearings, on its website, and at events like the Vendy Awards it maintains the clear message that street vending is an integral part of New York's economy and history that serves as an economic stepping stone for immigrants and the urban poor, and should therefore be encouraged rather than discouraged. In the introduction to a proposal for new vending regulations submitted to the City Council, the Street Vendor Project reminded politicians that

> wave after wave of immigrants and entry level entrepreneurs have used vending as a steppingstone to success on their way to realizing the American Dream. The primarily Jewish and Italian peddlers of yesteryear have today been replaced by Egyptians, Chinese, Mexicans, African Americans and many others—but vendors continue to be a symbol of our city's ambition and cultural vibrancy.[6]

This line of argument gets to the heart of why discourses of immigrant advancement are so compelling and resonate with the public and local politicians: they are rhetorically nested within broader myths and ideologies that legitimate capitalist regimes of accumulation. Also profoundly localized, these myths intertwine with long-standing historicized notions of New York as a city of immigrant opportunity and capitalist ambition. In a sense, the Street Vendor Project's discursive claims appeal to what people would like to believe about capitalism and New York—that every group of newcomers has the opportunity to succeed, that hard work is rewarded, and that New York is an especially hospitable environment for ambitious immigrants willing to work their way to the top. This framing is often echoed and reinforced by the local media. For example, a public interest article on street vending in the *New York Daily News* opened with familiar rhetorical overtones of bootstrap capitalism and immigrant entrepreneurship:

> [Street vendors] are the ultimate New York small business operators, selling their wares from stainless steel carts as iconic as the yellow cab or the Brooklyn Bridge. ... Street vending has historically been dominated by immigrants. Their stories often evoke themes of hard work and sacrifice, struggling at a menial job in order to give their children a better life. (Levisohn 2007)

By contrast, the actions of BIDs and other business and property interests disconcertingly reveal less seemly sides of free-market capitalism: the imperative to maximize profits at the expense of smaller, less powerful entities, and large corporations' tendency to protect their interests and ensure continuing growth by gaining undue influence over the state. By framing their struggle as one that pits small-scale immigrant entrepreneurs against powerful, wealthy real estate and business interests, vendors establish themselves as relatively sympathetic figures and provide themselves with a sort of political bulwark against further restriction. Politicians in New York, many of whom are eager to appear immigrant-friendly—or at the very least not hostile to the ideal of immigrant entrepreneurship—are often reticent to support explicitly anti-vendor legislation. In the words of a lobbyist for local business interests, "[politicians] are afraid of fallout, the anti-immigrant, anti-small entrepreneur stuff. [They're] all progressives you know, so they don't see political capital in [placing more restrictions on vending]."[7] In this way, discursive struggle over the right to public space and its proper use becomes an important political asset for street vendors who lack conventional political power.

The potency of this discourse is revealed in part by the vigor with which business and property interests attempt to contest and discredit the "David versus Goliath" narrative. Large-scale property interests constantly attempt to portray vendors as big businesses disguised as individual entrepreneurs. Donald Trump, whose disdain for vendors is well known in the city, accused them of being "a small band of extremely wealthy people...[with]...homes in New Jersey and Connecticut" (Blauner 1987). Others in the real estate industry claimed (without providing any evidence) that "the people on the street are largely employees";[8] that "vendors aren't the struggling little man, they are working for big corporations,"[9] and that "it's not just the little guy selling his wares—it's run by a few guys who have 50, 60, tables each. It's a regular underground economy" (Molloy 1988).

The periodic accusations that vendors are big businesses in disguise have gained little traction in the public discourse. In one interview performed for this study, leaders of BIDs lamented their inability to gain control of the discourse. For instance, during one interview, the director of public safety of a major Manhattan BID reflected on how frustratingly engrained street vending was in the city's history and cultural landscape, even relating his own personal experiences:

> Somebody from Wisconsin comes and says, "I ate a hot dog on the streets of New York and I got a pretzel! I was sick to my stomach three hours later but..." [laughs] You know that has nothing to do with it, and I think that's part of the experience. I mean, it's ingrained in our culture here in the city. Everybody knows a family who had a grandfather or a great grandfather who was a street vendor in New York. I know people who knew people, so it's, you know, a part of the culture. I mean, I lived in Flushing [Queens] and the guy would come up the block ringing the bell selling fruits and vegetables. It's not like you go to Beverly Hills where if you have a street vendor on the street it's an aberration. Here you have, you know, "Oh my grandfather used to sell apples!"[10]

An official in another Manhattan BID related a similar frustration, pointing to the BIDs' need to actively reshape public opinion and discourse:

> The other issue is that people like the vendors, they like a bargain. The press also. They love stories about the poor little guy. And this creates a real problem, you know?... So it's really up to us [BIDs] to market the idea of how detrimental vendors can be to the city and make people realize they're hurting the city by patronizing vendors.[11]

One strategy that business interests are developing to contest populist vendor discourse came to light in a leaked 2007 e-mail from Richard Lipsky, a lobbyist for retail businesses who has consistently taken anti-vending stances. In a memo addressed to the directors of two major BIDs, one of whom is also the head of the New York City BID Managers Association, Lipsky suggested that anti-vending activities and lobbying needed to be spearheaded, at least publicly, by a multiethnic front of immigrant small business owners "in order to effectively challenge the peddler status and the concomitant mythology that surrounds their activity" (Paybarah 2007). That is, the only way to effectively counter vendor discourse was to cloak anti-vending arguments in the same rhetoric of immigrant entrepreneurship while "underscor[ing] the extent to which the peddlers do not represent a true entrepreneurial class" (Paybarah 2007). Lipsky closed the e-mail by laying out his plan to use immigrant small business owners as the public face of anti-vending campaigns:

> It would be my suggestion that we look to create a diverse umbrella coalition that has the financial support of the major real estate organizations. In this way we will be able to generate strong public support for beleaguered (and often minority) shopkeepers while at the same time generating enough resources from larger behind-the-scenes business interests. (Paybarah 2007)

After the memo was leaked and published in the *New York Observer,* the BID officials to whom the memo was addressed issued statements that they had no official connection to Lipsky, an independent lobbyist, and did not necessarily agree with the proposals made in the letter.[12] Nevertheless, the memo demonstrates the extent to which business interests feel they are at a discursive disadvantage compared to the vendors and wish to regain control over discourse. It also further reinforces the fact that the ability to shape discourse and public opinion is a key source of the political power held by street vendors.

In the introduction to their edited volume *Cities and Citizenship,* Holston and Appadurai argue that "citizenship concerns more than rights to participate in politics. It also includes other kinds of rights in the public sphere, namely, civil, socioeconomic, and cultural. Moreover, in addition to the legal, it concerns the moral and performative dimensions of membership that define the meanings and practices of belonging in society" (Holston and Appadurai 1999: 14). The discourses put forth by vendors inscribe them in the cultural landscape of New York. In effect, they become alternative claims to urban citizenship based not on formal membership but on active participation in, and contribution to, the urban fabric. They are attempts to expand the notion of citizenship to a "new social basis" (Holston 1999: 170) rooted in lived experience rather than formal rights.

Alternative claims to citizenship provide vendors with significant political leverage, but there are drawbacks to this approach. First, this discourse is most effective when utilized defensively, that is, to contest and discourage the city's attempts to enact further restrictions against vending. Vendors have had little success persuading city politicians to enact new laws in their favor, that is, to ease restrictions, increase the number of licenses available, or open more streets to vending. This is not for lack of trying. Vendor organizations often hold protests on the steps of City Hall, where vendors chant and carry signs attempting to appeal to the sympathies of New Yorkers. Many signs and slogans convey explicitly liberal notions of free markets, entrepreneurship, and the virtues of work over welfare or crime. In April 2009, for instance, in the midst of the economic crisis and soaring unemployment rates, the Street Vendor Project organized a protest by unlicensed vendors demanding that the city lift the cap on licenses in order to create jobs. Vendors carried signs that read "Create Jobs not Criminals!" and "I want to work!" Evoking the language of economic stimulus, the co-director of the Street Vendor Project, Michael Wells, told the *New York Times* that "this initiative [of lifting the license cap] is 'shovel-ready' to provide jobs for New Yorkers" (Lee 2009). Yet seldom have these and other, similar protests succeeded in encouraging legislators to introduce and support pro-vendor legislation. Most politicians strive to remain relatively neutral on the issue—neither explicitly anti-vendor nor actively championing vendor rights. Discourse, then, is a relatively effective and meaningful hedge against further marginalization but has proved less effective at actively producing positive legislative changes.

Also, limits and contradictions inhere in much of the Street Vendor Project's discourse. The arguments put forth by vendors are a double-edged sword. On the one hand, vendors exert a powerful critique: by holding liberalism accountable to its promises, they effectively destabilize an exclusionary regime of spatial regulation and call into question top-down representations of space created by property interests. At the same time, however, these discourses reinforce and operate through a particular idea of legitimacy and rights. The right to space claimed by vendors at the Street Vendor Project is derived from, and legitimated by, notions of individualism, entrepreneurialism, and self-reliance. Possession of these virtues helps vendors inscribe themselves into New York's landscape. Taken to their logical conclusion, however, vendors' claims become discourses of exclusion as well, as they implicitly delegitimize claims to substantive citizenship and urban space made by groups that do not exhibit the same entrepreneurial traits. Indeed, vendors commonly define themselves in opposition to groups implicitly or explicitly deemed less worthy, such as the unemployed, the homeless, or the welfare-dependent. The following example is a quote from a Bangladeshi hot dog vendor near City Hall:

> America good, in my heart. I can't move back, Bangladesh. America good country, good future everything. But, this tickets [for vending violations], and this city close [streets]? Big problems for me right now. I no ask for help, no welfare. I take care my family, man, but very hard right now. They give this license, but one by one these streets they close. Why this vendor license if no streets open? You close everything! Ok New York, you close everything? Help, give me this government help, this welfare help for everything I need. That's it. Close streets? Ok Bloomberg, pay my house. That's it. Close everything? Ok. Bloomberg pay my food. That's it. But I no bum. I no ask city [for] money, I work, for family, for my family.[13]

An Egyptian coffee vendor also working in Lower Manhattan echoed these notions of legitimacy through self-reliance:

> Which one you rather to do as a city, as an official? Would you rather for me to give you money or take money from you? Take public assistance? I don't want you—I don't need your money. I just need you to give me a chance to work. I don't ask you to feed my child, I want to work. My child's got to eat. Whether you let me work or not as a city, my child will eat, whether you like it or not.[14]

Conclusion

As this chapter has demonstrated, lack of traditional political power does not necessarily mean lack of political action. Through the Street Vendor Project, vendors organize and actively engage in discursive politics, demanding that New York live up to its mythical narrative of rewarding the hard work of entrepreneurial immigrants by including them in public space based on the demonstration of these values. However, precisely because the discourse operates through liberal notions of self-reliance, it is difficult to read these vendors' claims as a demand for the "right to the city" — in a pure sense, that is — for they do not necessarily place the use value of public space above its exchange value. For most vendors, the right to public space is a means to an end. They do not value public space outright for its open and inclusive nature; rather, they see access to public space as a vehicle for their individual ambitions. For the most part, the Street Vendor Project's claims are not necessarily based on radical or insurgent notions of spatial inclusion. They can be read as insurgent in that they destabilize elite representations of public space, expose contradictions within liberalism, and hold it to account, but these actions ultimately occur at the cost of potentially reinforcing neoliberal notions of legitimacy and rights, and tend to close the door on more radical reimaginings of New York's sidewalks as inclusionary spaces.

Ryan Thomas Devlin is currently Professor of Public Administration at John Jay College of Criminal Justice (CUNY) in New York City.

Notes

1. New York State General Business Law prevents municipalities in New York from denying an honorably discharged military veteran a vending license. Originally created in the late nineteenth century, the law was likely intended to help Civil War veterans get back on their feet economically. As a result of the law, veterans in New York are exempt from the local cap on vending licenses. The same year the city capped licenses, 1979, it also placed all of Midtown Manhattan off limits to general merchandise vending. New York State law, however, allows sixty military veterans to vend in Midtown despite the city-imposed geographic restrictions. These sixty vendors are chosen based on a seniority system.
2. For a more detailed discussion of this group of vendors, see Stoller (2002).
3. In 1979, the city capped the number of general merchandise licenses at 853. Despite heavy demand for these licenses, the cap has never been adjusted.

Vendors selling books and other printed material have been exempt from the cap since 1982, on the grounds that the city should not limit the sale of material deemed free speech. The sale of artwork gained exempt status in 1997, when a federal court ruled against the Giuliani administration's attempt to limit art vending, finding that artwork and other visual matter should also be considered protected speech under the First Amendment and are therefore exempt from the city licensing requirement and street restrictions.
4. One need not be selling one's own original artwork to be granted First Amendment protection. Just as the sale of newspapers or books is considered protected speech, even if the vendor is not the author, the sale of reproduced photos or prints is also protected.
5. See Smith (1996) for an account of the conflict.
6. "The Street Vendor Opportunity Bill: A Proposal to Increase Economic Development and Promote Small Business Growth by Revising NYC Laws on Street Vending," http://docslide.us/documents/vendor-opportunity-bill-memo.html.
7. Interview with lobbyist for retail business community, February 2008.
8. Tom Cusick, President of Fifth Avenue Association, quoted in Levine (1990).
9. Ibid.
10. Interview with the director of public safety of a Manhattan BID, July 2005.
11. Interview with high-level official in a Midtown BID in Manhattan, April 2008.
12. It should be noted that Lipsky's leaked memo gained the most attention not for its exposé of anti-vending strategies, but for a section where Lipsky listed several City Council members, evaluating their level of sympathy to the cause, political effectiveness, and legislative competence. Lipsky's bluntly worded negative assessments of a few City Council members drew the most attention from political insiders and the press.
13. Interview with Bangladeshi hot dog vendor, July 2005.
14. Interview with Egyptian coffee vendor, August 2005.

Bibliography

"A Bad Year for Pushcarts." 1984. *New York Times*, 11 November.
Beauregard, Robert A. 2003. *Voices of Decline: The Postwar Fate of U.S. Cities*. New York: Routledge.
Blauner, Peter. 1987. "Out of Africa: The Senegalese Peddlers of New York." *New York Magazine*, 16 February, 42–46.
Blomley Nicholas. 2004. *Unsettling the City: Urban Land and the Politics of Property*. New York: Routledge.
Bluestone, Daniel. 1991. "The Pushcart Evil: Peddlers, Merchants, and New York City's Streets, 1880–1940." *Journal of Urban History* 18 (1): 68–92.
De Soto, Hernando. 1989. *The Other Path: The Economic Answer to Terrorism*. New York: Harper & Row.
———. 2000. *The Mystery of Capital: Why Capitalism Triumphs in the West and Fails Everywhere Else*. New York: Basic Books.

Devlin, Ryan Thomas. 2010. *Informal Urbanism: Legal Ambiguity, Uncertainty and the Management of Street Vending in New York City.* PhD dissertation, University of California, Berkeley.
Duneier, Mitchell. 1999. *Sidewalk.* New York: Farrar, Straus and Giroux.
Holston, James. 1999. "Spaces of Insurgent Citizenship." In *Cities and Citizenship,* ed. James Holston. Durham, NC: Duke University Press.
Holston, James, and Arjun Appadurai. 1999. "Cities and Citizenship." In *Cities and Citizenship,* ed. James Holston. Durham, NC: Duke University Press.
Lee, Jennifer. 2009. "Street Vending as a Way to Ease Joblessness." *CityRoom.com,* 29 April. cityroom.blogs.nytimes.com.
Lefèbvre, Henri. (1970) 2003. *The Urban Revolution.* Minneapolis: University of Minnesota Press.
Levine, Richard. 1990. "On the Sidewalks, Business is Booming." *New York Times,* 24 September.
Levisohn, Benjamin. 2007. "Pushcarts: Vendors Work in the City's Small Business Trenches." *New York Daily News,* 30 April.
Mele, Christopher. 2000. *Selling the Lower East Side: Culture, Real Estate, and Resistance in New York City.* Minneapolis: University of Minnesota Press.
Mitchell, Don. 1996. *The Lie of the Land: Migrant Workers and the California Landscape.* Minneapolis: University of Minnesota Press.
———. 2003. *The Right to the City: Social Justice and the Fight for Public Space.* New York: Guilford.
Molloy, Joanna. 1988. "Selling Off the Books." *New York Magazine,* 17 October, 33.
Paybarah, Azi. 2007. "An Easy Guide to Racial Politics on the Council." *New York Observer,* 14 March.
Smith, Neil. 1996. *The New Urban Frontier: Gentrification and the Revanchist City.* New York: Routledge.
Stoller, Paul. 2002. *Money Has No Smell: The Africanization of New York.* Chicago: University of Chicago Press.
Vitale, Alex S. 2008. *City of Disorder: How the Quality of Life Campaign Transformed New York Politics.* New York: New York University Press.

CHAPTER 3

Creative Resistance
The Case of Mexico City's Street Artisans and Vendors

Veronica Crossa

Recent work on urban economic restructuring has shed light on the exacerbation of socio-spatial exclusion produced by neoliberal forms of urban governance (MacLeod 2002; Smith 2002; Ward 2003; Belina and Helms 2003). Authors have gone to great lengths to explore the multiplicity of ways in which urban governance has followed a face-lift approach characterized by urban boosterism, image-making, physical regeneration, and gentrification while leaving aside the more fundamental problems of poverty, inequality, and other forms of injustice (M. Davis 2007; Del Casino and Jocoy 2008). This literature argues that under neoliberal forms of governance, acquisition of basic services is no longer a right that urban citizens are entitled to, but rather a luxury that only some can afford (Mitchell 2003). Although it has addressed the consequences of global economic restructuring for disenfranchised groups, it remains dominated by top-down analyses with limited sense of the agency of the individuals and groups experiencing socio-spatial exclusion. Work in critical urban studies has recently critiqued the top-down narratives that characterize much of the work within urban political economy, emphasizing the importance of grassroots mobilizations' role in undermining hegemonic political economic systems. These bottom-up analyses have shown how individuals or groups who partake in so-called informal activities are engaging in "everyday" practices that challenge exclusionary urban policies (Swanson 2007; Bayat 2000, 2004; Lindell 2008, 2010).

My chapter seeks to add to these theorizations by thinking about resistance, particularly how place matters to the creation of specific resistance strategies. Drawing from Doreen Massey (1994) and using Tim Cresswell's (1996) notion of "sense of place," I show how connections to place shape strategies for defending elements and relations that are central to the very definition of those places. Empirically, the essay examines the neoliberalization of Latin American urban public space, particularly plazas, and its implications for street vendors who rely on these spaces for their material and nonmaterial lives. I focus on the case of Mexico City and its city authorities' attempt to promote it to both local and global audiences, especially investors. At the heart of this promotion strategy are efforts to "beautify" and "revitalize" the city's streets and public plazas, a process officially called the Recuperacion de Espacios Públicos (Recovery of Public Spaces) but popularly renamed Plazas Limpias (clean plazas). In the city's most vibrant plazas and tourist areas, this sanitization process has meant the removal of street vendors and artisans.[1]

In this chapter I focus specifically on the case of Coyoacán, a tourist-oriented neighborhood in the south of Mexico City that is known for its historical richness and aesthetic beauty. I will show how street vendors and artisans who were removed from the public spaces of Coyoacán engaged in a range of resistance strategies that exemplified their commitment to place—a commitment resulting from the economic importance of place as well as the particular cultural and social processes that produced this form of public space. Elsewhere (Crossa 2009, 2010), I have described how street vendors in other parts of Mexico City dealt with similar exclusionary policies through strategies of association and mobility. In the case of Coyoacán, vendors and artisans fought a long and arduous public battle against the exclusionary nature of the Plazas Limpias policy. They resisted not only because they were excluded from the area's economic spaces but also because the policy sought to undermine their sense that Coyoacán is and can be a space where an alternative lifestyle is possible.

Devotion to creativity was a particularly striking aspect of their resistance. The oppositional character of their battle drew on particular notions of Coyoacán as a place of and for creativity but also as a space that challenges the dominant political-economic system in Mexico. By "creativity" I mean two interrelated things. First, I use the term to refer to the nature of the tactics employed by vendors and artisans who relied primarily on artistic forms—painting, music, performance—to engage in a resistance movement. Second, I use "creativity" more generally to refer to how vendors and artisans found ways to resist the sorts of constraints the policy imposed on their everyday life (Ettlinger 2010). Hence, "creativity" attains a double meaning in this essay. The artistic tactics employed in the resistance movement were creative, as was the act of managing to find ways around the constraining forces of Plazas Limpias.

The essay draws on research I began in 2009, which involved intensive fieldwork in the summer of 2009 and a follow-up process during shorter visits to Mexico City. The fieldwork entailed open-ended and semi-structured interviews with thirty street vendors and artisans, authorities from the Coyoacán Delegación (borough), visitors to the area, and local residents.[2] In the case of the artisans and street vendors, I made some initial contacts and then, through a snowball method, was referred to other vendors in the area. To avoid speaking only to vendors located within the same network, I randomly selected and approached vendors who I identified as part of other organizations. Further, I conducted participant observation at demonstrations and protests organized by vendors and artisans. The fieldwork was complemented with analysis of newspaper reports and informal conversations with vendors who gave retrospective accounts of their struggles in the aftermath of the implementation of the Plazas Limpias project.[3]

In the next section of this chapter, I introduce the theoretical perspective on resistance to urban neoliberalism in Latin America, which serves as the framework for the empirical case study. I then provide general context relating to Mexico City's Plazas Limpias program and examine the case of Coyoacán as an emblematic illustration of city authorities' intentions to attract global and local capital by reinventing and marketing certain parts of the city. Following a brief overview of the policies, I use material from my research to show how street vendors and artisans' use of place enabled them to engage in a resistance movement through two interrelated practices. The first I call *bounded resistance,* in reference to the scalar dimension of the vendors' resistance movement. The term seeks to capture the way in which vendors, aiming to scale up their movement, mobilized the support of visitors to the plazas. Even though their movements remained localized in the plazas, the vendors used visitors' national and international networks to mobilize support and exert pressure on the local authorities. The second practice, which I term *creative resistance,* describes the tactics used by vendors that draw on the symbolic characteristics of Coyoacán as a place. This term seeks to both emphasize both the oppositional nature of the vendors and artisans' movement and simultaneously highlight the way they used creativity—through various art forms—to capture, engage, and nurture the resistance movement.[4]

Resisting Urban Neoliberal Policies

Latin American neoliberal policies have significantly altered the social fabric of cities, leading to new forms of socio-spatial exclusion (Radcliffe 2005). Some examples of these forms of exclusion are the proliferation of fortified enclaves and the systematic removal of poor sectors of the population from public spaces (Herzog 2006; Cordera, Kuri, and Ziccardi 2008; Caldeira 2000 Duhau and Giglia 2008). More specifically, the privatization of public space in many Latin American cities has brought about the removal and prohibition of activities that are not deemed profitable and attractive, especially street vending activities.[5] In Latin American cities, street vending is a fundamental expression of the particular class/race relations of the region. As an urban activity, it is predominantly practiced by indigenous populations who are subject to different social constructions of race, a legacy of Latin America's colonial past. Hence, the mutually constitutive relation between race and class results in a highly racialized form of socio-spatial exclusion. Prohibiting street vendors from selling in the plazas, parks, streets and other public spaces of cities is not only about abolishing particular "informal" economic activities but is also tied, as Swanson argues, to a "whitening" process aimed at rendering indigenous street vendors invisible (Swanson 2007: 209).

An expanding literature focuses on how citizen groups struggle against and resist the rollout of neoliberalism in contemporary cities (Leitner, Peck, and Sheppard 2007; Radcliffe 2005). For example, the edited collection *Contesting Neoliberalism* highlights the geographies of neoliberalism, its multiple forms of contestation, and the potential implications of such actions for neoliberalism itself. It builds on the work of scholars who seek to unravel the tactics that different urban groups use to undermine the power of neoliberal strategies (Leitner et al. 2007). Their goal is to "destabilize the concept of neoliberalism … together with the necessitating politics of 'there is no alternative'" (Leitner et al. 2007: 325). Although this collection offers invaluable accounts of how different forms of neoliberalism are contested, it concentrates on the resistance strategies employed by officially recognized groups, particularly NGOs, residents' organizations, unions, and other oppositional groups. Underrepresented groups such as street vendors, slum dwellers, and others who partake in so-called informal activities are not incorporated into this analysis of contestation. This lack of acknowledgment of other groups is partly a product of the geographic scope of the collection, which deals predominantly with cases within the Western world and the way in which representative politics shapes these contexts.

An analysis of underrepresented groups in studies of resistance can provide novel insights into how resistance is practiced under conditions of informality. Recent literature on informal actors argues that those involved in the informal economy are agents who actively participate in a form of exchange that provides them a daily income. Moving beyond earlier structuralist perspectives on the politics of poverty and survival, proponents of this new perspective focus on the multiple ways in which informal workers engage in resistance practices that allow them to maintain a livelihood *despite* the structural constraints produced by neoliberal policies (Cross 1998; Crossa 2009; Lindell 2010). Cross's (1998) historical analysis of street vendors in Mexico City, for example, explores the importance of street vending organizations as political players whose power has undermined many exclusionary practices implemented by the local state. Agency in this case is practiced through collective forms of organization that help improve conditions for street vendors. At a more individual level, sociologist Asef Bayat argues that the politics of the "informal people" is characterized by a "quiet encroachment," that is, a spontaneous, unplanned, informal, and sometimes unarticulated way of fighting for redistribution while remaining autonomous vis-à-vis the forces of the state and the market (2000, 2004). Agency from this perspective is silent, atomized, and ordinary, practiced through everyday life.

Within the politics of informality, struggle and resistance are theorized not only as people opposing structures of constraints, but as their survival, and in some cases their prosperity, despite these constraints. Therefore, resistance is also about how individuals reconstitute their social networks and relations. Such forms of encroachment are, as Mike Davis (2007) argues, frequently synchronized among marginalized groups that refuse to accept their marginality. Noncollective everyday practices like those mentioned by Bayat have the potential to strengthen ties among individuals who, in a particular time-space, share similar concerns and aid in the construction of new resistance tactics. Because resistance entails the exercise of different forms of power, it can lead to reconstitutions of forms of social life. For example, with reference to social reproduction and global economic change, Cindi Katz (2004) offers lessons about children's creative and inventive responses to uneven structural changes and constraints. She suggests that responses to the injustices inflicted by global economic restructuring are not always just about resisting new power structures but rather can entail survival strategies that enable marginalized groups to get by in their daily life (Katz 2004: 246). Katz contrasts this type of everyday life "resilience" with practices of "reworking" that "attempt to recalibrate power relations and/or redistribute resources" (247). Resilience and reworking, however, involve a form of power that only enables survival, without altering fundamental structures. The classic sense of resistance aims at achieving emancipatory change (251–257). Such practices involve the development of what Jane Mansbridge has called "oppositional consciousness," which she defines as an "empowering mental state that prepared members of an oppressed group to act to undermine, reform, or overthrow a system of human domination" (2001: 4–5).

The development of an oppositional consciousness is a socio-spatial process linked to a dynamic connection to place (Mansbridge 2001: 1). Resistance movements draw from and are shaped by place and people's sense of place. Place has a particular connotation throughout this essay. Rather than looking at places as temporally fixed and circumscribed locations, I understand places as products of social relations practiced both within a particular location and also beyond (Massey 1994). A major aspect of the production of place is the juxtaposition and coexistence of many different people, each with their own "sense of place," which produces multiple meanings and results in tensions. As Tim Cresswell notes, the fact that in most places all sorts of tensions result from this co-presence of people—each with their own understandings of "their" places—means that those very tensions and struggles have to be viewed as contributing to the production of place (Cresswell 1996: 59). To resolve these tensions, different actors deploy material and discursive practices that ascribe meanings to places. What, for example, is defined as in or out of place? What is welcomed and what is not? Moreover, the sorts of tensions sparked by co-presence and the multiple meanings of place they produce must also be seen as involving power—the power to define, to remove, or to resist. Inclusion of these aspects in theories of socio-spatial exclusion under neoliberal policies is useful because it tells us "something about who gets to participate in the construction and dissemination of meanings for places and thus places themselves" (Cresswell 1996: 60).

People's attachment to a place and their need to defend it are charged with material realities and symbolic associations that are crucial to understanding resistance movements. From the perspective of the informal agents who are denied access to urban public space, resistance is about more than recovering the economic relations they rely on for their daily survival: it is also about refusing to accept how others redefine who they are and what their sense of place should be. Therefore, a dynamic conception of resistance requires thinking about the multiple ways that people attach meaning to a place, for instance in the form of committing to rescuing it. As I will show in the next sections, street vendors' resistance strategies rest upon a specific connection and commitment to place.

"Plazas Limpias": Rethinking Urban Public Space

In the last decade, federal authorities and the government of Mexico City have collaborated in attempts to attract local and global investment by changing the image of the country and its capital city. This reimagining process has entailed both discursive and material practices that seek to represent Mexico City as a "good" place in which to live, visit, and invest. Under the rubric of "Recovery of Public Spaces," authorities have applied a diverse toolkit of actions meant to change the image of specific spaces within the city. The focus on *urban public space* indicates that the management and regulation of interaction in these spaces –the streets and plazas—is essential to realization of the city's economic development strategy. The "recovery" of public space in Mexico City has entailed physical and social transformations of the city's most important historic areas, particularly tourist destinations, which are typically tied to an important public *plaza* or public space. The objective of the policy is therefore to

> a) recover green spaces through their maintenance and rehabilitation; b) guarantee public security through the constant surveillance of public space, c) promote physical, cultural and other leisure activities in public space; d) elevate the quality of life for the local population; e) improve the image through infrastructure improvements; f) generate a positive impact in the quality of life of the local population. (Gobierno del Distrito Federal 2007)

The implementation of the policy signified a reversal of a citywide program for reorganizing street vendors that was developed and implemented by the first democratically elected city government in 1997. That program granted permits to street vendors throughout the city and enabled authorities to regulate the nature of the stall, the products sold, and so forth. The older policy remains effective in some parts of the city, but in the context of Coyoacán the new policy revokes those efforts .

Implementation has varied depending on the area undergoing "recovery." In areas where tourism is important, however, the recovery program has taken a very particular form. Tourist zones in Mexico City are primarily linked to historical areas, which share common characteristics as far as public spaces are concerned. The majority of Mexico City's colonial sites have a public square or *plaza*. As in other Latin American contexts, these plazas are multi-functional, symbolic spaces where diverse publics—street vendors, businesspeople, state authorities, tourists, residents, artisans—come together in both harmonious and conflicting ways. For centuries they have been the most important public spaces of the city (Carrion 2005; Pareyón 2002; Silva 2001), especially in the formation of local and national identities. Physically, they house major political, economic, and religious powers materialized in state buildings, marketplaces, and churches. They are centers of life and work for much of the urban population (Hardoy and Gutman 1991; Kuri 2009; Low 2000; Scarpaci 2005). Further, as places to purchase goods or services, often at relatively low prices, they are valuable economic spaces for vendors and artisans. Plazas also function as arenas of public protest where different social organizations congregate to challenge authority.

Mexico City's largest plaza is the Zócalo, located in the heart of the city, its historic center. But the city also has a network of many smaller plazas that, like the Zócalo, are historically, culturally, socially, and economically significant and vital to the city's tourism industry. The Centenario and Hidalgo Plazas, located in the Delegación of Coyoacán, stand out as two of them. Indeed, after the Zócalo, these two plazas in Coyoacán are the most popular tourist destinations in the city (Safa 1998). Part of their attraction lies in their location: Coyoacán's historic center, a place of fundamental value to the symbolic and material life of Mexico City. The area also holds very important meanings for individuals and groups that benefit from Coyoacán in their daily life. Many national celebrations such as Independence Day are commemorated in the historic center and the plaza. Coyoacán also serves as a social and economic hub for street vendors and artisans selling all manner of commodities. For inhabitants of the city and the area, it is a place to purchase art and crafts, walk around and enjoy oneself, relax, read, or play. Mexican tourist brochures and travel guides list the historic center of Coyoacán as a must-see because of its museums, colonial architecture, bookstores, and general bohemian ambiance (Kuri 2009).[6] In all of these ways, the streets and plazas of the historic center of Coyoacán operate as a place where families, neighbors, tourists, street vendors, artisans, and organizations mingle, interact, play, purchase goods, fight, and also challenge authority.

The Recovery of Public Spaces program (hereafter Plazas Limpias) was initiated in Coyoacán in March 2008. Costing approximately $4.5 million (U.S.), the plan had three phases. The first involved upgrades to underground infrastructure, such as the repair and replacement of almost a kilometer of water and sewage pipes, and installation of two kilometers of new telecommunications cable. In the second phase, the sidewalks of both plazas were renovated with new red and gray stone tiles. The final phase involved renovation and beautification of the plaza's visible infrastructure, including new street benches, lamppost and garbage can replacement, and revamped gardens.

Work during these three stages entailed the removal of more than five hundred street vendors and artisans from the Hidalgo and Centenario Plazas. The official justification for removing the artisans and vendors was twofold. First, the local authority accused vendors of using the public spaces illegally, even though all of these plazas' street vendors and artisans held permits issued by that same local authority. The second argument was behavioral: it portrayed vendors as central participants in illicit and antisocial acts, particularly alcohol and drug abuse. Both arguments built upon a prominent rhetoric in urban areas that depicts street vending as an "urban cancer" and street vendors as "a bunch of cockroaches."[7] The actual removal of vendors and artisans was accomplished through direct means, such as fencing off the plazas during the initial phase or ensuring the continuous presence of police and riot police at the corners of the plazas. The removal was also enforced indirectly through practices like not renewing permits that were about to expire and not recognizing permits that were legally valid, which effectively made the permits worthless.

In March 2008 all five hundred street vendors and artisans in the Centenario and Hidalgo Plazas witnessed the start of the Plazas Limpias program as local authorities fenced the plazas, barring their entry.[8] The objective of the policy was to re-create the image of Coyoacán's plazas as "clean spaces ... free of vendors so that foreigners and local people could enjoy the plazas. Coyoacán is a historically rich area. The idea of the program is to rescue that history," according to one of the directors of the borough, Jaime Zarza, (23 July 2009). Discourses of history and tradition were key to creating a perceived need to revamp public spaces and plazas throughout the city. Embedded within such discourse was a claimed sense of a loss of tradition associated with the growth of activities like street vending. The Plazas Limpias policy refers to the historic center of Coyoacán as a culturally and historically rich area that recalls traditional, potentially salvageable practices. Zarza continued: "After beautifying the plazas, we can't let vendors return, right? Some will be allowed to return. Only the traditional vendors like the *paperos*,[9] *globeros*,[10] *algodoneros*.[11] The rest will have to leave" (Zarza, 23 July 2009). For the borough of Coyoacán, history and tradition were physically defined by colonial buildings and architecture, and socially defined by the visibility of limited, selected economic actors, particularly "traditional" vendors. The policy has portrayed only selected images of the plazas and the traditional activities associated with them, images that do not include many street vendors and artisans.

Given these points, I argue that the policy was meant not only to physically transform public spaces but also, and more importantly, to alter social practices and interactions that are crucial to street vendors and artisans whose economic and social life relies primarily on the streets and plazas. The removal of artisans and vendors from the plazas implied a process of redefining both Coyoacán as a place and the street vendors' social, economic, and cultural networks, consolidated over the previous twenty years. However, as the following will show, street vendors and artisans resisted these actions.

Tactics of Resistance

Prior to the implementation of Plazas Limpias, the Centenario and Hidalgo Plazas were frequented by more than five hundred vendors and artisans organized into twenty-two organizations. Mostly created in the 1990s, the organizations shared the purpose of acquiring legitimacy and the power to negotiate with local authorities. But the organizations themselves and their memberships are far from homogeneous. For example, some artisan-based organizations only welcome members who are self-producers—that is, individuals who are intimately connected to the production and creative processes of the product—whereas others are internally diverse in terms of the products sold by their members. Some organizations have more than forty members, others as few as three. Within an organization, members are differentiated in terms of the diverse products they sell and, more importantly, the circumstances that led them to settle in Coyoacán and use it as their main working space. Many vendors in Coyoacán see street vending as the best way to make a living in difficult socioeconomic circumstances, whereas for others, like Samuel, it represents an explicit form of resistance. As Samuel recalled, "this is an activity to prove that it is possible to live at the margins of systems of exploitation and alienation imposed by the capitalist mode of production" (Samuel, 14 August 2009).

Street vendors and artisans' resistance to Plazas Limpias took various forms. Next I discuss two general tactics that show how resistance, more than just a territorial dispute, was a fight for their rights, as citizen-artisans, to remain members of the plazas of Coyoacán—a struggle that reflects their commitment to place. These tactics—bounded resistance and creative resistance—proved applicable in the case of street vendor resistance in Coyoacán.

Bounded Resistance

At the start of their resistance movement, the street vendors' and artisans' objective was to appeal to a wide area and audience. However, their mobilizing tactics were bounded in place. They made short videos documenting discussions with national and international visitors about their views on the Plazas Limpias policy and what they thought the plazas would look like if the vendors were removed. Many tourists were sympathetic to the vendors' struggles and expressed concern over their removal. Drawing from Coyoacán as a place that brings together a wide range of practices and interactions in conflicting but also cooperative ways, vendors and artisans made the place center stage in their resistance movement. As Jorge, a young vendor who has sold in Coyoacán for fifteen years, explained: "Our struggle was not only a struggle over a working space. We were defending a public space. A space of co-existence, a place of encounter ... because Coyoacán is precisely that: a place where multiplicity co-exists" (Jorge, 25 July 2009).

Upon the closure of the Centenario and Hidalgo plazas, vendors and artisans from different organizations came together in a peaceful resistance sit-in (*plantón de resistencia pacífica*) in 2008. Staged as an initial act of protest, the sit-in tapped into notions of belonging, identity, and commitment to place. Marcela, who has sold handmade shoes for nine years, stated: "We've been here twenty-five years making this space not my space but *our* space. We [referring to the vendors and artisans] made this place what it is.... I might not have a receipt to show ownership, but this is a place that we've made ourselves and we've made it for ourselves and others" (Marcela, 29 July 2009). Similarly, Rodrigo, a younger artisan who sells handmade notebooks, said: "Our place is here. This is where we have emerged from and grown. We could go elsewhere, but why should we? Our place is right here. Leaving would be accepting that we are not part of this anymore" (Rodrigo, 2 August 2009). Marcela's anger and frustration is directed at both the exclusionary nature of the policy and its underlying implications of ownership. She has been denied the right to be part of a place she believes she had an active role in building. Hence, for Marcela, as for other vendors and artisans, resistance is not just a territorial struggle but rather a larger struggle over their rights as citizens to remain a part of the representations of Coyoacán.

The sit-in started as a sporadic and informal protest against closure of the plazas, but it evolved into a larger, more organized set of practices that drew from and reacted to an already cemented geography of exclusion of vendors in Mexico City. Plazas Limpias policy had been successful in removing vendors from other important plazas of the city, particularly the historic center of Mexico City, where more than nine thousand vendors were relocated into enclosed markets (Crossa 2009). This practice became emblematic of the ethos of the new city government's policy toward street vending activities, which was based on Giuliani's implementation of Zero

Tolerance in New York City (D. Davis 2007: 639–640). The Plazas Limpias policy in Coyoacán had the same objectives.

In opposition, artisans and vendors sought to legitimize their presence in the plazas by re-creating their own image through discourses of difference and separation from the street vendors of the city's historic center. Rodrigo clarified that "we are being treated as if we were vendors from the Historic Center whose products are all Chinese or have dodgy origins. We are different. I'm not saying we are better or worse, we are just different" (Rodrigo, 2 August 2009). A collective identity formed among vendors and artisans based on the idea that vendors in Coyoacán were fundamentally different from those in other parts of Mexico City. As Fernanda, a young vendor selling silver jewelry, commented: "The nature of this place is entirely different. Coyoacán was born out of a countercultural movement. We started here because we were rebelling against a system. The vendors in the historic Center have a very different background" (Fernanda, 7 August 2009). The "different background" that Fernanda identifies was a discursive boundary expressed by many vendors and artisans in Coyoacán.

Many vendors and artisans emphasized that Coyoacán is a place that has given rise to a unique set of vending practices and nurtured a different kind of vendor. Adding to what Lindell (2010) identifies as the multiplicity of class relations and positions embedded within the informal economy, the case of Coyoacán shows the geographic nature of this multiplicity. The simultaneous construction of sameness among those within Coyoacán and differences from vendors outside it made Coyoacán central to its vendors' collective identity. According to Roberto, a shoemaking artisan who has been selling his products for twenty years, "government authorities think we do not deserve a working space out here. They say 'these guys are just a bunch of depraved druggies'" (Roberto, 19 July 2009). In the words of José Luis, a middle-aged vendor who sells T-shirts and women's bags: "The typical discourse of the government to disqualify our existence is to equate us with the vendors from the Historic Center. But they did damage, and ruin the place. We haven't. On the contrary, people come to visit Coyoacán to see us" (José Luis, 26 July 2009). The vendors from Coyoacán differentiated themselves from other vendors and other places of the city by appropriating the repeated government rhetoric about street vendors ruining the historic center. Thus, in trying to defend themselves from the characterizations typically made by government officials, they reproduced a politics of difference that in fact reproduced governmental discourses.

The Coyoacán vendors' binary creation of "us" and "them" also had a material dimension: they developed new resistance strategies as means of differentiating themselves from vendors in the historic center. For Edgar, a middle-aged artisan selling silver jewelry, "the reason why [Plazas Limpias] worked in the Historic Center was because vendors didn't have the support of the people. In fact, people were happy they were gone" (Edgar, 31 July 2009). Part of the perceived weakness and failure of vendors in the historic center was their lack of support from the local population, both residents and clients. However, vendors in the historic center had not reached out for support from their client base. In that area, the nature of street vending organization is such that most negotiation and resistance occur at the formal political institutional level (Crossa 2009; Cross 1998).

The distinctions that Coyoacán vendors drew between themselves and vendors from the historic center were reproduced internally, within Coyoacán. Existing divisions between artisans and vendors were heightened. According to Juan, an artisan, the local authorities treated all street vendors equally, irrespective of their differences. He stated, for example, that "the authorities told us 'You guys are vendors. I don't care if you sell the crafts you make or if you sell shoes made in China. You are occupying a public space, and that is all I care about.'" This approach by the authorities sparked outrage among organizations whose members identified as real artisans. Out of twenty-two such organizations, two attempted explicitly to separate themselves from the general consensus the remaining twenty organizations had built to deal with the exclusionary measures of Plazas Limpias. The self-proclaimed artisans divided themselves from the general resistance movement and developed their own sets of strategies to engage with the local authorities.

Seeking out local support was an essential component of the resistance movement established by the artisans and vendors of Coyoacán. The movement's success in obtaining support was due to the vendors' particular position within the local street economy: whereas vendors in the historic center sold products addressed to people's needs (e.g., clothes, school uniforms, school supplies), Coyoacán's vendors catered to discretionary spenders, tapping into people's disposable income to sell arts and crafts. Aware of their niche, vendors used it to justify their difference.

An estimated fifty thousand plus people visit the Centenario and Hidalgo Plazas every weekend (Robles 2008). The artisans and vendors strove to elicit support from that niche. Throughout the eight-month sit-in, they held a number of workshops and sessions to inform the population about their activities as vendors and artisans, and about the importance of Coyoacán to their constitution. The leaders of the organizations participating in the sit-in put together a petition calling for the defense of street vendors and artisans' right to remain in the public plazas. The petition was an idea broached by members of several organizations who realized that many visitors were unhappy with the policy and wanted to alleviate the vendors and artisans' plight. The petition gathered approximately 160,000 signatures from people who condemned their removal from the plaza. Physically this form of resistance was confined to the spaces of Coyoacán, but the tactic was about scalar networking, that is, scaling up to obtain the support of national and international visitors. Hence, Coyoacán's importance as a locus of national and international visitors is precisely what vendors capitalized on to fight for their right to remain on the streets and plazas.

Creative Resistance

I argue that Coyoacán's uniqueness within Mexico City was a dominant factor in shaping the vendors and artisans' resistance tactics. Indeed, they *creatively* used Coyoacán's image as a cultural and artistic hub to resist the Plazas Limpias policy. The creative element resulted from their desire for a style of resistance that attracted support while also reminding people of the cultural practices that constitute *their* livelihoods. As Rodrigo stated, "Coyoacán is an icon of art, crafts, and culture. We decided that our movement had to draw from that. We all used our different talents to make our movement an alternative one" (Rodrigo, 2 August 2009). Similarly, Jorge, a young artisan who sells handmade leather crafts, suggested that "our movement is of a different kind. Our motto is our hands. We create with our hands. Our movement was also based on creating with our hands" (Jorge, 25 July 2009).

Street vending in Coyoacán's historic center was established in the 1980s by approximately twenty vendors—the "group of twenty," as they became known—who settled in one of the plazas in search of an alternative way of life (Maria, 8 August 2009). Samuel, a middle-aged vendor on the streets of Coyoacán since the 1980s, recalled that "the group of twenty began as a counter-cultural movement. We were artisans who were here [in the plaza] not necessarily because of our economic circumstances, but rather for conviction; to look for an alternative economic life to the one offered by the capitalist system" (Samuel, 14 August 2009). Many who became artisans and settled in Coyoacán viewed the plaza as an alternative economic space. For many of the vendors and artisans, the resistance movement involved the preservation of a political project that for years had distinguished them from other vendors of the city. As Omar, a middle-aged artisan who has sold hand-made jewelry since the mid 1980s, pointed out: "For us this activity was more than just a way to make a living. It was the struggle for a specific identity. It was the struggle for freedom to be creative and not tied to the demands of a person or company" (Omar, 12 July

2009). These artisan-oriented alternative spaces multiplied and merged with the growth of vendors who resorted to street vending to deal with the unemployment and underemployment associated with the neoliberal economic reforms initiated in Mexico in the late 1980s, which boosted informal economic activities on the street (Biles 2008; Jaramillo 2007). At this time numerous parts of Mexico City, including Coyoacán, experienced rapid increase in street vendors and artisans on central plazas and thoroughfares. Coyoacán in particular gained an image and reputation—not only among street vendors and artisans, but more importantly among urban dwellers and visitors—as a fun place to visit, hang out, and buy and sell handmade crafts (Safa 1998).

When the plazas were fenced off, vendors and artisans used the construction site in creating what became an informal outdoor gallery displaying photographs, colorful banners, and video clips of their struggle. The exhibit's objective was to inform the public of how events were experienced through their eyes and "hands." The photographs documented different moments in their struggle against the Plazas Limpias implementation process, including their forced departure from the plazas, the marching-in of hundreds of police in riot gear to prevent their sit-in, their creation of a human chain to prevent police harassment, and other situations. The exhibition attracted attention from visitors and the media (Pantoja 2008). Information tables next to the exhibition conveyed the situation to people and were also used as a resource for reinvigorating their economic activities. More than two hundred vendors and artisans participated in this process, creating an extensive line of tables displaying products for sale to visitors, clients, or tourists. In addition, the tables were sites of free creative workshops that the vendors and artisans offered to teach children interested in arts and crafts how to make papier-mâché, maracas, piñatas, paintings, and kaleidoscopes. These workshops were extremely popular among families taking weekend strolls in Coyoacán. During the workshops, vendors and artisans would talk and answer questions about their struggle and the government's attempts to remove them from the plazas.

Creativity imbued many of the resistance acts performed by vendors and artisans. They invited a wide range of artists to their sit-in, including dancers, rock bands, singers, and drummers. Similarly, they organized a carnival march to the offices of the city government. Their goal was to situate their creative presence as the constitutive element of both their own livelihoods and those of the plazas (Barrera-Aguirre 2009). For Maria, who has spent fifteen years as a street vendor in the area, "Coyoacán is festive, and that was the goal of our struggle, to make it celebratory" (Maria, 8 August 2009). In the words of Mateo, one of the first artisans to settle in the area, the sit-in "was not only to defend an individual or collective workspace. We were also defending a way of being; a way of living that is part of the essence of Coyoacán" (Mateo, 25 July 2009).

Conclusions

The story of Coyoacán's vendors and artisans' resistance movement is ongoing. After the eight-month peaceful sit-in, the building work ended, and vendors negotiated their return to the plazas for seven months while an enclosed parking lot was renovated for their relocation. During this return to the plazas, the vendors and artisans concentrated their efforts on fighting against their relocation. The resistance tactics implemented after their removal exemplified their need to maintain the economic networks that supported their livelihoods, but they were also a way to sustain their commitment to the plazas as cultural and social sites of materialization and reproduction of many of their social relations. Creativity characterized their struggle as they set up resistance tents in the middle of the plaza, offering music, discussion tables, and dance. Despite their creative political efforts, most of them were forced out of the plazas into an adapted parking lot in September 2009. Their displacement into an enclosed space rendered them invisible, forcing them to redefine who they are and what they do.

As Lefèbvre (1991) stressed, places should be theorized as products of three mutually embedded moments: the experienced, the perceived, and the imagined. Places are constituted not only by experienced material spatial practices—understood as flows of goods, money, people, and labor, which are all fundamental processes of economic production—but also through the perceptions and imaginings of different actors who attach different meanings to places. The development and implementation of Plazas Limpias is emblematic of a wider set of national- and international-scale changes concerning efforts to exclude and displace individuals involved in so-called informal activities. Under the rhetoric of rescuing public spaces or revamping urban spaces, current neoliberal urban policies have been implemented with the goal of redefining the informal economy and its spaces. Rather than address the fundamental socioeconomic issues that often drive people to engage in informal activities on the streets, urban governments instead push them into spaces where they are less visible, not heard, smelled, and felt. Yet even as places are represented and constructed through the perspectives of planners, architects, bureaucrats, and the like, the practices and interactions of many different people are simultaneously challenging and reshaping these perceptions in their everyday lives. As this chapter has shown, street vendors and artisans in

Coyoacán have not remained silent during the implementation of policies aimed at their exclusion. Their determination to remain in the area's streets and public spaces sprang from their commitment to their particular understanding of Coyoacán. Their sense of Coyoacán as a place clashed with the representation of public space embedded within the Plazas Limpias policy. This contested sense of place reinforced the vendors and artisans' definition of Coyoacán as an alternative economic and symbolic space. For the street vendors, the plaza is not just the place where they work; it is also where their children are cared for, where they meet their friends, where new ideas are shared, where loving relationships flourish, where discussions take place. Through creative acts, vendors and artisans sought to re-emphasize that they were not just street vendors but creative contributors to Coyoacán. The message was clear: removing them from the plazas of Coyoacán meant removing their own and the area's creative life.

Veronica Crossa is a lecturer in urban studies at El Colegio de México in Mexico City. She is interested in power and resistance in cities of the Global South. Her work has centered mostly on the politics of urban public space, particularly with regard to the displacement of street vendors and artisans from key spaces in Mexico City. She has published in various journals within urban studies and geography, in both English and Spanish.

Notes

1. The difference between street vendor and artisan in Coyoacán concerns the nature of the production process of the commodities sold. Artisans primarily sell crafts they produced themselves. Street vendors resell crafts and other products they have bought. This distinction was clear among the vendors I interviewed.
2. All the interviews were carried out in Spanish. The translations are the author's.
3. For confidentiality purposes, I have changed the names of all the street vendors, as agreed on at the start of each interview.
4. The differentiation between tactics and strategy is based somewhat on De Certeau (1984). Accordingly, *strategy* implies power, that is, the practices applied by institutional and governmental structures as an exercise of their power. *Tactics,* as per De Certeau, has a more oppositional meaning. Tactics are practices that individuals or groups carry out to deceive and undermine power — clever everyday life practices, or "joyful discoveries," as he called them.
5. The removal of street vendors from urban public spaces is not confined to the Latin American context, as this book documents. My interest here is in

contrasting the particularities of exclusionary practices in Latin America with well-cited examples from old industrial cities, especially in the Global North. However, this does not imply that all cities in Latin America share this trend, or that cities in other regions of the so-called Global South do not experience similar processes of exclusion (see, e.g., Lindell 2008; Musoni 2010).
6. Including the house of Frida Kahlo and the Leon Trotsky museum.
7. Such terms arose repeatedly throughout my fieldwork and are a general way of discussing street vending in Mexico City. This specific sentence is based on a personal interview with the head of CANACO, a business lobby group in Mexico (23 November 2003).
8. Authorities of the Delegación of Coyoacán offered the vendors an alternative location: a largely abandoned, rarely used space approximately 8 km south of Coyoacán's historic center. Around twenty vendors made the move, but the majority decided to stay in Coyoacán and continue struggling to find a way to remain on the streets and plazas.
9. Vendors who sell potato chips.
10. Vendors who sell balloons.
11. Vendors who sell cotton candy.

Bibliography

Barrera-Aguirre, Juan Manuel. 2009. "Artesanos y Comerciantes Marchan al Zócalo." *El Universal* (Mexico), 24 March 2009.
Bayat, Asef. 2000. "From 'Dangerous Classes' to 'Quiet Rebels': Politics of the Urban Subaltern in the Global South." *International Sociology*, 15 (3): 533–557.
———. 2004. "Globalization and the Politics of the Informals in the Global South." In *Urban Informality: Transnational Perspectives from the Middle East, Latin American and South Asia*, ed. Ananya Roy and Nezar Alsayyad. Lanham, Maryland: Lexington Books.
Belina, Bernd, and Gesa Helms. 2003. "Zero Tolerance for the Industrial Past and Other Threats: Policing and Urban Entrepreneurialism in Britain and Germany." *Urban Studies* 40 (9): 1845–1867.
Biles, James. 2008. "Informal Work and Livelihoods in Mexico: Getting By or Getting Ahead?" *Professional Geographer* 60 (4): 541–555.
Caldeira, Teresa. 2000. *City of Walls: Crime, Segregation and Citizenship in São Paulo*. Berkeley: University of California Press.
Carrion, Fernando. 2005. "The Historic Centre as an Object of Desire." *City & Time* 1 (3): 1. Accessed January 2006. www.ct.ceci-br.org.
Cordera, Rolando, Patricia Ramírez Kuri, and Alicia Ziccardi. 2008. *Pobreza, Desigualdad y Exclusión Social en la Ciudad del Siglo XXI*. Mexico City: Siglo XXI.
Cresswell, Tim. 1996. *In Place/Out of Place: Geography, Ideology, and Transgression*. Minneapolis: University of Minnesota Press.
Cross, John. 1998. *Informal Politics: Street Vendors and the State in Mexico City*. Stanford, CA: Stanford University Press.

Crossa, Veronica. 2009. "Resisting the Entrepreneurial City: Street Vendors' Struggle in Mexico City's Historic Center." *International Journal of Urban and Regional Research* 33 (1): 43-63.

Davis, Diane. 2007. "El factor Giuliani: Delincuencia, la 'Cero Tolerancia' en el Trabajo Policiaco y la Transformación de la Esfera Pública en el Centro de la Ciudad de México." *Estudios Sociológicos* 25 (75): 639–668.

Davis, Mike. 2007. *Planet of Slums*. New York: Verso.

De Certeau, Michel. 1984. *The Practices of Everyday Life*. Los Angeles: University of California Press.

Del Casino, Vincent, and Christine Jocoy. 2008. "Neoliberal Subjectivities, The 'New' Homelessness, and Struggles over Spaces of/in the City." *Antipode* 40 (2): 192–199.

Duhau, Emilio, and Angela Giglia. 2008. *Las Reglas del Desorden: Habitar la Metrópolis*. Mexico City: Siglo XXI.

Ettlinger, Nancy. 2010. "Bringing the Everyday into the Culture/Creativity Discourse." *Human Geography* 3 (1): 49–59.

Gobierno del Distrito Federal. 2007. *Manos a la Obra 2007–2009: Programa de Recuperación de Espacios Públicos*. Gobierno del Distrito Federal

Hardoy, Jorge, and Margarita Gutman. 1991. "The Role of Municipal Government in the Protection of Historic Centers in Latin American Cities." *Environment and Urbanization* 3 (1): 96–108.

Herzog, Lawrence A. 2006. *Return to the Center: Culture, Public Space and City Building in a Global Era*. Austin: University of Texas Press.

Jaramillo, Norma Angélica. 2007. "Comercio y Espacio Público: Una Organización de Ambulantes en la Alameda Central." *Alteridades* 17 (34): 137–153.

Katz, Cindi. 2004. *Growing up Global: Economic Restructuring and Children's Everyday Lives*. Minneapolis: University of Minnesota Press

Kuri, Patricia R. 2009. *Espacio Público y Ciudadanía en la Ciudad de México: Percepciones, apropiaciones y prácticas sociales en Coyoacán y su Centro Histórico*. Mexico City: Miguel Angel Porrua.

Lefèbvre, Henri. 1991. *The Production of Space*. Cambridge, MA: Blackwell.

Leitner, Helga, Jamie Peck, and Eric Sheppard. 2007. *Contesting Neoliberalism: Urban Frontiers*. New York: Guilford Press.

Lindell, Ilda. 2008. "Multiple Sites of Urban Governance: Insights from an African City." *Urban Studies* 45 (9): 1879–1901.

———. 2010. "Informality and Collective Organising: Identities, Alliances and Transnational Activism in Africa." *Third World Quarterly* 31 (2): 207–222.

Low, Setha. 2000. *On the Plaza: The Politics of Public Space and Culture*. Austin: University of Texas Press.

MacLeod, Gordon. 2002. "From Urban Entrepreneurialism to a 'Revanchist City'? On the Spatial Injustices of Glasgow's Renaissance." *Antipode* 34 (3): 602–624.

Mansbridge, Jane. 2001. "The Making of Oppositional Consciousness." In *Oppositional Consciousness: The Subjective Roots of Social Protest*, ed. Jane Mansbridge and Aldon Morris. Chicago: University of Chicago Press.

Massey, Doreen. 1994. *Space, Place and Gender*. Minneapolis: University of Minnesota Press.

Mitchell, Don. 2003. *The Right to the City: Social Justice and the Fight for Public Space.* New York: Guilford Press.

Musoni, Francis. 2010. "Operational *Murambatsvina* and the Politics of Street Vendors in Zimbabwe." *Journal of Southern African Studies* 36 (2): 301–317.

Pantoja, Sara. 2008. "Se reinstalan solo 6 artesanos en Coyoacán." *El Universal* (Mexico), 30 March 2008.

Pareyón, Alejandro Suarez. 2002. "El Centro Histórico de la Ciudad de México: presente y futuro." In *Los Centros Vivos: La Habana, Lima, México, Montevideo,* ed. Rosendo Mesías and Alejandro Suarez Paredón. Lima: Red XIV.

Radcliffe, Sarah. 2005. "Neoliberalism As We Know It, but Not in Conditions of Its Own Choosing: A Commentary. *Environment and Planning A* 37: 323–329.

Robles, Johana. 2008. "Depurarán padrón de comerciantes." *El Universal* (Mexico), 28 March 2008.

Safa, Patricia. 1998. "Identidades locales y multiculturalidad: Coyoacán." In *Cultura y Comunicación en la Ciudad de México. Modernidad y Multiculturalidad: La Ciudad de México a Fin de Siglo,* ed. Nestor Garcia Canclini. Mexico: Grijalbo.

Scarpaci, Joseph. 2005. *Plazas and Barrios: Heritage Tourism and Globalization in the Latin American Centro Histórico.* Tucson: University of Arizona Press.

Silva, Armando. 2001. "Algunos imaginarios urbanos desde centros históricos de América Latina." In *La Ciudad Construida: Urbanismo en América Latina,* ed. Fernando Carrión. Ecuador: FLACSO.

Smith, Neil. 2002. "New Globalism, New Urbanism: Gentrification as Global Urban Strategy." *Antipode* 34 (2): 427–451.

Swanson, Kate. 2007. "Revanchist Urbanism Heads South: The Regulation of Indigenous Beggars and Street Vendors in Ecuador. *Antipode* 39 (4): 708–728.

Ward, Kevin. 2003. "Entrepreneurial Urbanism, State Restructuring and Civilizing 'New' East Manchester." *Area* 35 (2): 116–127.

Crossa, Veronica. 2009. "Resisting the Entrepreneurial City: Street Vendors' Struggle in Mexico City's Historic Center." *International Journal of Urban and Regional Research* 33 (1): 43-63.

Davis, Diane. 2007. "El factor Giuliani: Delincuencia, la 'Cero Tolerancia' en el Trabajo Policiaco y la Transformación de la Esfera Pública en el Centro de la Ciudad de México." *Estudios Sociológicos* 25 (75): 639–668.

Davis, Mike. 2007. *Planet of Slums*. New York: Verso.

De Certeau, Michel. 1984. *The Practices of Everyday Life*. Los Angeles: University of California Press.

Del Casino, Vincent, and Christine Jocoy. 2008. "Neoliberal Subjectivities, The 'New' Homelessness, and Struggles over Spaces of/in the City." *Antipode* 40 (2): 192–199.

Duhau, Emilio, and Angela Giglia. 2008. *Las Reglas del Desorden: Habitar la Metrópolis*. Mexico City: Siglo XXI.

Ettlinger, Nancy. 2010. "Bringing the Everyday into the Culture/Creativity Discourse." *Human Geography* 3 (1): 49–59.

Gobierno del Distrito Federal. 2007. *Manos a la Obra 2007–2009: Programa de Recuperación de Espacios Públicos*. Gobierno del Distrito Federal

Hardoy, Jorge, and Margarita Gutman. 1991. "The Role of Municipal Government in the Protection of Historic Centers in Latin American Cities." *Environment and Urbanization* 3 (1): 96–108.

Herzog, Lawrence A. 2006. *Return to the Center: Culture, Public Space and City Building in a Global Era*. Austin: University of Texas Press.

Jaramillo, Norma Angélica. 2007. "Comercio y Espacio Público: Una Organización de Ambulantes en la Alameda Central." *Alteridades* 17 (34): 137–153.

Katz, Cindi. 2004. *Growing up Global: Economic Restructuring and Children's Everyday Lives*. Minneapolis: University of Minnesota Press

Kuri, Patricia R. 2009. *Espacio Público y Ciudadanía en la Ciudad de México: Percepciones, apropiaciones y prácticas sociales en Coyoacán y su Centro Histórico*. Mexico City: Miguel Angel Porrua.

Lefèbvre, Henri. 1991. *The Production of Space*. Cambridge, MA: Blackwell.

Leitner, Helga, Jamie Peck, and Eric Sheppard. 2007. *Contesting Neoliberalism: Urban Frontiers*. New York: Guilford Press.

Lindell, Ilda. 2008. "Multiple Sites of Urban Governance: Insights from an African City." *Urban Studies* 45 (9): 1879–1901.

———. 2010. "Informality and Collective Organising: Identities, Alliances and Transnational Activism in Africa." *Third World Quarterly* 31 (2): 207–222.

Low, Setha. 2000. *On the Plaza: The Politics of Public Space and Culture*. Austin: University of Texas Press.

MacLeod, Gordon. 2002. "From Urban Entrepreneurialism to a 'Revanchist City'? On the Spatial Injustices of Glasgow's Renaissance." *Antipode* 34 (3): 602–624.

Mansbridge, Jane. 2001. "The Making of Oppositional Consciousness." In *Oppositional Consciousness: The Subjective Roots of Social Protest*, ed. Jane Mansbridge and Aldon Morris. Chicago: University of Chicago Press.

Massey, Doreen. 1994. *Space, Place and Gender*. Minneapolis: University of Minnesota Press.

Mitchell, Don. 2003. *The Right to the City: Social Justice and the Fight for Public Space.* New York: Guilford Press.
Musoni, Francis. 2010. "Operational *Murambatsvina* and the Politics of Street Vendors in Zimbabwe." *Journal of Southern African Studies* 36 (2): 301–317.
Pantoja, Sara. 2008. "Se reinstalan solo 6 artesanos en Coyoacán." *El Universal* (Mexico), 30 March 2008.
Pareyón, Alejandro Suarez. 2002. "El Centro Histórico de la Ciudad de México: presente y futuro." In *Los Centros Vivos: La Habana, Lima, México, Montevideo,* ed. Rosendo Mesías and Alejandro Suarez Paredón. Lima: Red XIV.
Radcliffe, Sarah. 2005. "Neoliberalism As We Know It, but Not in Conditions of Its Own Choosing: A Commentary. *Environment and Planning A* 37: 323–329.
Robles, Johana. 2008. "Depurarán padrón de comerciantes." *El Universal* (Mexico), 28 March 2008.
Safa, Patricia. 1998. "Identidades locales y multiculturalidad: Coyoacán." In *Cultura y Comunicación en la Ciudad de México. Modernidad y Multiculturalidad: La Ciudad de México a Fin de Siglo,* ed. Nestor Garcia Canclini. Mexico: Grijalbo.
Scarpaci, Joseph. 2005. *Plazas and Barrios: Heritage Tourism and Globalization in the Latin American Centro Histórico.* Tucson: University of Arizona Press.
Silva, Armando. 2001. "Algunos imaginarios urbanos desde centros históricos de América Latina." In *La Ciudad Construida: Urbanismo en América Latina,* ed. Fernando Carrión. Ecuador: FLACSO.
Smith, Neil. 2002. "New Globalism, New Urbanism: Gentrification as Global Urban Strategy." *Antipode* 34 (2): 427–451.
Swanson, Kate. 2007. "Revanchist Urbanism Heads South: The Regulation of Indigenous Beggars and Street Vendors in Ecuador. *Antipode* 39 (4): 708–728.
Ward, Kevin. 2003. "Entrepreneurial Urbanism, State Restructuring and Civilizing 'New' East Manchester." *Area* 35 (2): 116–127.

PART II

Street Vending and Ethnicity

CHAPTER 4

Metropolitan Informality and Racialization
Street Vending in Berlin's Historical Center

Noa Ha

Walking the streets of the historical center of Berlin in the year 2014, one notices few street vendors operating at specific spots—Alexanderplatz, Checkpoint Charlie, and the area near Berliner Dom, for example. But right after the reunification of Germany in the 1990s, a lot more vendors were claiming public space. This change in the geography of street vending resulted from the urban planning, administrative regulation, and aesthetic envisioning of the German capital at the end of the Cold War and during its aftermath, when the informal practice of street vending challenged the formal purpose of Berlin's historical center as a particular site of national representation. Berlin had become the capital of reunified Germany, proclaiming itself a "European City" in search of a new identity. This urban vision, debated by architects, urban planners, and urban sociologists, was concretized in urban planning documents. Meanwhile, a new administrative regulation of public space was introduced, leading to substantial restriction of street vending areas in Berlin's historical center.

The few vendors in the limited areas remaining to them nowadays operate under strong surveillance and constant controls of the police and the municipal public order office. Street vendors in these areas sell food, jewelry and souvenirs, and a few newspapers. Each of these types of street vending is precisely regulated and falls into a hierarchy: food vending, for example, demands a higher deployment of knowledge and technology than does the sale of other goods. The subjectivities of the vendors reflect this hierarchy: food vendors are mostly white German; jewelry and souvenir vendors are mostly men of color.[1]

At the core of this essay is the question of the so far untold story of the racialization and ethnification that is rendered invisible by policies of urban aesthetization implemented via urban planning and design. To address this question, I consider the practice of street vending in the historical center of Berlin as a case study, relating planning discourses and local regulations to the spatial practice of street vending. This chapter examines the history of urban development in the formerly divided city of Berlin from a postcolonial perspective, focusing on its relations to the subjectivities of men of color engaging in street vending practices in Berlin's public space. This perspective incorporates the notion of racialized exclusion from public space that is implicit in the narrative of the European City that dominates planning discourses. Within this framework I understand street vending as a form of *metropolitan informality* that includes both the story of racialized vendors and the story of becoming the nation's capital.

Conceptualizing a Postcolonial Perspective on Metropolitan Informality

Over-regulation of petty entrepreneurial activities has become a global phenomenon because in the modern understanding of the city, street vending is not an appropriate use of space (Cross and Karides 2007: 30). Cross and Karides point out that as the informal economy of street vending has become less problematic in terms of urban policymaking, the focus of contention has moved from the vending activity to the urban places. Vendors' struggles have intensified in urban areas that are of particular interest to the tourism and financial sectors. Hence, the discussion on street vending shifts from the question of how they vend and to whom, to the issue of the territory on which vending takes place. Local discussions on urban development, focused on the aesthetics of public space and its adequate uses, have obscured the social strata of vendors and the necessity of street vending (Anjaria 2006; Bromley and Mackie 2009; Bromley 2000; Crossa 2009; Donovan 2008). Here, I take up the concept of urban informality, which Ananya Roy and Nezar AlSayyad developed for the Global South (2004), and explicitly contextualize it for the Global North, theorizing it as metropolitan.

The term informality, which can be thought of as the opposite of formality, refers to the field between the formal (the right) and the illegal (the wrong). It was introduced to describe the urban economies of so-called developing countries in particular as the "informal sector" (Hart 1973), but this classification has been a subject of fierce debate since its introduction (Rakowski 1994). The notion of the informal sector produced an understanding of a self-contained economic space in which standardized and formalized labor relations neither apply nor exist. In this sense, the practice of street vending has become an iconic informal-sector practice, despite the fact that many regulations exist. Contemporary ideas of informality relate to the production of formality and regard this relationship of dependency between the informal and the formal as crucial to understanding the growth of the informalization of labor and space (Altvater and Mahnkopf 2002). Contemporary labor relations have changed in industrialized countries, leading globally to growth in informality due to the dominance of a neoliberal form of capitalism and the globalization of the economy (Jütting and Laiglesia 2009; Blanchflower 2000).

Informalized and precarious labor and living conditions are consequently on the rise in the cities of the Global North, affecting women and people of color in particular. The neoliberalization of economies produces social injustice along the lines of race, gender, and class (Castro Varela 2005; Lewed 2005) and produces multidimensional, interrelating effects of discrimination (Crenshaw 1991; Winker and Degele 2009). Informality in the neoliberal era is no longer reserved for the Global South, since after a century of efforts by the regulatory state, it is increasingly a condition in the Global North. Saskia Sassen has observed that it is "a systemic feature of advanced capitalism, rather than an importation of the Third World" (Sassen 2005: 85). Therefore the global dimension of informality—notwithstanding its very different shapes and practices worldwide and in various cities—has become a constitutive feature in the understanding of urbanity in the twenty-first century.

David Harvey has argued that "the fundamental mission of the neoliberal state is to create a 'good business climate' and to optimize conditions for capital accumulation no matter what the consequences for employment or social well-being are" (Harvey 2006: 25). Such an understanding exposes the state as a producer of informality, as its "mission" entails a structural transformation of previous labor relations through such means as rolling back labor rights, applying technologies of self-entrepreneurialism, and allowing different forms of subcontracting (Mayer 2007). Mediating the global spread of neoliberal ideology were the "magic" words *deregulation* and *flexibility*, used to camouflage the growth of precarious workplaces and spaces (Butterwegge, Lösch, and Ptak 2008: 83ff.). Ananya

Roy, analyzing the role of urban planning in such a "mission," coined the term *urban informality* (Roy 2005). Her analytical perspective identifies urban planning as an instrumental force working to shape the city in conformance with the neoliberal logic of consumption and commodification of urban and public spaces. The conceptual framework Roy proposes for the interplay of informality and urbanity "rejects the notion of an informal sector and instead views informality as a *mode* of urbanization," assuming that "this notion of informality … helps reveal some key trends of urbanization" (Roy 2005: 148). Thus she understands urban informality as a fundamental intertwining of a relation between the state and the globalized economy in the production of urban development. Roy's approach takes into account critical research on informality that has focused on the diverse and dynamic relations between the formal and the informal (Centeno and Portes 2006; Sassen 1996; Portes, Castells, and Benton 1989; Roy and AlSayyad 2004).

Roy emphasizes a paradox in the literature: whereas much of the urban growth in the twenty-first century is taking place in the "developing" world, most theories of how cities function are rooted in the "developed" world (Roy 2005: 147). Because the dominant model for the production of knowledge in urban studies remains fixed within an imagination of cities of the Global North, the scholarly discipline of urban studies—embedded in a specific environment of understanding the world and producing specific forms of knowledge that are situated in the Global North—can therefore be understood as a transatlantic exchange focused on theorizing cities of North America and Europe (Robinson 2002). Although Roy reflects on the dominance of the "First World" in urban studies, she asserts that urban informality is a "mode of metropolitan urbanization" without explicitly discussing the colonial aspects of the notion of what is considered metropolitan (Roy 2005: 148).

The concept of the metropolitan in urban studies in North America implies a critical and analytical approach to urban developments in the postmodern era and addresses globalization and economic restructuring, the rescaling of higher-level state functions to local and regional levels, and pressing problems such as social injustice and segregation (Mayer 2006; Soja 2001). When illuminating the notion of the metropolitan in the dominant discourses, however, it is equally important to consider the concept within European knowledge production. Farías and Stemmler (2006) critique the European concept of the metropolis as historically rooted within a colonial geography of the world (e.g., "non-métropolitaine" for French colonies overseas versus "France métropolitaine"). Over time, the notion of the metropolis morphed into its contemporary usage as not only an advertising message in city marketing but also a normative, positive, descriptive term in urban studies. Farías and Stemmler note that "the contemporary metropolitan turn, or in other words, the inflationary use of the word *metropolis*, both in city marketing and in urban studies, is striking" (2006: 12). The present chapter attempts to reconsider the colonial continuities of the metropolis against the backdrop of processes understood as urban informality. It critically interrogates the affirmative usage in contemporary urban studies by defining informality from a postcolonial perspective as metropolitan. When conceptualizing and analyzing metropolitan informality, the dimensions of ethnicity and racialization are pivotal theoretical questions that have to be considered. Here I invoke a concept of metropolitan informality informed by postcolonial intellectuals like Homi Bhabha, who argues that

> The Western metropole must confront its postcolonial history, told by its influx of postwar migrants and refugees, as an indigenous or native narrative internal to its national identity. … Postcoloniality, for its part, is a salutary reminder of the persistent "neo-colonial" relations within the "new" world order and the multinational division of labour. (Bhabha 1994: 6)

Postcolonial studies address the interrelation of racialization and socialization in the making of modern societies. A postcolonial perspective questions the epistemological implications of scientific knowledge production and particularly addresses racialization in this process of knowledge production. The origins of postcolonial thinking lie not only in the anti-colonial and anti-imperial struggles of colonized countries in the Global South, but also in the metropolises of the Global North. A major consideration of postcolonial epistemology is the legacy of Western philosophy, including the European humanism and philosophical heritage of the Enlightenment, which enable a universalizing narrative of global history (Chakrabarty 2000). The universalism anchored in this tradition of philosophy has been deconstructed as a particular position of white,[2] male, bourgeois subjectivity. In his pathbreaking postcolonial critique in literature studies, Edward Said analyzed the canonized literature in colonial Britain, tracing the imagination of the Orient as the Other of the West and hereby coining a new term to understand colonial cultural production (Said [1978] 2003). Feminist postcolonial thinkers have challenged the male centrism in postcolonial studies, calling for critical reflection on different regimes of discrimination affecting women of color (Mohanty 1988). In particular, feminist postcolonial thinkers have pointed out the intersections between oppression and the multifaceted dimensions of different oppressive regimes, such as sexism, racism, and classism. These regimes of oppression do not operate separately; rather, they are intertwined and inscribed in history and place too.

The term *postcolonial* indicates the historical phase after the formal end of colonialism, but it also implies the political and critical production of knowledge as practice of resistance against (neo-)colonial mastery and its consequences (Castro Varela and Dhawan 2005: 24). It positions racialized subjects as the point of reference, set against universalizing Enlightenment discourses (Castro Varela, Dhawan, and Randeria 2009: 312). Analysis of spatial practices from such a postcolonial perspective aims to contest hegemonic knowledge about spatial practices by linking the representations of space to the positions of racialized subjectivities. This approach enables critical reflection about the contents and forms of representations as well as the positions from which specific spatial practices are produced.

The Daily Practice of Street Vending in the Historical Center

Street vending in Berlin was not always as marginal in urban space as recent decades' different episodes of street vending suggest. It was a common and visible feature in the city from the 1920s[3] up until shortly after World War II (Zierenberg 2008). In the years of economic growth in the 1950s and 1960s, street vending was regarded as an economy of the poor, especially war veterans; later, it almost disappeared in West German cities as years of general social prosperity allowed the integration of the poor into a fairly comprehensive German welfare system.[4] Shortly after the wall separating East and West Germany came down in 1989, however, urban street vending became a daily feature in the formerly divided city. In Berlin's historical center it reached a peak in the mid 1990s (1994/95), when Christo and Jeanne-Claude wrapped the Reichstag,[5] and when a huge market was formed in front of the Brandenburg Gate by about 150 vendors, some of whom are still operating on the street. So-called *Polen-Märkte* (Polish markets) emerged on different vacant lots in the inner city but soon were pushed from one area to another (Weber 2002). Entrepreneurial activities blossomed, for a short time transforming the public space into huge informal markets because currency rates between the two German states[6] and Poland were good for business[7] (Gnauck 2009). Ambiguous regulation of police powers diminished the local police's authority, and urban space came to be commonly used for semi-legal practices. The practice of street vending expanded rapidly, becoming a daily feature and turning the imaginations of a modern city upside down.

Street vending in Berlin is regulated along two lines. The first concerns the process of licensing and approval, and issuance of the permits needed to conduct a formally acknowledged street vending business. In 1998, the local administration passed a tiny but far-reaching amendment to the Executive Code (*Ausführungsvorschrift*) of the Street Law of Berlin (*Berliner Straßengesetz*),[8] introducing the so-called *Negativkatalog*, a list of streets declared no-vending areas. This new policy has essentially banned street vendors, whose interests were seen as opposed to national and local interests, from almost every street in the historical center by forbidding peddling and hawking there (N. K. Ha 2009: 79ff.).

The second line of regulation applies to vending practices and modes of operating while selling on the streets, particularly hygienic standards for selling foods. Sale of items on streets and squares is limited to selling from a portable tray that must be raised off the ground while vending (*Bauchladenhandel*). This regulation has spawned a variety of new human-machine complexes such as vendors wearing cooking grills around their bodies, as well as deviant selling from a standing tray with the inevitable hide-and-seek between local authorities and the vendors. Vendors who install or rest a tray on public ground violate this rule, and local authorities frequently enforce it and regularly fine violators. This particular guideline puts great stress on the vendors in their daily practice, who must choose between selling from a standing tray on the ground and thus having to evade the authorities, or complying with a regulation that forces vendors to carry a heavy weight on their shoulders when engaging in street selling. Either way, this rule is incompatible with contemporary selling practices and products, which differ from those of former times, when stamps and cigarettes made up the bulk of the street vending commerce.

Sellers of souvenirs, jewelry, hats, and snacks cater mostly to tourists. Such vending takes place in a few spots at Alexanderplatz, near the Berliner Dom and Checkpoint Charlie, and on the bridge close to the Museumsinsel—that is, at the margins of the no-vending area defined by the amendment of the executive code. The regulation divides the vendors into two main groups according to their wares: food vendors and sellers of souvenirs, hats, jewelry, sunglasses, and other items. The vendors operate on a daily basis and produce a spatial practice. Other practices, like the selling of homemade souvenirs, handicraft jewelry, balloons, and art, can be observed at random but are more prevalent on weekends, when vendors sell such items for additional income or to experiment with new sales ideas.

Food vending is precisely regulated and limited to two items—pretzels and sausages.[9] (Different regulations apply to selling ice cream, the only item that can be sold out of a vehicle while vending in public space[10] or from a bike in the parks.) Competition between the sausage sellers is intense because good locations are few, owing to the containment of street vending and the vying among different companies in the field. Sausage sellers are organized in companies with their own logos, colors, and names. As pushcarts are not allowed for street vending, the company lends portable grills to vendors, who operate in teams of two at their spot. These grills weigh about twenty kilograms (forty-four pounds) and may not be placed on the ground. The company also tracks the profitability of the various vending spots and consults food vendors about their business. The vendors themselves must obtain personal permits and work together in a team: one grills the sausages while the other brings buckets of bread and sausages and attends to other supplies; then, after two hours, they switch positions because of the grill's heavy weight.

The main anxiety faced by people of color who sell souvenirs and jewelry concerns the likelihood of being fined, even though they all obtain and carry official papers and permits. Like food vending, the practice of street vending is subject to policing that enforces the holding of trays off the ground and penalizes violations like putting down the tray. Souvenir and jewelry vendors respond to this specific control in different ways. One way is to follow the regulation, which means holding the tray all day long. Vending trays are typically very heavy (from 15 kg/33 pounds up to 25 kg/55 pounds) and cumbersome, and a day of work is at least four hours and up to eight or more hours long. Compliance with this regulation is hindered not only by the physical load but also by the way it impairs communication between vendor and customer. For example, vendors wearing the heavy tray have difficulty handling the items being shown and offered. Deviant practices therefore rely on permanent observation of the surroundings to avoid getting a ticket while the tray is standing on the ground. Some vendors alert each other via mobile phone when control personnel approach, holding the tray for some time or covering it with a sheet to signal the closure of the business for a while. Folding chairs are rarely seen on the streets, as such practices as sitting and "parking the tray" have been increasingly policed in the past years.

Some of the people I talked to had worked as street vendors since before or right after reunification. To this day, vendors who share origins in Pakistan or Turkey work next to each other at specific spots and help each other during their daily routine, sharing food and beverages, looking after trays, and watching out for police, for example. Vendors who speak the same language, mostly Urdu or Turkish, tend to stay close to one another and form cooperative working relations. Cooperation across communities is not directly preferred, but street vendors respect each other's vending spots and share the scarce available public space. Considering the different regulations attached to street vending, the practice is also economically precarious, prone to insecurities stemming from lack of income generation at times of illness or inability to work, harshly regulated working conditions, and exposure to changing weather conditions. Moreover, street vending has become a very narrow, highly regulated path of self-employment, as practices other than vending from a portable tray are criminalized. The Street Law of Berlin—the legal basis of the rules and penalties applicable to street vending—generates exhausting working conditions harmful to the body and frustrating for the people concerned.

Street Vendors Experiencing Racialization

Food vendors are generally men and mostly white Germans, whereas jewelry and souvenir sellers are mostly men and some women of color. The clerk at the municipal department of streets and parks confirmed this observation when he stated, "Germans apply for permits to sell sausages and foreigners for souvenirs and jewelry" (Interview, 19 March 2010). This racialized division of street vending practices hints at inequality of opportunity among the different groups participating in the urban economy.

Based on ethnographic data collected in 2008, 2009, and 2010 via unstructured interviews and participant observation conducted with about twenty different street vendors at various spots within the historical district, the present study applies the concept of *quiet encroachment* to the specific case of post-unification Berlin. Most of the vendors I talked to are men of color who immigrated to Germany from Pakistan or Turkey. They perceived my own position as that of a paid researcher and woman of color. Our different positions enabled some connections and disabled others. Within the process of research, we inhabited positions of privilege and disadvantage shaped by various cultural, economic, and social capital (Bourdieu 1983). Having or lacking these sorts of capital came into play during the process of building trust and sharing information.

The souvenir and jewelry vendors distinguish themselves as the ones with "black hair" (*Schwarzhaare*) who are perceived not as German citizens but as "foreigners" (*Ausländer*), even though some of them hold German citizenship. The public rhetoric and debate of migration and integration in Germany very much concerns questions of assimilation, integration, and conformance of "Others" who are not German or German-looking. Therefore these debates lead to the ethnification and racialization of those considered "foreigners," "guest workers," and nowadays "persons with a background of migration." After reunification in 1989, the cultural climate was dominated by celebration of the German nation (*Volk*), a development that migrant communities observed with suspicion because they were treated as foreigners and lacked access to German citizenship, despite having borne and raised their children in German society.[11] Following reunification, migrants were hit hard by the structural transformation of German society as large industrial sectors fell away in the cities and labor regulations preferred German and EU citizens in new jobs. The growth of unemployment and precarious work is particularly pronounced amongst migrants (OECD 2005: 35ff.).

For the most part, racism in Germany is perceived as being located at the margins of German society. Efforts to counter it are focused on the violence of the extreme right, and it is seldom analyzed in terms of its structural and institutional heritage and legacy (Osterkamp 1997; Terkessidis 2010: 88ff.).[12] In view of Germany's history and the Holocaust, racism and anti-Semitism are officially ostracized and banished to the past. Therefore, the story of migration and discrimination against migrants has been analyzed and covered in terms of xenophobia (*Fremdenfeindlichkeit*) and hostility towards foreigners (*Ausländerfeindlichkeit*) rather than considered as modified contemporary racism. But Black Germans and "Othered" Germans tell a very different story about continuities in racist practices in German society and culture (Oguntoye, Ayim/Opitz, and Schultz 1986; Mecheril 1994). In his book *Interkultur* (2010), Mark Terkessidis addresses the call to sensitize German society by trying to develop an intercultural "literacy" program for Germany as an immigration-receiving country. Terkessidis defends his program by asserting that structural racism is still very much a part of German society, especially as it translates into debates of migration and integration. Further, he sees his program as especially important in the context of cities (2010: 16): for migrants, cities are sites of contestation, representation, and the possibility of survival, so urban development entails precisely these questions of inclusion and exclusion.

Speaking about the prejudice of the local authorities on patrol, one souvenir vendor of color complained, "that all street vendors are foreigners, this is not true—look—the sausage seller and the balloon seller and the pretzel seller, they are all German. This is quite a simplification!"[13] (Interview, Rahul, 9 May 2009). This impression results from the frequent controls by local authorities and the vendors' own comparing of daily observations during business time on the street. Another vendor maintained that a German woman who sold sausages without a permit had never had any problems with the police or others from the municipal public order office (Interview Mohamed, 27 May 2009). He offered this observation as proof of different levels of contact between various groups of vendors on one hand and the police and municipal authorities on the other.

The frequent controls imposed not only by the police but also by the municipal public order office are particularly stressful and frustrating for Berlin's vendors of color. These encounters are largely perceived as personal attacks against the vendors and their right to work. The vendors understand that setting a tray down is not allowed and that by doing so they are taking advantage of a deviant practice. But against the backdrop of a dearth of alternatives, such as a job in the formal labor market or the option to receive welfare benefits instead of working, this labor is a legitimate income-generating practice. Furthermore, as Aman stated, "one feels like a criminal, despite not having committed a crime" (Interview, Aman, 4 June 2010),[14] so the vendors do not regard their entrepreneurship as illegitimate. The contradiction between the city's enforced criminalization of street vending practices and the vendors' own right to work is regularly manifest, as controls are carried out several times a week.

The experience of becoming a subject of delinquency heightens feelings of powerlessness and anger. Especially after severe flooding in Pakistan in the summer of 2010, the vendors expressed outrage: "Our country is under water and we want to work, we want to support, but we are not allowed—they are pigs!"[15] (Interview, Amir, 30 August 2010). This anger was expressed after the police had requested that vendors seen with their trays standing on the ground close down their business. These confrontations contribute to the adverse perceptions of local authorities among the vendors, who constantly confront the unequal relationship between themselves and the police. Rahul, for example, reflecting on the relationship and the police's lack of understanding about their work, working conditions, and backgrounds, suggested that "the police should do a practical training on the street. They have their position above and have clean toilets and everything is dry. And the more tickets are issued the better is the chance to improve their careers. But we are the little poor men who finance their careers"[16] (Interview, Rahul, 9 May 2009).

Resisting the Confinement: Quietly Encroaching on Public Space

How can the politics of the vendors understood in such a space of daily territorial contestation? Asaf Bayat (2004), in his inspiring piece on the "politics of the informals in the Global South," argues that the new global restructuring reproduces subjectivity, social spaces, and a new terrain for political struggle that current theoretical perspectives cannot account for, and thus proposes an alternative outlook. In contrast to binary conceptualizations of the poor as either revolutionary or passive subjects (2004: 83), he offers the concept of the "quiet encroachment of the ordinary," which "describes the silent, protracted, but pervasive advancement of ordinary people in relation to the propertied and powerful in order to survive and improve their lives" (90). He discusses similar activities in industrialized countries that, albeit limited and confronted by restrictive states, are better equipped to regulate such practices with ideological, technological, and institutional tools (95). Although Bayat develops his thoughts about the "politics of informals" for the Global South, his theoretical claims can well be applied to the Berlin case. Bayat points out that as long as broader society fails to integrate the "ordinary," identified here as male vendors of color, the vendors' practices can be seen as "quiet encroachment." In his analysis of the daily practices of the informals, he distinguishes their resistance as a survival strategy from their own politics of self-organization and self-representation, arguing that "the poor struggle not only for survival, they strive in a life-long process to improve their lot through often individualistic and quiet encroachment on the public goods and the property of elite groups" (Bayat 2000: 553). Through this differentiation, he avoids essentializing the politics of the informals, referring to an important article in which Janice Perlman developed her critique of marginality (Perlman 1975), and concludes that the "marginalized poor were, in fact, a product of capitalist social structure" (Bayat 2004: 83).

The daily practices of vendors of color are mostly based on deviant practices, direct negotiations with local authorities, and collective communication, rather than on political action to alter their situation. Although Bayat developed the concept of quiet encroachment in reference to practices in the so-called developing world, his analytical approach is relevant to the case in question and to souvenir and jewelry vendors of color in particular. Moreover, I regard quiet encroachment as a postcolonial practice of the vendors and refer here to the continued encounter between white people furnished with power and poor persons of color who are denied access to cultural, economic, and social capital. This encounter takes place in a social and cultural environment where public space is constructed as a clean, safe space dedicated to traffic uses or consumption practices, but not as a space for micro-business opportunities. Simultaneously, however, the practice of food vending as described above has developed into a professionalized technique of selling adjusted to local regulations. I consider the practice of food vending in Berlin to be one of quiet encroachment by the somewhat better equipped. In the street vending business, food vending remains a highly contested economic niche in which some companies profit from the stringent regulations. However, as vendors of color must contend with the social reality of having very little access to formal labor markets, forms of low-level self-employment opportunities, though very rare, are important.

Street Vending as Berlin Becomes the German Capital

In the early days following reunification, a coalition of architects, urban planners, urban sociologists, and urban development administrators debated new urban forms to represent Berlin's new role in the global landscape after the end of the Cold War. Just after reunification in 1989, parliament voted to make Berlin the capital of the Federal Republic of Germany. Formerly, (East) Berlin[17] had been the capital of the German Democratic Republic, while Bonn was the seat of government in the Federal Republic.[18] Against the backdrop of the historical reunification, the city's architectural and urban design was negotiated in architecture competitions and peer-reviewed processes, and the urbanists' visions were circulated in the local media and displayed in exhibitions (Binder 2009: 130ff.).

The former district of Mitte[19] gained importance as a symbol of the new center of a reunified nation. This area contains many prominent historical buildings of neoclassic design, as well as many institutions of government and high culture, and is also a site of many of the ruptures that came to characterize Berlin's urban form due to competing urban planning ideologies in the two Germanys. The Palace of the Republic, the seat of parliament of the former GDR, was located here and torn down after reunification. In the year 2007 the national parliament has voted to rebuild the castle of Berlin on this site and since 2014 a castle is build as "Humboldtforum", though this topic remains hotly debated among urban scholars and the people of Berlin. Further urban developments in this district, which has a pivotal role in representing the nation, were disclosed in the 1999 *Planwerk Innenstadt,* the plan for the inner city.

Both this plan and its implementation were discursively negotiated through the hegemonic narrative of the European City. Architects, urban planners, and the urban development administration generated a discourse and image of the European City with theoretical underpinnings in urban sociology. In her essay "The Cultural Production of Locality: Reclaiming the 'European City' in Post-Wall Berlin," Virag Molnar describes the process of defining the European City as "the constant mixing of empirical reality, conceptual constructions and normative representations" (Molnar 2010: 285). The urban narrative of the European City correlated with bourgeois imaginations of a specific urban form in Wilhelminian style and thereby made strong historical reference to the period of "promoterism" (*Gründerzeit*) that shaped German and Austrian cities at the turn of the twentieth century in particular. The reference to a supranational identity and a historical era prior to the World Wars situates this image of the future in the past, before the era of the Nazi regime and the later competition between two Germanys. The appeal to this history constructed a bourgeois identity that enabled a leveling of differences in the German cultural self-conception.

In the era of globalizing economies and lifestyles, this image was carefully contrasted to the "American City" (Häußermann and Siebel 1987;

Häußermann, Läpple, and Siebel 2008; Siebel 2006), depicted as a commodified city lacking public space due to an urban infrastructure of individual traffic, suburban living, and shopping malls. Public space in the European City, however, was conceptualized as a location for a diversity of people and the unfolding of public life on the streets and in the squares (Molnar 2010: 287). Here public space was associated with "the ideal of the bourgeois public," promoted as representing democracy and benefiting integration in a society that respects differences (Siebel 2006: 15). Public space became an important feature in planning the new area housing government and parliament in Berlin. On the one hand, the area is designed as a walkable space, particularly with an eye to tourism. On the other hand, it serves as a stage for the reunified nation (Vaz et al. 2006). Meanwhile, the overarching discourse on public space in the European City relies on a rhetoric of encounter and leisure, whereby the regulatory regime imposed on street vending dramatically confines the spatial territory for such practices in public space.

The Marginalization of Street Vending in the German Capital

The aim of this chapter has been to discuss racialization as an untold, (in)visible notion within urban development policies. Those who engineered the transformation of Berlin after the fall of the Wall aimed not only to adopt and adapt to neoliberal processes of globalization but also to formulate Berlin's new role as the capital of reunified Germany. In the aftermath of reunification, this transformation induced a paradigmatic shift in the regulation of the use of public space. Vendors conducting business in a public space where high-end consumerism, leisure, and tourism shape the image of the neoliberal city must navigate daily challenges. Today, the few vendors still operating in public space contest the cultural representation of the European City, which regards them as disturbing and out-of-place. Therefore I argue that the representation of the European City reproduces a bourgeois imaginary of the urban and leads to the prohibition of specific practices in public space.

The cultural representation of the future urban form was legitimized as a "democratic" locality in the invented tradition of the European City. The broader discourse on modernity and urbanity, portrayed in particular as "European," poses the question of why street vending is perceived as an immigrant economy of "Others" incompatible with a modern image of the city. The construction of the European City reproduces hegemonic ideals of space and place and applies not only to urban planning but also to the careful selection of allowed and forbidden uses of urban space. It therefore deepens social difference in Berlin's urban geography by depicting discrimination in economic opportunity as an incidental byproduct.

The case of street vending in Berlin exemplifies how the cultural practice of urban planning and regulation is complicit in amplifying structural discrimination and neglecting the challenge to produce cities of equity and shared commons. The details of the regulatory regimen show the contradictions of an economic practice assumed to be "informal" and illustrate how the assiduous regulation of street vending in Berlin leads to precarious working conditions. Though street vending as such does not raise the question of origin and migration, street vending as an urban practice calls for economic participation and provides people with low-capital business opportunities. Therefore, the harsh regulation of low-capital businesses mainly targets those who are socially marginalized due to structural discrimination, and particularly affects communities of color. Reducing spatial access to economic opportunity at the low-capital level applies a criminalizing logic to urban poverty and perpetuates the society's racial division of labor and wealth. Against this backdrop, the spatial practice of street vending contests hegemonic notions of bourgeois public space and quietly encroaches on public goods for the needs of the ordinary, analyzed here as metropolitan informality. Processes of racialization need to be rendered visible in their historical continuity, for they underpin the location and dislocation of people in urban geography based on categories of race, gender, and class. The specific spatialized and racialized form of urban discrimination is fundamental to the issue of social justice and action against discrimination in the city.

Noa Ha holds a PhD in Architecture from Technical University Berlin and is currently a postdoctoral researcher at the Center for Metropolitan Studies, Technical University Berlin. Her research interrogates the production of space from a feminist, de-colonial, critical race theory perspective and was funded by the Rosa-Luxemburg-Foundation and the Technical University Berlin. Currently she is conducting a study on the spatial production of Asian diasporas in European cities.

Notes

1. Here I use the term people of color—which has been introduced to the German context and adapted—to address experience of racialization and racist exclusion. It is used to discuss alliances between groups targeted for racist discrimination and to strengthen strategies of self-representation (K. N. Ha, Lauré al-Samarai, and Mysoreka 2007: 37). Referring to vendors as people of

color reflects an understanding of the history of migration to Germany as involving not just movement and integration but also structural racial discrimination in labor markets and institutions.
2. The term *white* refers to the political and social construction of *whiteness*. Critical whiteness studies scrutinize the construction of the unmarked "self," regarded as "normal." Critical whiteness studies, developed in Anglophone sciences since the 1990s, have entered into debates in Germany as well (Eggers et al. 2005).
3. See the writings of Erich Kästner and Alfred Döblin, with their descriptions of daily life in 1930s, which provide insight to the vibrant presence of street vending (Döblin 1929; Kästner 1931). Further evidence can be found in 1933 administrative handbook "Der Straßenhandel in Berlin und seine gesetzliche Regelung" (Viseur 1935).
4. For a "renewed discussion" on poverty after the 1960s, see also Leibfried and Tennstedt (1985: 14ff).
5. Interview with German street vendor who operated from 1993 until 1998 in front of the Brandenburger Tor, 28 May 2009.
6. The currency union of the former East and West Germany came into force on 1 July 1990.
7. „Polenmarkt verboten", DIE ZEIT, 30. Juni 1989.
8. The *Berliner Straßengesetz* (BerlStrG) has been in effect since after 28 February 1998 and renewed 13 July 1999.
9. In 2010, two young men attempted to obtain a permit to sell sandwiches at Alexanderplatz. Although the administration signaled its intent to issue the permit, the young men were informed just before launching their business that sandwich sales would not be allowed at Alexanderplatz. The launch of this business was documented and followed by the TV series *Plan B — Ich werde selbstständig* (*Plan B – I start my own business,* translation by the author). As the municipal administration explained to me, the regulations limit the sale of food to two items to prevent the growth of food vending under a more or less informal agreement within the administration (Interview at Municipal Street and Parks Department, 19 March 2010).
10. Food truck vending has become a feature of the urban economy, offering new variations of food vending; however, these trucks operate only on private territory. Food vending from a truck on public territory is allowed only for the selling of ice cream or at farmer's markets.
11. In 2000, the citizenship law was revised: whereas citizenship previously was based solely on blood and German origin, the law now acknowledges immigrants as residents and potential citizens. This reformulation of the citizenship law opened up a new discussion of integration policies and particularly language courses, an aspect that had been neglected in preceding years, when migrants, thought of as "guests," were not perceived as either immigrants or rightful citizens.
12. The report of the European Commission against Racism and Intolerance (ECRI Secretariat 2009) details discrimination in various fields, especially housing, education, and employment. The ECRI emphasizes the structural

discrimination faced by immigrants in Germany and critically reviews their opportunities for access and participation. Reviewing the politics of gaining equality, the ECRI discovered, and not for the first time, serious failures: "ECRI strongly recommends that, as part of their ongoing efforts towards creating a workplace free of racism, the German authorities launch an awareness-raising campaign aimed specifically at changing employers' attitudes towards persons with an immigrant background" (2009: 23). In particular, the ECRI recommendations address the high barriers that cultural, religious, and/or ethnic differences pose to access to the labor market, calling for an active anti-discrimination policy. The ECRI report demonstrates the urgent need for increased awareness of racist discrimination within German society.
13. "Und es gibt dieses Vorurteil, dass die Straßenhändler alle Migranten wären, aber das stimmt gar nicht, denn die Grillwalker und Luftballonverkäufer und der Brezelverkäufer, das sind alles Deutsche. Das ist doch eine Reduzierung."
14. "Man fühlt sich wie ein Krimineller, obwohl man eigentlich nichts verbrochen hat."
15. "Unser Land steht unter Wasser und wir wollen hier arbeiten, wir wollen unterstützen, aber wir dürfen nicht — das sind doch Schweine."
16. "Ach, die Polizei soll doch mal ein Praktikum auf der Straße machen, sie sind da oben und hätten ihre saubere Toilette und alles ist trocken. Und je mehr Bußgelder sie verteilen, desto besser würden sie aufsteigen. Und es sind wir die kleinen armen Männer, die deren Karrieren finanzieren."
17. East Germans referred to their capital city as "Berlin," thereby neglecting its division into East Berlin and West Berlin.
18. In all the years of the division, the West German government carefully avoided claiming Bonn as its capital, regarding it instead as a temporary seat of government.
19. As of 2001, the former twenty-three districts were newly composed into twelve districts, some of them renamed. The former district of Mitte was fused with the two former districts of Wedding and Tiergarten to become one of two districts straddling the former border between East and West Berlin, the other being Friedrichshain-Kreuzberg.

Bibliography

Altvater, Elmar, and Birgit Mahnkopf. 2002. *Globalisierung der Unsicherheit: Arbeit im Schatten, schmutziges Geld und informelle Politik*. Münster: Westfälisches Dampfboot.
Anjaria, Jonathan Shapiro. 2006. "Street Hawkers and Public Space in Mumbai." *Economic and Political Weekly* 41 (21): 2140–2146.
Bayat, Asef. 2000. "From Dangerous Classes to Quiet Rebels: Politics of the Urban Subaltern in the Global South." *International Sociology* 15 (3): 533–557.
———. 2004. "Globalization and the Politics of the Informals in the Global South." In *Urban Informality*, ed. Ananya Roy and Nezar AlSayyad. Lanham, MD: Lexington Books.

Berliner Straßengesetz (BerlStrG), 13 July 1999. Berlin: Senatsverwaltung für Stadtentwicklung und Umwelt
Bhabha, Homi K. 1994. *The Location of Culture*. London and New York: Routledge.
Binder, Beate. 2009. *Streitfall Stadtmitte: historische Erzählungen, geschichtspolitische Interventionen und die Produktion von Lokalität; stadtethnologische Perspektiven auf ein Berliner Konfliktfeld*. Cologne and Weimar: Böhlau Verlag.
Blanchflower, David G. 2000. "Self-Employment in OECD Countries." *Labour Economics* 7 (5): 471–505.
Bourdieu, Pierre. 1983. "Ökonomisches, kulturelles und soziales Kapital," trans. Reinhard Kreckel. In *Soziale Ungleichheiten*, ed. Reinhard Kreckel. Göttingen: Schwartz: 183–198.
Bromley, Ray. 2000. "Street Vending and Public Policy: A Global Review." *International Journal of Sociology and Social Policy* 20 (1/2): 1–28.
Bromley, Rosemary D. F., and Peter K. Mackie. 2009. "Displacement and the New Spaces for Informal Trade in the Latin American City Centre." *Urban Studies* 46 (7): 1485–1506.
Butterwegge, Christoph, Bettina Lösch, and Ralf Ptak. 2008. *Kritik des Neoliberalismus*. Wiesbaden: VS Verlag.
Castro Varela, María do Mar. 2005. "Prekarität für alle?! Zur differentiellen symbolischen und faktischen Deklassierung von „Migrantinnen." Eine transnationale Perspektive." *ZtG Bulletin* 29/30: 90–102.
Castro Varela, María do Mar, and Nikita Dhawan. 2005. *Postkoloniale Theorie: eine kritische Einführung*. Bielefeld: Transcript-Verlag.
Castro Varela, María do Mar, Nikita Dhawan, and Shalini Randeria. 2009. "Postkoloniale Theorie." In *Raumwissenschaften*, ed. Stephan Günzel. Frankfurt a. M.: Suhrkamp.: 308-323.
Centeno, Miguel Angel, and Alejandro Portes. 2006. "The Informal Economy in the Shadow of the State." In *Out of the Shadows: Political Action and the Informal Economy in Latin America*, ed. Patricia Fernández-Kelly. University Park: Pennsylvania State University Press.
Chakrabarty, Dipesh. 2008. *Provincializing Europe: Postcolonial Thought and Historical Difference*. Princeton, NJ, and Oxford: Princeton University Press.
Crenshaw, Kimberlé. 1991. "Mapping the Margins: Intersectionality, Identity Politics, and Violence against Women of Color." *Stanford Law Review* 43 (6): 1241–1299.
Cross, John C., and Marina Karides. 2007. "Capitalism, Modernity, and the 'Appropriate' Use of Space." In *Street Entrepreneurs: People, Place and Politics in Local and Global Perspective*, ed. John Cross and Alfonso Morales. London and New York: Routledge.
Crossa, Veronica. 2009. "Resisting the Entrepreneurial City: Street Vendors' Struggle in Mexico City's Historic Center." *International Journal of Urban and Regional Research* 33 (1): 43–63.
Döblin, Alfred. 1929. *Berlin Alexanderplatz: Die Geschichte vom Franz Biberkopf. Novel*. Frankfurt a. M.: S. Fischer.
Donovan, Michael G. 2008. "Informal Cities and the Contestation of Public Space: The Case of Bogota's Street Vendors, 1988–2003." *Urban Studies* 45 (1): 29–51.

ECRI Secretariat. 2009. *ECRI Report on Germany, European Commission against Racism and Intolerance, ECRI Secretariat Directorate General of Human Rights and Legal Affairs Council of Europe.* http://www.institut-fuer-menschenrechte.de/de/menschenrechtsinstrumente/europarat/europaeische-kommission-gegen-rassismus-und-intoleranz-ecri.html.

Eggers, Maisha M., Grada Kilomba, Peggy Piesche, and Susan Arndt, eds. 2005. *Mythen, Masken und Subjekte.* Münster: Unrast Verlag.

Farías, Ignacio, and Susanne Stemmler. 2006. "Deconstructing 'Metropolis': Critical Reflections on a European Concept." *CMS Working Paper Series,* No. 004-2006.

Gnauck, Gerhard. 2009."Geschichte: So bezwangen Polen die Berliner Mauer." Berlin: *Welt Online,* 4. May.

Ha, Kien Nghi, Nicola Lauré al-Samarai, and Sheila Mysoreka, eds. 2007. *re/visionen — Postkoloniale Perspektiven von People of Color auf Rassismus, Kulturpolitik und Widerstand in Deutschland.* Münster: Unrast Verlag.

Ha, Noa K. 2009. *Informeller Straßenhandel in Berlin: Urbane Raumproduktion zwischen Störung und Attraktion.* Berlin: wvb Wissenschaftlicher Verlag Berlin.

Hart, Keith. 1973. "Informal Economy Opportunities and Urban Employment in Ghana." *Journal of Modern Africa Studies* 11 (1): 61–89.

Harvey, David. 2006. *Spaces of Global Capitalism: Towards a Theory of Uneven Geographical Development.* London: Verso.

Häußermann, Hartmut, Dieter Läpple, and Walter Siebel. 2008. *Stadtpolitik.* Frankfurt: Suhrkamp.

Häußermann, Hartmut, and Walter Siebel. 1987. *Neue Urbanität.* Frankfurt: Suhrkamp.

Jütting, Johannes, and Juan R. de Laiglesia. 2009. "Is Informal Normal? Towards More and Better Jobs in Developing Countries." Paris: OECD Publishing.

Kästner, Erich. 1931. *Pünktchen und Anton. Novel.* Hamburg: Atrium Verlag.

Leibfried, Stephan, and Florian Tennstedt. 1985. *Politik der Armut und die Spaltung des Sozialstaats.* Frankfurt a. M.: Suhrkamp.

Lewed, Karl-Heinz. 2005. "Ausschluss und Zwang – Migration, Rassismus und prekäre Arbeitsverhältnisse." *LabourNet.de Germany.* http://labournet.de/diskussion/arbeit/realpolitik/prekaer/karlheinz.html.

Mayer, Margit. 2006. "Metropolitan Research in Transatlantic Perspective." *CMS Working Paper Series,* No. 002-2006.

———. 2007. "Contesting the Neoliberalization of Urban Governance." In *Contesting Neoliberalism: Urban Frontiers,* ed. Helga Leitner, Jamie Peck, and Eric S. Sheppard. New York: Guilford Press.

Mecheril, Paul. 1994. *Andere Deutsche.* Berlin: Dietz.

Mohanty, Chandra Talpade. 1988. "Under Western Eyes: Feminist Scholarship and Colonial Discourses." *Feminist Review* 30: 61–88.

Molnar, Virag. 2010. "The Cultural Production of Locality: Reclaiming the 'European City' in Post-Wall Berlin." *International Journal of Urban and Regional Research* 34 (2): 281–309.

OECD. 2005. *Die Arbeitsmarktintegration von Zuwanderern in Deutschland—The Labour Market Integration of Immigrants in Germany.* Berlin: OECD Publishing.

Oguntoye, Katharina, May Ayim/Opitz, and Dagmar Schultz, eds. 1986. *Farbe bekennen: Afro-deutsche Frauen auf den Spuren ihrer Geschichte*. Berlin: Orlanda Frauenverlag.

Osterkamp, Ute. 1997. "Institutioneller Rassismus. Problematik und Perspektiven." In *Psychologie und Rassismus*, ed. Paul Mecheril and Teo Thomas. Reinbek bei Hamburg: Rowohlt.

Perlman, Janice E. 1975. "Rio's Favelas and the Myth of Marginality." *Politics & Society* 5 (2): 131–160.

Portes, Alejandro, Manuel Castells, and Lauren A. Benton, eds. 1989. *The Informal Economy: Studies in Advanced and Less Developed Countries*. Baltimore, MD: John Hopkins University Press.

Rakowski, Cathy. 1994. *Contrapunto: The Informal Sector Debate in Latin America*. Albany: State University of New York Press.

Robinson, Jennifer. 2002. "Global and World Cities: A View from Off the Map." *International Journal of Urban and Regional Research* 26 (3): 531–554.

Roy, Ananya. 2005. "Urban Informality: Toward an Epistemology of Planning." *Journal of the American Planning Association* 71 (2): 147–158.

Roy, Ananya, and Nezar AlSayyad, eds. 2004. *Urban Informality: Transnational Perspectives from the Middle East, Latin America, and South Asia*. Lanham, MD: Lexington Books.

Said, Edward W. (1978) 2003. *Orientalism*. London: Penguin Books.

Sassen, Saskia. 1996. "Rebuilding the Global City: Economy, Capital and Culture in the 21st Century Metropolis." In *Re-presenting the City: Ethnicity, Capital, and Culture in the 21st-century Metropolis*, ed. Anthony D. King. Houndmills: Palgrave Macmillan.

———. 2005. "Fragmented Urban Topographies and their Underlying Interconnections." In *Informal City. Caracas Case: Urban Think Tank*, ed. Alfredo Brillembourg and Kristin Feireiss. Munich: Prestel.

Siebel, Walter. 2006. *Die europäische Stadt*. Frankfurt a. M.: Suhrkamp.

Soja, Edward W. 2001. *Postmetropolis: Critical Studies of Cities and Regions*. Oxford: Blackwell.

Terkessidis, Mark. 2010. *Interkultur*. Berlin: Suhrkamp.

Vaz, Lilian Fessler, et al., eds. 2006. *Der öffentliche Raum in der Planungspolitik: Studien aus Rio de Janeiro und Berlin*. Weimar: Verlag der Bauhaus-Universität.

Viseur, Max le. 1935. *Der Straßenhandel in Berlin und seine gesetzliche Regelung*. Berlin: Industrie- und Handelskammer.

Weber, Ursula. 2002. *Der Polenmarkt in Berlin*. Neuried: Ars Una.

Winker, Gabriele, and Nina Degele. 2009. *Intersektionalität: zur Analyse sozialer Ungleichheiten*. Bielefeld: Transcript.

Zierenberg, Malte. 2008. *Stadt der Schieber: Der Berliner Schwarzmarkt 1939–1950*. Kritische Studien zur Geschichtswissenschaft BD. 179. Göttingen: Vandenhoeck & Ruprecht.

CHAPTER 5

Selling Memory and Nostalgia in the Barrio
Mexican and Central American Women (Re)Create Street Vending Spaces in Los Angeles

Lorena Muñoz

> I still vividly remember the smell of *comida típica* [traditional foods] sold by the street vendors in my small town of Rosario, Sinaloa ... not only did the vendors sell food but candy, that was my favorite. ... My mother used to take us to the plaza on Sundays, we went right after Sunday mass. ... The smell of *tamarindo* [tamarind] takes me back to my childhood, where our Sunday treat was not only to buy food from the vendors but also listen to live music, play with our friends and occasionally get a new or used toy from the toy vendor.[1]
> —Milagro (a Mexican street vendor)

Sidewalks, predominantly those in immigrant neighborhoods in Los Angeles, are where immigrants actively (re)produce street vending landscapes from "back home." Food vendors in particular sell "typical" foods from their own cultures, each invoking memories of home for purveyors and consumers alike. Furthermore, the vendors bring common law expectations with them: Latino immigrants typically claim special rights in their vending areas, a process that further shapes the way that street vending (re)creates culture.[2]

Milagro, a Mexican-born street vendor, makes her living selling traditional Mexican food in Los Angeles. She immigrated to the United States from Mexico in 1996, shortly after her mother passed away. The journey was her own, but she followed a route first traveled by her brothers a couple of years prior. These men made their move during the 1994 economic crisis that devaluated the peso. With political instability rife and President Carlos Salinas de Gortari's power waning, the Zapatista Army of National Liberation warred against the oppressive Mexican government.[3] These factors cost Milagro's brothers their jobs in the tourist city of Mazatlan and, ultimately, their homes. At first they returned home to neighboring Rosario to find work, but after these attempts failed they decided to cross the U.S.-Mexico border to Los Angeles and so far have not returned. Not long after, Milagro, her sisters-in-law, and her two nephews made their way as well. The family reunited early in 1997 and moved into a three-bedroom house in an immigrant community at the southern end of the Garment District. While her brothers secured stable employment in a pseudo-pharmaceutical company that makes vitamins and other health products in Southeast Los Angeles, Milagro worked first as a domestic and then as a janitor before becoming a street vendor. Despite being communicative and animated in general, she describes the domestic work she did as "solitary" and "depressing." In contrast, she is excited about street vending, saying that, for her, it is a very good fit:

> I talk a lot. If I am working alone, I get depressed. I am not happy if I cannot talk to people; I will talk to anyone. My mother used to say that I had no shame; I can walk up to anybody and start a conversation ... well, they have to speak Spanish [laughs]; well, even in English I try.[4]

As one of the estimated ten thousand vendors operating on the streets of Los Angeles on any given day (Hamilton and Chinchilla 2001), she cites her flexible hours, networking opportunities, ability to care for children, and proximity to family (i.e., her sisters-in-law) as reasons she prefers vending to low-wage employment in the service sector. Milagro recalls, "I grew up with street vendors, it is a part of my home-town's life ... when I make tamarind water, it brings memories of my town, my mother and childhood."[5] Although Milagro did not work as a street vendor in Mexico, she states that when she was growing up, street vendors became part of her happy childhood memories. For Milagro, buying from street vendors in the park after church on Sundays was a treat.

This essay qualitatively explores the ways in which immigrants, Latinas(os) in particular, re-create their home-culture street vending practices. I also examine the role of nostalgia, a factor that influences both vending practices and consumer tastes, in turn transforming Latino urban neighborhoods in Los Angeles. The data in this research are sourced from participant observation, interviews, photo-documentation, and photo-elicitation conducted from 2003 to 2007 within two predominantly Latino neighborhoods in Los Angeles. I myself am a U.S. citizen raised in Mexico and thus share a language, experience, and culture with the interview participants, so reflexivity, positionality, and situated knowledge also informed the fieldwork (Gilbert 1994; McDowell 1992; Katz 1994; Rose 1997). Over the course of the study, sixty vendors were interviewed—thirty at each site—as were ten state agents (code enforcers, police, and city employees) and six business owners.

"Placing" Immigrant Labor in Los Angeles

Not unlike Milagro, the thousands of immigrants arriving in Los Angeles in the 1990s found themselves amidst the global economic phenomena driving the restructuring of Southern California's economy (Muñoz 2010), that is, the replacement of the manufacturing sector with the rise of a regional service economy (Ibarra 2007; Torres Sarmiento 2002; Soja and Scott 1996). Currently, the Los Angeles economy mirrors the bifurcated national economy, with high-wage, highly skilled labor on top and low-skilled, low-wage, marginalized workers on the bottom, the latter being primarily in the service sector (Soja and Scott 1996). The demand for unskilled service workers attracts Latino immigrants to serve as the main source of this labor pool. Poverty wages and scarce benefits ensure a large population of working poor. Low-skilled immigrant laborers often resort to taking additional jobs in the informal economy to survive and sustain their families.[6]

According to Sassen, immigrants increasingly participate in the informal economy since they tend to form communities that "may be in a favorable position to seize the opportunities presented by informalization, [though] immigrants do not necessarily *create* such opportunities" (1998a: 154). There are several advantages to supplementing income by working in the informal economy; for example, the income earned, though taxable, is easy to hide from the Internal Revenue Service; work hours are flexible; and in some cases, laborers do not have to report to supervisors (Hamilton and Chinchilla 2001; Zlolniski 2006).[7] In this economic context, street vendors use informal economic opportunities to create both place and a sense of place, and to transform public spaces into vending spaces.

Space as a concept is socially constructed. It can refer to physical entities such as location, land, regions, cities, city blocks, sidewalks, or even mountain ranges, but one constant remains: space has boundaries. These vendors transform the intended meanings and use of space (i.e., those intended by the State) through "place"-making mechanisms such as imposing alternative meanings and uses on public space (Muñoz 2008). Place, as a concept, is created through a process by which various social and cultural phenomena interlink everyday life experiences. In other words, place is vibrant and dynamic. It is a socially constructed process through which imagination, memories, and experiences form specific place-based identities that remain fluid even across social and physical boundaries (Jackson and Penrose 1993; Massey 1997). "Sense of place" emerges from "places" where individuals or a group of people experience deep connections or emotive feelings attached to place. Sense of place is both a personal and a collective phenomenon experienced through a sense of attachment to and meaning of a place. It is created by memory, experiences, and desires that are individual or shared, and often the result is ultimately articulated by the way people use, understand, and create a specific place. Sense of place is constructed through unbound, unfixed emotive feelings that are constantly informed by memory, images, photographs, stories, personal histories, and experiences. Sense of place is therefore a subjective psychosocial process triggered by feelings of familiarity: the smell of food, sounds of music, language, dress, behaviors. These concepts are thus vital elements of vending spaces in Los Angeles. In this way, street vendors create "place" not only in the carrying out of their daily informal economic practices, but also in the way that they perform these duties. The specific types of wares they sell, to whom, and where—these all become meaningful to vendors as well as to customers, neighborhood residents, business owners, and local state enforcers (see Crossa in this anthology).

Selling "Authentic" Experiences: Nostalgia, Memory, and Place

Vendors physically transform the streets into public markets, utilizing sidewalks, fences, walls, parking lots, and benches. Some vendors use shopping carts taken from local grocery stores to carry and distribute their food. Vendors transform public space into informal marketplaces and in doing so stake claims to perceived cultural rights (as well as space) in Latino neighborhoods in Los Angeles. The vendor's and the consumer's memory and nostalgia aid in this transformation of space and its resulting use. Alison Blunt calls nostalgic processes that actively change physical space as beyond memories, which "often invoke but also extend far beyond spaces of home" whereas "nostalgia invokes home in its very meaning (2003: 717)". She further describes nostalgia as spatial and memory as temporal, noting that the former can take shape as an emotive desire for home, rather than a "desire for desire" (720). She further postulates that productive nostalgia is beyond that of mere imagination because it is recalled through an "embodiment and enactment of practice" (717). Rather than a sense of a lost past, where one mourns something one no longer has, it is an actual representation of past memories, present conditions, and future desires. For example, Latina/o street vendors utilize productive nostalgia to change, reconfigure, or claim urban space, creating informal commercial spaces in Latino neighborhoods in Los Angeles.

This is not far-fetched, as nostalgia is generally part of what is consumed on the sidewalks of Latino neighborhoods, a trend that Hughes (1995: 781) terms the "social construction of authenticity." With the move toward homogenization and place-less spaces[8] in modern times, the representation of "local" is increasingly in the hands of large, nonlocal corporations:

> The collective of globalization theories suggests that various economic, information, and population flows have profoundly influenced the ways in which cultures have become represented. In a traditional view, authenticity is validated by kinship with its conceiving culture and discernible from its especial characteristics that have been preserved through territorial separation. But the global extension of commodification, and the forms through which it is represented, homogenize this cultural differentiation of territory by drawing actors into consumption practices which are largely manipulated by, and for, corporate economic interests. The standardizing effect of this, frequently given labels like "Coca-Colaization," carries over onto cultural meaning and erodes the territorial integrity of cultures. The commodification perspective, therefore, conceives cultural parameters to be increasingly framed by corporate interests, which transgress territorial demarcations, in their search for profitability. (Hughes 1995: 783)

In Los Angeles, a global city, we find that urban spaces are (re)inscribed by both homogenized global capitalist cultures and local economic place-based practices—what Hughes (1995) calls traditional cultural practices that are reinforced by territorial separation. Thus, spatial cultural practices are fluid, dialectical, and flexible, allowing traditional cultural economies to thrive across territories. These forms of cultural economies often cater to immigrants' reconstructions of home-culture practices.[9] This is not to say that the actual wares are recalling actual memories; rather, tourists, non-native customers, or second- or third-generation immigrants, for example, are prompted to imagine what they perceive to be traditional Latin American food to be—reminding them of blanketed imaginaries of packaged "authentic Latino Immigrant cultural experiences." That is, nostalgia is formed by both the collective and individual memories and past experiences of customers and vendors. For example, Milagro's memory (or even her nostalgic imagination) of her childhood in Rosario becomes more than just a yearning for something in the past, because in effect, she uses it to re-create a modern form of entrepreneurship in the streets of

Los Angeles. As a result, these neighborhoods are layered with actively produced, changing interpretations of space. Some Latina vendors even use this method to establish new business strategies and models, such as making traditional tamales in addition to their branded tamales (with "secret" ingredients). Milagro's entrepreneurial strategies are shaped by the larger economic context and her own lived places and worlds. It is not only the past that is accessed to create a present, but a collection of multiple experiences, memories, and nostalgic practices from her own life and her customers' lives as well. In other words, the production of place is more than simply a survival strategy; it is a marketing mechanism used to build a business, predominantly by offering customers innovative ways to access the products/food they want to purchase (Spalter-Roth 1988).

Street vending customers are also motivated by connections to the past. On occasion their food purchases are motivated by a desire to "remember" their homes. For example, Mexican immigrant Juanito says that it is not only easier to buy Milagro's tamales before work, but also more experiential, as they are a comfort to him: "sometimes I go to McDonalds and buy breakfast, but I feel that tamales or tacos are more filling to my stomach and to my soul." Linda, an area supervisor for a garment factory and another of Veronica's daily customers, described her reasons for patronizing the street vendors:

> Well [food], it's cheap, good, and it's a way for our community to make a living. It is what we know, what we feel comfortable with, in my shop, we also play Latino music in the radio, it's a way to make sure we know that we all belong here, and the shock for some [recent immigrants] is not that big … well it is; but at least there are things in the neighborhood and at work that one remembers as being part of who we are and that is not just back home but it is here where we live and work.[10]

Linda's words describe this sense of place—a space created less by memories from back home than by current Latino immigrant experiences in Los Angeles. Similarly, the vendors who had permits in McArthur Park[11] intentionally planned their open marketplace as a community, as was evident in the way they sold, packaged, and conducted their business. For example, they used uniformed carts resembling vending carts in traditional *zocalos* (plazas), ultimately romanticizing street vending representations reminiscent of Latin America.

Latina Street Vendors in Los Angeles?

Veronica, a mobile street vendor, pushes a *tamal* and *champurrado* cart in the mornings and then sells the same in front of her daughter's elementary school after school. Vendors like Veronica use colorful umbrellas and plastic crates to sell in public space that is restricted for commercial use. Like Veronica, most vendors sell what they know—what they are familiar with acquiring and preparing. This goes beyond the actual items, as the food items are often announced with a distinct jingle unique to the seller. When asked why, the reply was consistent among vendors: "That is the way you sell tamales." This marketing technique is particularly relevant for mobile vendors, whose less permanent visibility in high-traffic areas forces them to compete by other advertising means, such as honking horns for attention while selling from cars. Most of the interviewed mobile vendors traveled established routes every day or on a rotating basis, but some switched routes to cover more territory and gain new customers.

Vendors also capitalize on seasonal traditions to sell items besides food. Holidays include Christmas, Halloween, Valentine's Day, Mother's Day, Catholic religious holidays, and Mexican and Central American national holidays. In the Christmas season, vendors often sell homemade products like Christmas stockings, floral arrangements with poinsettias (*nochebuenas*), and religious artifacts featuring the baby Jesus and *reyesmagos* (the three kings). Homemade goods are just one type of inventory, though; some vendors stock items normally found in 99-cent stores, such as Christmas lights, plastic Christmas trees, and small toys. Mother's Day in the United States, which is also the official Mother's Day in Mexico and some Latin American countries, is marked with traditional floral arrangements as well as anything that can honor the concept of motherhood, from La Virgen de Guadalupe products to plastic jewelry boxes that display *madre* (mother) for mother's day.

Vendors also claim territory, even though they are using public space. For example, stationary vendor Teresa stands on a busy street corner with her distinctive red grocery cart, offering the convenience of a drive-through for people in cars on their way to work. In the morning, a line of cars waits to purchase *tamales* and/or *champurrado* from Teresa. Not unlike Teresa, Lupe sells food from her car, storing her wares in the trunk and parking in the busiest locations in terms of time of day and foot traffic. When she began as a vendor, she used a grocery cart but kept having trouble with police. To avoid legal troubles, she bought a car and became more mobile and discreet. Selling from her trunk allows Lupe to travel to various locations outside garment factories during breakfast and lunch. Should there happen to be a police raid, she can close her trunk and drive off. Otherwise, she is able to display her food—*comida típica* (traditional)—in an attractive way in her trunk. Teresa's and Lupe's productive nostalgia informs their entrepreneurial vending practices as they actively change and reconfigure their approach in order to increase revenue.

Cultural Citizenship: Street Vending Spaces as Lived Home Places

By bringing their culture (i.e., vending tactics) to the city, these vendors carve out an economic and cultural niche on the sidewalks of Latino neighborhoods, even though such practices are prohibited in Los Angeles. In this way, noncitizens inadvertently support a social movement by making alternative claims to space (Rosaldo 1999; Flores and Benmayor 1997). These particular cultural spaces appear strongly constituted by nostalgia, memory, identity practices, and well-worn business practices. Concerned with visibility, being heard, and belonging, noncitizen vendors impose their own cultural understandings in a traditional manner despite what the host country's culture denies them. As Castañeda states, "the history and stories of Mexican migrants in the U.S. illustrate how belonging is encoded in citizenship. As migrants create a transnational citizenship, marked by translocal and/or transnational practices within a scenario of contrasting political cultures, legal notions of citizenship are articulated with practices of belonging" (2004: 73).

Traditional citizenship means that people must gain membership in order to claim political, social, and civil rights (Marshall 1950). In practice, nations grant this "full citizenship" based on a set of standards; for instance, U.S. citizenship is granted by birth or application. However, many who feel they are unable to gain citizenship in the traditional manner seek alternatives, trying to exercise rights and meet obligations to the state as illegal residents. Social citizenship, Castillo (2007) claims, has enabled noncitizens to participate in the social economic system as full citizens: "Illegal immigrants both benefit from the social services of the host country and fulfill the duty of full citizens to create tax revenues through their labor to pay for these services" (2007: 95). Yet in some cases these policies affect Latino immigrants regardless of their citizenship status. The English-Only movement,[12] for example, limits language rights and castigates vulnerable populations regardless of their citizenship by not allowing them to preserve or choose to speak their home language at school or work. Yet noncitizens have resisted these categorizations of citizenship by carving out their own spaces, where they claim rights and exercise alternative forms of citizenship on the local scale and simultaneously on the scale of the body.

Not unlike Milagro, Veronica, and Lupe, Sara is a street vendor who sells in the MacArthur Park area. Calling "Tres paletas por un dollar" (three popsicles for a dollar), she sells homemade frozen treats and used clothing, vying to be heard at a noisy intersection on a busy sidewalk by the park. She arranges the used clothing on a rack on top of a rug on the sidewalk and displays the bright-colored flavored ices signs on top of a large cooler where she stores them. She actively shouts, trying to gain customers. Short, brown-skinned, and now aged thirty-six (though she looks much older), she came to the United States from Guatemala eighteen years ago because her family and two children were destitute—"We were starving and the political situation did not help"[13]—bringing her street vending knowledge with her. She says her dream was to open up a corner store, what she calls a "legitimate business," but like many women in her town, she was unable to pursue formal employment because of the economic climate: "There weren't even enough jobs for the men, as a woman, what kind of job could I expect?"[14]

Sara came alone through Mexico to Los Angeles. She joined a family friend who had left Guatemala for a better life in America two years prior. She left her two children with her parents, promising to return in a couple years with enough savings for them to open up a corner grocery store. However, Sara has not returned to Guatemala once in the eighteen years since she left. Her eyes fill with tears as she explains the situation with regard to her children: "My parents raised them, I talk to them on the phone often."[15] Sara became a legal resident five years ago, but the residency she worked to gain came too late. Though she now is able to visit Guatemala, she has little reason to do so, as her parents do not want her to bring her children to Los Angeles at this point. For the past five years she has lived in Korea Town in Los Angeles. Five days a week, from seven in the morning to six in the evening, she works as a domestic, cleaning houses and taking care of children, but on Saturdays and Sundays she is a vendor in MacArthur Park. Employed as a domestic since her arrival, thirteen years ago she started supplementing her income by selling food with a friend on the weekends. Street vending was something Sara was familiar with, for in her hometown she had been a vendor, selling prepared food alongside her mother. Unfortunately, she has never been able to send back enough money to finance the envisioned grocery store, but she proudly affirms that she religiously sends money to Guatemala for her family's medicines and food.

Sara feels better selling on the weekends than at her regular domestic job. She feels "at home" in the park, explaining that "aquí todos somos Latinos y hablamos Español, conosco a varios vendedores que tienen vendiendo aquí muchísimos años," which translates as "here we are all Latinos and we speak Spanish; I know some vendors that have been selling here for years." In addition to being a vendor, Sara also shops for Guatemalan products in the park and says that she, like the rest of the people who frequent the park, prefers to spend weekends enjoying a day with good music, food, and friends. For Sara, the meanings that produce street vending spaces go beyond economic strategies by creating meaning, especially in regard to the way vendors use public spaces in Latino immigrant neighborhoods. Sara does just this when she claims and constructs her own place in the urban landscape; that is, she is exercising an alternative form of citizenship, what Flores and Benmayor (1997) call "Latino cultural citizenship."

Flores suggests that Latinos transform space by "obtaining space, keeping it, and being free to use it as they see fit which often requires these groups to organize themselves and make demands in society" (2003: 89). These vending strategies break down myths about informal vending as markets that just "pop up" in unregulated spaces. The simplistic notion that vending is an unorganized economic survival strategy practiced by people operating at the margins of society—as in Latin America—does not explain vending practices in Los Angeles, where in fact vending is organized at the street level and varies by block. Some vendors in Los Angeles even pay local gang members "rent" for the use of sidewalk space and protection from business owners, neighborhood residents, other gangs, and law enforcement. Street vendors, in this study often paid gang members five dollars a day for protection and security whenever they sold on a particular block. It is unclear how many vendors pay rent to gang members because the subject is not one most vendors want to talk about. Rents charged by gang members are considered illegal and extortion by the LAPD. Yet for some vendors, paying rent can be a convenience, since gang members can remove non-paying vendors to avoid competition. Vendors who pay rent to local gang members for protection, illustrate how, systematically, they navigate spaces in which restrictions imposed by the local government are layered with resistance to the local government (e.g., paying dues to gang members who protect them from police raids and potential competition). Thus, Latina street vendors are clearly navigating and negotiating local government restrictions even as they agree to participate in protection mechanisms with gang members in order to claim public space as their own.

Perhaps most beneficial to established vendors is the gang's "barrier to entry," imposed when competition tries to open in a paying vendor's location. This is why some new vendors choose to push their food carts around the neighborhood instead of parking in a specific spot. Lizette, a Mexican immigrant mobile vendor, says: "I go to my customers, instead of waiting for the customers to come to me." She has been a street vendor for approximately six months, preferring move through the neighborhood, calling "Tamales…Tamales…Tamales…" She works only in the morning, from 5 A.M. to 9 A.M., traveling thereafter to her full-time job. She reports making a good living from her job in the formal economy and describes her part-time vending as supplementary. The four hours she works every morning, according to Lizette, are equal to a full day stationed on a street corner. With regular customers who buy tamales from her almost every day for breakfast, she makes about fifty dollars a morning. In addition to her regulars, she says, she always has new customers willing to try her tamales. However, she avoids certain streets in the neighborhood where she has been slightly harassed by *cholos* (gang members) and other vendors. She learned quickly how to navigate the streets of the neighborhood while building her clientele, accomplishments she attributes to starting early in the day (before people go to work). Holding down a regular full-time job and a part-time vending business, she considers herself successful.

As "cultural citizens," vendors create and impose their own self-organizing and regulating mechanisms. They also organize, resist, and demand spaces in the city by imposing their own meanings on the streets via their everyday performances and reenactments of memory and nostalgia on the streets of Los Angeles. Vendors like Milagro and Sara claim and reconfigure spaces in the city by imposing their own meanings on the streets through their reenactments of memory and the "productive" nostalgia that informs their entrepreneurial vending strategies. The sense of place that transforms the space emanates from their own histories while also reflecting customers' preferences and a desire to connect to "authentic" nostalgic representations from back home. What is more, their brand of street vending is systematically organized on the avenues of Los Angeles and therefore should no longer be seen as unorganized economic survival strategies practiced by immigrants operating on the margins of society. In fact, Latina/o immigrant street vendors create sophisticated forms of informal work and exercise agency in re-creating and organizing public space on the streets of Los Angeles.

Lorena Muñoz is an assistant professor in the Department of Geography, Environment and Society at the University of Minnesota. She is also affiliate faculty of the Department of Chicano and Latino Studies and the Department of Gender, Women and Sexuality Studies. Her research focuses on the intersections of place, space, gender, sexuality, and race. Through qualitative frameworks she examines the production of Latina/o informal economic landscapes in trans-border spaces. Her research has been funded by the National Science Foundation, the National Institute of Health, and the University of Minnesota's, Global Spotlight Major Faculty Grant.

Notes

1. Original in Spanish: "Todavia me acuerdo el olor de la comida tipica que vendedlos vendedores ambulantes en my pueblo de Rosario, Sinaloa...no solo venden comida pero dulces, esos eran mis preferidos...My mama nos llevaba a la Plaza los Domingos, ibamos despues de misa...El olor a tamarindo me lleva a mi infancia, cuando no solo el domingo era comprarle comida a los vendedores pero tambien escuchar musica en vivo, jugar con nuestros amigos y en algunas ocaciones nos tocaba un juguete usado que le comprabamos a los vendedores." All interviews were recorded and conducted in Spanish. As I am fluent in both Spanish and English, it was not necessary to translate all the interviews.
2. This chapter stems from my research exploring the production of Latino vending landscapes in Los Angeles, where I gathered ethnographic data over the course of three years at two different street vending sites. The fieldwork process consisted of participant observation at the two selected sites; photo-documentation and photo-elicitation; oral histories; interviews; and secondary sources.
3. Street vending in the United States has been described as a consequence of waves of immigration from Central America and Mexico to the United States, and Los Angeles in particular, from the nineteenth century to the present day (Sanchez 1993). However, the street history of Los Angeles has been documented only in the last twenty-five years. Few sources describe street vending activities in Los Angeles prior to the 1890s, which were mostly dominated by Mexican and Chinese immigrants selling agricultural goods door-to-door and in the Plaza of La Reina de Los Angeles (Sanchez 1993: 72; Hayden 1995: 112–118). As such, street vending practices have been part of the daily economic life of immigrant neighborhoods in Los Angeles since the nineteenth century. Street vending (practiced mostly by Mexicans) was widespread in the area prior to the 1890s, according to Hamilton and Chinchilla (2001), but once whites (i.e., Anglo-Saxon racialized white populations) became dominant in Southern California, they cracked down on the practice by passing and enforcing restrictive legislation—prohibitions that exist to this day. Nonetheless, the rapid growth and greater visibility of Latino vendors since the 1980s have drawn more attention to these particular informal economic practices. Street vending continues to be popular in areas such as East Los Angeles, where the majority of the population is of Mexican origin. During the 1980s, street vending also became popular among newly arrived Central American populations.
4. "Yo hablo mucho, y si trabajo solita me agarra la depression, no estoy contenta si no puedo estar platicando. You hablo con cualquiera, my madre me decia que no tenia verguenza, que puedo parar a qualquiera en la calle y empezar a platicar, bueno tienen que hablar Español [risas] bueno hasta en Ingles trato." (Interview and translation from Spanish to English by author, 24 June 2007).

5. "Yo creci comprandole a vendedores, es parte de la vida cotidiana de mi pueblo...cuando hago agua de tamarindo, be recuerda a mi pueblo, am mi mama y a cuando era chamaca."
6. The informal sector, once considered a natural consequence of underdeveloped economies, is rapidly growing in industrial countries (Portes, Castells and Benton 1989). Global economic restructuring practices, such as the global division of labor, reorganizes and redistributes labor sectors from the United States to other countries in search of cheaper labor. Global market competition creates demand for cheaper unskilled labor, especially in global cities like Los Angeles. Hence, producers take advantage of available lower-cost labor in order to compete in global markets. According to Sassen (1998a), the globalization of production is partly responsible for the growth of the informal economies of leading postindustrial countries. She adds that the decline of manufacturing and the growth of the service sector increased temporary and part-time jobs and weakened job protections. What Sassen calls "casualization" of the labor market "has facilitated the absorption of rising numbers of immigrants during the 1970s and 1980s—a growing Third World immigrant work force in what is supposedly one of the leading post-industrial economies" (Sassen 1998b: 34).
7. According to the Economic Roundtable (a Los Angeles–based, nonprofit, public benefit corporation organized to conduct economic, social, and environmental research that contributes to the sustainability of individuals and communities), on any given day in Los Angeles, there are approximately 670,000 informal workers (Flaming and Haydamack 2005). However, the number of informal workers who are street vendors remains unclear because studies on the informal economy of Los Angeles have not included street vendors. The focus has been mainly on manufacturing- and service-sector informal employment, including household and landscape services. Immigrant and noncitizen participation in informal employment is at the forefront of these studies, highlighting the fact that immigrants make up 65 percent of this informal labor force.
8. Place-less landscapes refer to uniform global brand franchises, such as Starbucks, where one can feel a sense of familiarity with other Starbucks around the globe. These global franchises transform commercial space to resemble a global brand, so the aesthetic changes in line with that of the entire chain, regardless of whether the particular location is a locally owned franchise (Bale 1996).
9. Shopping centers that cater to global brands typically conduct their business with a place-less aesthetic, whereas diverse neighborhoods that organically cater to immigrants are qualitatively distinct from each other.
10. Interview conducted in English by author, 12 April 2007.
11. MacArthur Park, the only legal vending district in the city, is in one of the most densely populated areas in the City of Los Angeles. The neighborhood is a predominantly Latino residential and Korean business community. Currently targeted for private development and investment, it is changing fast.

What once was known as the place with the highest murder rate in the city is now an oasis for young urban professionals. Gang members, the homeless, drug dealers, and *miqueros* (people who sell work documents or *micas*) had frequented this particular site, which was also home to unlicensed vendors in the 1970s and early 1980s. In 2002, local government and state enforcers, in collaboration with local business owners and residents, fought to change the meaning of the park. They sought to create a historical, passive, green space accessible to all. The city installed cameras to enhance its aggressive surveillance effort to reduce and deter crime in the park and the area. This enforcement and surveillance program is part of a revitalization of the area by developers and business leaders in partnership with the City of Los Angeles. In 2005, the park boasted the most drastic crime rate reduction rate in Los Angeles. Redevelopment projects are transforming the area's historical buildings into trendy lofts for yuppie dwellers. Until 2005, MacArthur Park was a site for legal vending. Unfortunately, permits were not renewed in 2005 because the vendors did not have enough capital to continue operating.

12. The "English-Only" movement is a historical and contemporary movement to establish national policies making English the official language. As of 2010, twenty-eight states have passed state laws declaring English the official state language. This policy unequally affects non-native English speakers by raising a barrier to full citizenship: all legal materials and communication with state entities must be in English, which in effect bars ESL individuals from civic participation.
13. "Nos estábamos muriendo de hambre y la situación política no ayudaba la situación de uno." (Interview translated by author, 2007.)
14. "No había ni siquiera trabajo para los hombres como mujer, que tipo de trabajo podría esperar a encontrar?" (Interview translated by author, 2007.)
15. "Mis papas los criaron, yo hablo con ellos por telefono seguido." (Interview translated by author, 2007.)

Bibliography

Bale, J. 1996. "Space, Place and Body Culture: Yi-Fu Tuan and a Geography of Sport." Geografiska Annaler Series B. Human Geography. 78(3): 163–171.

Blunt, Alisson. 2003. "Collective Memory and Productive Nostalgia: Anglo-Indian Homemaking at McCluskiegani." *Environment and Planning D: Society and Space* 21: 717–738.

Castañeda, Alejandra. 2004. "Roads to Citizenship: Mexican Migrants in the United States." *Latino Studies* 2: 70–89.

Castillo, Adelaida R. Del. 2007. *Illegal Status and Social Citizenship: Thoughts on Mexican Immigrants in a Postnational World.* Durham, NC, and London: Duke University Press.

Flaming, Daniel, and Brent Haydamack. 2005. *Hopeful Workers, Marginal Jobs: LA's Off-The-Books Labor Force.* Los Angeles: Economic Roundtable.

Flores, William V. 2003. "New Citizens, New Rights: Undocumented Immigrants and Latino Cultural Citizenship." *Latin American Perspectives* 30 (2): 87–100.
Flores, William V., and Rina Benmayor, eds. 1997. *Latino Cultural Citizenship: Claiming Identity, Space and Rights.* Boston: Beacon Press.
Gilbert, Melissa. 1994. "The Politics of Location: Doing Feminist Research at 'Home.'" *Professional Geographer* 46 (1): 90–95.
Hamilton, Nora, and Norma S. Chinchilla. 2001. *Seeking Community in a Global City: Guatemalans and Salvadorans in Los Angeles.* Philadelphia: Temple University Press.
Hayden, Dolores. 1995. *Power of Place: Urban Landscape as Public History.* Cambridge: MIT Press.
Hughes, George. 1995. "Authenticity in Tourism." *Annals of Tourism* 22 (4): 781–803.
Ibarra, Maria de la Luz. 2007."Mexican Immigrant Women and the New Domestic Labor." *Women and Immigration: In the U.S.-Mexico Borderlands.* Durham, NC, and London: Duke University Press.
Jackson, Peter, and Jan Penrose, eds. 1993. *Construction of Race, Place, and the Nation.* Minneapolis: University of Minnesota Press.
Katz, Cindi. 1994. "Playing the Field: Questions of Fieldwork in Geography." *Professional Geographer* 46 (1): 67–72.
Marshall, H. Thomas. 1950. *Citizenship and Social Class and Other Essays.* Cambridge: Cambridge University Press.
Massey, Doreen. 1997. "Power-Geometry and Progressive Sense of Place." *Mapping the Futures: Local Cultures, Global Change.* New York: Routledge.
McDowell, Linda. 1992. "Doing Gender: Feminism and Research Methods in Human Geography." *Transactions of the Institute of British Geographers* 17 (4): 399–416.
Muñoz, Lorena. 2008."'Tamales…Elotes…Champurrado…' The Production of Latino Vending Street-Scapes in Los Angeles." PhD dissertation, University of Southern California: Los Angeles.
———. 2010. "Brown, Queer and Gendered: Queering the Latina/o 'Street-Scapes' in Los Angeles." In *Queer Methods and Methodologies,* ed. Kath Browne and Catherine J. Nash. Surrey: Ashgate Press.
Portes, A. Castells, M. and Benton L. (eds). 1989. *The Informal Economy: Studies in Advanced and Less Developed Countries.* Baltimore: John Hopkins University Press.
Rosaldo, Reynaldo. 1999. "Cultural Citizenship, Inequality, and Multiculturalism." In *Race, Identity and Citizenship: A Reader,* ed. Rodolfo D. Torres, Louis F. Miron, and Jonathan Xavier Inda. Blackwell Press: New Jersey.
Rose, Gillian. 1997. "Situating Knowledges: Positionality, Reflexivity and Other Tactics." *Progress in Human Geography* 21 (3): 305–320.
Sanchez, George. 1993. *Becoming Mexican American: Ethnicity, Culture, and Identity in Chicano Los Angeles 1900–1945.* New York: Oxford University Press.
Sassen, Saskia. 1998a. *Globalization and Its Discontents: Essays on the New Mobility of People and Money.* New York: The New Press.
———. 1998b. "The Informal Economy: Between New Developments and Old Regulations." *Yale Law Journal* 103 (8): 2289–2304.

Soja, Edward W., and Allen J. Scott. 1996. "Introduction to Los Angeles: City and Region." In *The City: Los Angeles and Urban Theory at the End of the Twentieth Century,* ed. Edward W. Soja and Allen J. Scott. Berkeley and Los Angeles: University of California Press.

Spalter-Roth, Roberta M. 1988. "Vending on the Streets: City Policy, Gentrification, and Public Patriarchy." In *Women and the Politics of Empowerment,* ed. Ann Bookman and Sandra Morgen. Philadelphia: Temple University Press.

Torres Sarmiento, Socorro. 2002. *Making Ends Meet: Income-Generating Strategies among Mexican Immigrants.* LFB Scholarly: El Paso, Texas.

Zlolniski, Christian. 2006. *Janitors, Street Vendors and Activists: The Lives of Mexican Immigrants in Silicon Valley.* Berkeley, Los Angeles, and London: University of California Press.

CHAPTER 6

Ethnic Contestations over African American Fiction
The Street Vending of Street Literature in New York City

Kristina Graaff

Since the early twentieth century, the outdoor selling of goods from street stands has been a common practice in Black low-income neighborhoods in U.S. cities. To this day it allows for the provision of products that are either unavailable or unaffordable in fixed store locations.[1] One of these products is street literature, currently the most widely read genre of Black popular fiction. By the late 1990s, it was being sold on the streets of various East Coast cities.[2] Predominantly written by African Americans,[3] many of them first-time authors, the novels usually narrate coming-of-age stories set in low-opportunity areas like those where the novels are sold. Unfolding in urban neighborhoods in the 1980s and later, the plots revolve around postindustrial struggles for daily survival through illicit practices, especially involvement in the local drug trade. The glossy covers of the books often show men with scantily dressed women and common items associated with the drug business: weapons, crack vials, yellow crime scene tape, prison bars. Though most of the novels are legitimately criticized for their patriarchal and misogynistic overtones and focus on drug-related violence (Chiles 2006; Fugate in Weeks 2004: C01; Jones 2008),[4] they nevertheless provide insights into the persistence of racial biases, especially as they play out in the nation's justice system and labor market. The primarily male protagonists, having failed to obtain employment due to labor discrimination, eventually engage in illicit street-level economies, described as the most accessible source of income. Street literature's portrayal of the streets as being under constant police scrutiny speaks to the discriminatory surveillance and arrest practices that target especially low-income minority populations and are common in today's U.S. justice system (Alexander 2010). The novels also address the obstacles faced by former convicts. Many of the books' characters spend time in prison and return to street economies upon their release because their prison record limits their chances on the labor market even further.[5] Street literature is thus infused with entrepreneurial practices on both an imaginative and a physical level. Street entrepreneurship is central to the genre's distribution as well as the actions that structure its plots—the former merely informal, the latter also illegitimate.

Despite the criticism often voiced against the popular narratives, they have taken an important place in the American book industry since their emergence. Primarily self-published in the beginning, today they are produced by self-publishing authors, independent African American publishers, and mainstream presses like Random House, Warner, and St. Martin's Press alike. Taken up by numerous mainstream publishers, the novels are now also available in chain bookstores such as Barnes & Noble and from online retailers like Amazon. The yearly revenue generated by the genre is not known. Considering, however, that the popular novels dominate most African American literature sections in chain bookstores, it can be assumed that a considerable share of the over 320 million dollars that Black readers have recently spent on books goes toward street literature (Target Market News 2010).[6]

The outdoor vending of street literature from street stands began in Harlem at the turn of the twenty-first century and is mainly based in New York City's low-income neighborhoods. Nationwide, New York City possesses the highest density of street literature vendors, located mainly on Harlem's 125th Street, Fordham Road in the Bronx, and Fulton Street in downtown Brooklyn. Sometimes a single block features numerous book vendors.[7] This density is explained by New York City's long legacy of street vending, highlighted by Naison in this anthology. Also beneficial are the vitality and heavy foot traffic of most New York City neighborhoods, not to be found in the deserted cores of numerous other postindustrial cities like Detroit, Saint Louis, or Baltimore, or in spread-out, car-centered cities like Los Angeles. The abundance of book vendors relates also to the fact that printed matter is considered a work of expression. Street literature thus falls under the First Amendment of the U.S. Constitution, so no license is needed to sell it; moreover, local government cannot impose a license ceiling to regulate the number of vendors selling books.[8] This is backed up by the New York Department of Consumer Affairs, whose regulations state that books are "associated with right to free speech" (New York Department of Consumer Affairs 2010). Nevertheless, First Amendment vendors must comply with other regulations, for example a list of restricted streets and vending days (New York Department of Consumer Affairs 2010; New York City Council 2013), as well as copyright laws (Benson 2006: 7; Improta cited in Dawkins 2005: 46). Generally, however, the compliance of daily vending routines with, say, requirements for sizes or positions of tables, is under less scrutiny in disadvantaged neighborhoods than in the city's "high-value" areas—at least, until city planning shifts its attention to a neighborhood's "potential" for gentrification. The informalized practice of outdoor distribution of street literature has therefore developed relatively freely over the past ten years, and anyone with sufficient capital can establish his or her own stand.

The novels are sold from folding tables that are positioned close to the street at the sidewalk's outer edge and taken down at night.[9] Outdoor selling takes place in all seasons, usually starting around noon and ending slightly after the regular closing time of indoor stores around 8:30 P.M. so as to serve late customers and employees of adjacent businesses. All street vendors that I observed during my research in New York City are people of color. The majority of them are immigrants from Francophone West African countries, especially the Ivory Coast, Ghana, and Senegal. In the early 1980s, economic problems in West Africa, in particular the devaluation of the West African franc (Stoller 2002: 17), triggered an immigration wave from the region. Since then, West Africans have dominated the street vending business in all of New York City. They met the new product of street literature with an established selling network that was readily adaptable to carrying the books.[10] An increasing number of African American vendors, however, are currently entering the book selling business, claiming a financial share in the distribution of a product that they consider "theirs," given that street literature is not only written but also published and read predominantly by African Americans.

For this case study, I selected two vendors to illustrate the importance of street vending in the emergence of street literature, its development over the past years, and the present-day contestations over the selling business that are inextricably linked to questions of ethnic and national origin. The first vendor, 43-year-old Imara Adeyemi,[11] is originally from the Ivory Coast. One of Harlem's first street literature vendors, he has managed to expand his book distribution business significantly. The second is Darius Jackson, a 41-year-old African American native of the Bronx who entered the street literature vending business rather late, in 2006, and currently sells at two spots in the Bronx. The data were collected during several guideline-based, in-depth interviews; informal talks; and participant observation in the years 2009 and 2010. They were conducted at various indoor and outdoor vending locations, including the corners of 125th Street and 7th Avenue in Harlem, and Westchester and Longwood Avenues in the South Bronx, as well as two bookstores located in these neighborhoods.[12]

As the case studies illustrate, the two vendor groups operate under very different selling conditions that not only depend on when they entered the business and whether networks are available to them, but also are linked to differing entrepreneurial experiences and social positioning in the United States. Moreover, the study indicates, collaboration between the two groups is impeded by mutual distrust, usually expressed in stereotypical assumptions about the respective other party.

Both of the vendors I interviewed are men, reflecting the prevalence of male sellers in the outdoor book selling business. I encountered only two women vendors in downtown Manhattan and Brooklyn. Women are under-represented among both African and African American sellers on the street literature vending scene for several reasons. First of all, most West African immigrants come to the United States as single men, leaving behind families to whom they send remittances (Stoller 2002: 21). The predominance of male African Americans may be explained by the fact that they are the demographic most strongly affected by discrimination and recent job cuts in the labor market, which more often compel them to enter the informal(ized) labor market.[13] One of the female vendors, when asked to explain the scarcity of women in the business, said most females are deterred from the outdoor selling business by the toughness of the vending scene, especially "the cops [that] are threatening you" (Grace, personal communication, 30 June 2010).

Street Literature Vending and "Black Entrepreneurialism" in the United States

Before examining the backgrounds, motivations, and practices of West African and African American street literature vendors as well as the relations among them, it is useful to have a closer look at the tradition of entrepreneurial practices carried out by both groups in the United States in order to better understand their positioning in the country's entrepreneurial sector. In the following, I use phrases such as "Black" or "African American entrepreneurialism" without perceiving these economic activities as natural or embodied practices. Though I drop the quotation marks around the terms henceforth, I understand ethnic entrepreneurship as a construction conceptualized by academia and also often used strategically by entrepreneurs to a specific end.[14]

The first African American entrepreneurial practices can be traced back to the time of chattel slavery, when slaves sold surplus products generated from "provision grounds," plots of land assigned to them so that they could grow their own food and minimize the master's "maintenance" cost (Walker 2009: 31f.). Occasionally, slaves were able to purchase their freedom with money earned from selling their produce, usually at marketplaces (Rodriguez 2007: 428f.). During the Antebellum Period many slave entrepreneurs were bondsmen, mostly from urban areas, who hired their own time from the owner in order to establish their own businesses (Walker 1997: 220). They commonly worked in the food, craft, building, and service industries but also in unskilled occupations such as street vending, using the profits to purchase freedom for themselves and their relatives (220f.). Also after Emancipation, both in the South and increasingly, with the Great Migration, in the urban North, African Americans founded their own enterprises, which were usually concentrated in the retail and service sector and included restaurant, funeral, barbershop, and beauty salon businesses (Green and Pryde 1997: 21; Tabb 1970: 45).[15]

From the very beginning, however, African Americans' entrepreneurial experiences differed from those of other ethnic groups in the United States because they were historically impeded by a variety of barriers. In the immediate post–Civil War era in the South, alongside the Black Codes that circumscribed African American mobility and entrepreneurial participation, the fact that most whites still associated African Americans with "a life of servitude and exploitation" also challenged "their legitimacy as economic actors and existence as equal humans" (Young 2007: 168). Lack of financial capital was largely what limited the foundation and expansion of African American businesses: most lending institutions refused to grant loans or provided them only at high interest rates, a problem that still confronts many Black businesses today (Bates 1997: 189f.). African American entrepreneurs are also frequently limited to low-income neighborhoods because, for the reasons previously mentioned, they cannot compete with larger businesses located in more affluent areas. As a consequence, they must also cope with limited purchasing power (Young 2007: 171; Tabb 1970: 44). Other likely reasons for the continuing low rate of African American self-employment refer to the scarcity of business role models, low asset levels, and limited access to business, social, and family networks (Fairlie 1999: 82; Fratoe 1988: 35–36, 48–49). Due to these various factors, not only is the percentage of entrepreneurs among African Americans the lowest for any ethnic group in the United States,[16] but the obstacles to and rarity of successful Black businesses have also brought about "negative attitudes regarding entrepreneurship" among large parts of the African American population (Austin 1995: 245).[17]

Although America's Black immigrants are also subjected to racial discrimination, they traditionally had better entrepreneurial opportunities that engendered a more positive attitude toward the practice. In the case of Harlem, immigrants from the Caribbean were among the neighborhood's most successful businesspeople by the early twentieth century, with occupations ranging from major positions in import-export trades to illicit businesses like the lottery numbers game (Watkins-Owens 1996: 173).[18] Several factors contributed to their advantaged access to the entrepreneurial sector and still apply today. In comparison to African Americans, most Black immigrants have not faced "virulent competition from a hostile white majority" in their home countries (173). Instead, they often arrive with trade skills and business connections to their countries of origin. Once in the United States, many also maintain helpful business networks with other immigrants of the same cultural and religious background (127). To this day Black immigrants have a large share in the American entrepreneurial economy, in particular in the informal(ized) sector. Thus West African immigrant merchants control most of New York City's vending business, including that of street literature, even though African Americans have a long tradition of participating in this business as well (Bluestone 1991: 80, 86; Duneier 1999: 120). As the following two case studies illustrate, however, the street literature vending business can currently be considered a terrain in flux, a contested territory where the interests of Black immigrants and African American entrepreneurs overlap and compete.

"Books Were Selling Like Cake"—Establishing Street Literature through the Practice of Street Vending

Imara Adeyemi's arrival in New York City in 1999 coincided with the emergence of street literature. Established publishers at the time rejected this form of writing because they did not consider it commercially viable, so the first street literature authors started to self-publish and distribute their books out of car trunks, at car washes and beauty salons, and most notably on street corners—a method also known as "bootstrapping."[19] As self-published novels grew in number, existing street book vendors who had previously sold novels by Toni Morrison, Donald Goines, Maya Angelou, and Terry McMillan began to add the new genre to their selection (Grace, personal communication, 30 June 2010; Keita, personal communication, 30 June 2010). At the same time, new entrepreneurs like Adeyemi entered the business. These vendors acted as intermediary dealers for the authors, allowing them to distribute their novels on a larger scale and only occasionally "hit the streets" themselves. Setting up bookstalls on street corners where pedestrian traffic is densest, these "intermediary vendors" began to offer a variety of titles by different authors and soon focused predominantly on the genre of street literature.[20]

Having amassed capital of six hundred dollars by working as a cab driver and jewelry store employee in Harlem, Adeyemi, who also resides in Harlem, opened his first book table in 2000 at 125th Street and 7th Avenue. It is still one of his main vending spots. Especially in the first years, Adeyemi enjoyed unexpected demand for the popular novels, which none of the local Black-owned bookstores offered at the time. Initially, he says, "books were selling like cake. ... I was selling cases, people were making lines at the stands" (Adeyemi, personal communication, 10 January 2009), which testifies to the enormous street literature consumption, especially in the first few years. As he claims, he commonly sold two hundred titles per day, back then still at the rounded-up cover price of $15.[21] Considering that he received the copies directly from the authors, usually at a cost of $7.50, and paid no overhead costs,[22] Adeyemi made a daily net profit of $1,500. In the first months of street selling, Adeyemi's collection consisted of only several dozen titles,[23] but it soon became impossible for him to keep track of all the new authors and publications. A constantly growing selection of books emerged in a relatively short time frame, reflecting the avid demand for the popular novels and the creative potential of the community. Although by now the market has reached saturation,[24] which finds expression in the price decline examined further below, Adeyemi confirms that the output, especially of self-published novels, is unceasing: "Now we got thousands of them, thousands of titles. *Every* single day, there are new books out. *Every* single day" (personal communication, 10 January 2009).

From the beginning, his main customers have been African American females—daily passers-by from the community ranging from teenagers to women in their 50s.[25] Discussions with or among his customers about topics, narrative strategies, or personal connections to the storylines are common at his table, making it a center of attraction as a public spot for meeting and debate. Adeyemi's participation in these discussions and the fact that, at least in the beginning, he was very familiar with all the narratives he was selling can be regarded as atypical for West African vendors of street literature, most of whom—lacking language skills and cultural connection to the stories—have not read the narratives and sell the books as simply another product, hardly different from a watch or umbrella.

Having entered the street literature outdoor vending business at its most prosperous time, Adeyemi was able to build on and expand from his first entrepreneurial activity. Apart from the six tables he currently maintains in most of New York City's boroughs,[26] he also opened an indoor bookstore in 2006. Located on Frederick Douglass Boulevard close to 125th Street, it functions as both a retailer and wholesaler of street literature, providing books not only to other street vendors but also to bookstores outside the city. Today, in contrast to the boom times, it is much more difficult to accumulate enough capital from the outdoor selling of street literature to expand beyond the street vending business. Many sellers indeed "acquire the skills and resources that it takes to operate at a fixed location" (Austin 1994: 2127). Nevertheless, most never manage to eventually "upgrade" to their own stores, even though such a move would be welcomed by local government, which in the case of New York City tried several times to promote the shift from outdoor to indoor vending (Williams 2008: B2; Zukin 1995: 241f.).[27] Adeyemi is aware of his exceptional status, having experienced firsthand the difficulty, particularly for small Black-owned enterprises, of obtaining credit. The challenges of expanding local low-capital businesses seem to affect West African immigrants and African Americans alike. As Adeyemi confirms, the situation has only changed for the worse since the latest economic recession.

Contesting the Territory: West African and African American Street Literature Vendors

Although most street literature vendors do not proceed into the formal economy, Adeyemi contributes to expanding a local type of informalized entrepreneurialism by hiring vendors for his bookstalls. Most of them come from African Francophone countries and usually do not possess sufficient English skills or the higher education that would allow them to enter the "regular" labor market. His vendors start at a weekly salary of $250 dollars and receive periodic raises, provided they have worked satisfactorily for three to five months. Their salaries peak at $400 dollars a week (Adeyemi, personal communication, 10 January 2009). Vendors who prove to be reliable employees for several years eventually receive their "autonomy" (ibid.); in other words, Adeyami signs their book tables over to them so they can work as independent, self-employed sellers, which allows Adeyemi to hire new vendors. During the approximately five years

of exponential growth of the street literature selling business, this practice led to a comprehensive supply of popular African American novels, even in areas that lack the cultural infrastructure of bookstores.

As Adeyemi's hiring practice indicates, not all members of Harlem's community, from which he recruits his vendors, have equal access to his vending operation. His choice indeed confirms observations about the close-knit ties and networks between West African immigrants in the United States, particularly in the informal sector of street vending (Stoller 2002: 6–7, 80). Adeyemi's statement that "every two or three days there are people coming from Africa" (personal communication, 10 January 2009) who approach his stand in search of work also testifies to the permanent influx of immigrants from that region to Black urban working-class neighborhoods in particular (Stoller 2002: 6). This mutual support among West Africans in the street literature vending business cannot be explained by common language and shared cultural and religious backgrounds alone: it is also motivated by a general distrust of U.S. society, expressed by various immigrant vendors and attributable to the "sociocultural, legal and political tensions" (23) that vendors, especially undocumented ones, are subjected to. Despite possessing the status of a permanent resident,[28] Adeyemi shares this impression: "There are no *honest* people here. There is *no way* in America. There is no honesty. It's all about the Benjamins, it's about the money…" (personal communication, 10 January 2009). This dismissal of a system that is considered ruthless, morally depleted, and money-oriented is often projected onto African Americans, who have increasingly entered the street literature selling business. Adeyemi's prejudices against African American vendors refer mainly to their supposed striving for "fast money" and alleged lack of a work ethic (ibid.). His views tap into centuries-old stereotypes that depict African Americans as incapable of maintaining a job—claims that have been used to justify systems of enforced labor such as chattel slavery, debt peonage, and convict leasing. By holding African Americans personally responsible for their diminished social and economic mobility, Adeyemi ignores the many forms of structural racism they are still subjected to. Factors like urban segregation, underfunded city schools, employment discrimination, and the system of mass incarceration are often unknown to or ignored by recent immigrants.

However, it is not only the prejudices African Americans encounter that impede their participation in the vending business. Due to their late entry, they are also those most affected by the shrinking profit margins brought about by the commercialization of street literature.[29] Darius Jackson, who began selling the popular novels in 2006 at two locations in the Bronx that are still his main selling spots,[30] testifies to the various obstacles that individual African American vendors face who have entered the business rather late. Jackson did not purposefully plan his entry into the street vending business but began out of necessity, when it became apparent that the bookstore his mother had established in 2006 in the South Bronx would not survive without additional outdoor selling. Whereas the bookstore carried educational, religious, and self-help publications, Jackson's stand exclusively offers street literature. Although the stand did steer people's attention to the store, which was located in a low-traffic area right next to an elevated subway line, and was profitable enough to cofinance the overhead costs that the fixed location could not cover by itself, the bookstore had to close its doors in 2011. The fact that street vendors are apparently the most suitable distributors for books in the South Bronx is an indicator of the area's economic conditions. In the Bronx, which has the highest unemployment rate in New York City and New York state,[31] cultural infrastructure is generally scarce, particularly in the southern part. Until Jackson's mother's shop opened, there were no bookstores in the South Bronx, a community of over half a million people. As the failed retail store exemplifies, books are too expensive and not high in purchasing priority for the many dwellers who live below the poverty line and thus must deal with more existential concerns. The visually conspicuous street literature stands that nowadays offer novels at reduced prices are therefore the best alternative book distribution platform in this area.

In contrast to Adeyemi, who spent several years selling the novels at their cover price, Jackson entered the business after the genre had already been commercialized. Despite the popular novels' wide availability at independent and chain bookstores as well as online retailers, street vendors are in a favored position in that they do not have to pay overhead costs and can sell books at rates distinctly below the cover price to continue to attract customers. It is precisely the continuous decline in prices that is the main obstacle to Jackson's establishing himself as a street vendor. Beginning around 2005, when the genre reached its saturation point, books began to fetch only seven to ten dollars and were increasingly sold at even lower prices. Several factors apart from the above-mentioned commercialization and the growing number of street literature suppliers are responsible for this price decline. With street literature having become so popular, massive numbers of first-time authors are entering the scene on a daily basis, many hoping to quickly acquire a share of the market before the novels' potential loss of popularity. In these circumstances, numerous writers are willing to sell their books for five dollars directly to the vendor, thereby earning approximately three dollars per book.[32] Additionally, the greater affordability of producing books has led to a steady output of new titles, which in turn makes street literature novels more short-lived. The scene is also increasingly dominated by authors who consider writing just another business—an additional source of income to cover immediate costs—and who do not invest in a long-term writing career. These authors, as Darius Jackson terms it, "fly by night": "Today you are writing a book, tomorrow you are not. Today, you got hardship, so now you are trying to get rid of your book dirt cheap," a practice that, according to Jackson, "just hurts the game" because it contributes to the growing deflation of book prices on the streets (personal communication, 1 November 2009).

Jackson deplores the embrace of this business practice by many vendors, especially those who are already established in an extensive network and can claim a monopoly over New York's outdoor street literature vending business, as is the case for most booksellers on 125th Street. Generalizing this group of well-connected vendors as "African immigrants," Jackson ignores their diverse countries of origin, though he does acknowledge that they "have been in the game longer than [him]", "stick together," and have the power to exert price pressure (ibid.). As part of a larger vendor network, the better-established street literature sellers can distribute larger quantities of books over wider areas, and can use this argument to convince authors to sell their books at a lower price because earnings are achieved through the sheer volume of books sold. As an individual seller, Jackson can generate only a limited profit of two dollars per book, which is why he rejects the practice of price dumping and accuses West African vendors of only being after "the fast dollar" (ibid.), reflecting the same prejudices expressed by Adeyemi. Finally, customers are more and more unwilling to pay more than seven dollars per book, having become used to the lower prices and often expecting to receive an even higher discount. Although Jackson still makes a small profit selling in the South Bronx, his experience shows that many customers do not consider expenses on the vendors' side and in fact try to determine the book prices themselves. Customers also use the vendors' origin to pit vendors against each other, as in the case of a reader who, unwilling to accept Jackson's price, proclaimed: "I got an African. He *give* me books" (ibid.).

Jackson, however, is convinced that the use of alternative selling strategies and networks will also allow African American newcomers to the business to establish themselves as vendors. Key to his approach is to build connections with independent street literature publishers and individual authors who, unwilling to sell their novels at deflated prices, instead actively participate in marketing their books via events such as readings and book signings—prerequisites for Jackson's continued selling of books at prices of ten or twelve dollars.[33] By establishing direct connections with these types of publishers and authors, all of whom are African American, Jackson also seeks to build an alternative network that allows him to circumvent business with West African vendors with the aim of eventually breaking their monopoly. By repeatedly mentioning that he and his business partners share an upbringing in New York City's Black low-income neighborhoods, Jackson implicitly claims a close proximity to and ownership of the street literature product that recent immigrants do not possess. Emanating from this shared experience, his business connections also harbor collective resentment against West African vendors, clearly expressed by one of the publishers Jackson works with: "Honestly. I sweat their game. They don't give a rat's ass about Americans, Black Americans. They think they are way above us. 'I am king. You are a slave child.' You know? That's really how they treat us, I feel." Recalling hierarchies that reflect West African traders' participation in the transatlantic slave trade—over 73 percent of Africans transported to America were shipped from West Africa, and large numbers were sold by African traders (Walker 2009: 24)—the publisher's statement illustrates that the current hostilities in play in the street literature vending scene have deep historical roots. From an African American vendor's perspective, West African immigrants are intruders who—economically, but also culturally, socially, and spatially— appropriate a territory claimed by African Americans.

Conclusion

Street vending's importance to street literature lies not only in its role in establishing the genre but also in its essential function of offering the popular novels to low-income neighborhoods that have no indoor bookstores. Today's vending scene, having reached its saturation point, is characterized by contestations between the vendor group of West African immigrants, who still dominate the business, and African Americans, most of whom entered the street vending scene after others had taken the most lucrative vending spots, established close-knit networks, and determined pricing policies. West African vendors justify their predominance by citing their perseverance and work ethic, attributes they do not assign to African Americans. The latter, meanwhile, observe with suspicion those first-generation immigrants who have achieved comparatively greater economic mobility in a shorter time thanks to their supportive networks, even though they often also lack higher education.

When claiming their share in the street literature business, African American vendors frequently refer to the novels as "theirs," as they depict experiences not shared by recent West African immigrants. In light of the disproportionately high unemployment rate among African Americans, however, their rising numbers among street literature vendors also demonstrates that "a good share of the informal sector is not [merely] the result of immigrant survival strategies, but also an outcome of structural patterns of transformations in the larger economy" (Sassen 1988: 15). The practice of street literature selling thus occupies an ambiguous position. On the one hand, given its persistence over the past ten years, bookselling may begin to look like a steady occupation to those who initially saw it as a short-lived practice carried out primarily by immigrants, most of whom eventually return to their home countries. From this angle, booksellers, and especially those who lack higher education, may acknowledge their practice as an alternative to the short-term, part-time, low-paid jobs usually available to them on the "regular" labor market. On the other hand, substantial changes in the street literature selling business over the past years, particularly in regard to pricing policies, have transformed it into a more flexible and consumer-friendly practice, negatively affecting individual vendors who are trying to enter the business after the genre's first selling wave. The quarrel between the two seller groups is thus indicative of larger conflicts between immigrant and African American populations, which have intensified with recent immigration waves and cannot be attributed to language and cultural barriers alone, but also reflect the harsh competition in today's neoliberal labor market.

Although many obstacles—such as obtaining credit or facing new restrictions in view of Harlem's gentrification and rezoning for redevelopment[34]—affect both vendor groups alike, current tendencies confirm that the two groups prefer to work in separate networks rather than creating a united workforce. Taking into account the differences in the challenges each group has historically faced in the U.S. entrepreneurial sector, the outdoor vending of street literature so far rather confirms the advantaged position of immigrant groups and the secondary role that African Americans play in entrepreneurial ventures. How the economic terrain of street literature vending will be negotiated and divided in the near future remains to be seen. It will, however, be closely related to the overall development of the genre, especially its further differentiation into subgenres and the number of persisting authors.

Kristina Graaff received her PhD in American Studies from Humboldt University of Berlin, Germany, where she is currently an assistant professor of (African) American literature and culture. She has been a fellow at the Transatlantic Graduate Research Program Berlin-New York and a visiting scholar at Fordham University's African American Studies Department, the Bronx African American History Project and the University of Washington's Honors Program. Her areas of research include Black popular culture and its relationship to the U.S. justice system, critical race theory, law in literature, and the interplay between literary and entrepreneurial practices.

Notes

1. Taking today's street vending scene in Harlem as an example, vendors cater to members of the Black community with goods like CDs, movies, jewelry, and beauty products. An increasing number of products also target visitors drawn to Harlem as a tourist site; these include pictures, bags, and shirts showing Martin Luther King, Malcolm X, or President Obama. Additionally, one can find goods also offered by street vendors elsewhere in New York City such as fruit, coffee, hot dogs, and kebabs, usually sold from so-called pushcarts.
2. Other common names for the genre are "urban fiction" and "hip-hop lit." However, since the streets are not only a central narrative location in the novels but also a major physical location for the genre's distribution, I will use the term "street literature" throughout this essay.
3. The expansion of what is called Latina/o street literature has increased the number of writers who are also of Latin American descent.
4. For a close reading of selected novels that elaborates on the criticism voiced against street literature, see Graaff (2013).
5. For the relationship between street literature and the prison system, see Sweeney (2010) and Graaff (2015; 2010).
6. This is just an estimate; reliable figures are unavailable due to the large number of novels sold on the streets. The estimate takes into account that African American readers do not exclusively read books by African American authors, and that other reader groups likewise also purchase Black popular fiction.
7. According to my repeated observations over a three-year time frame, up to eight book stands usually operate on Harlem's 125th Street between Morningside Avenue and Park Avenue. On Brooklyn's Fulton Street between Flatbush Avenue and Court Street, there are usually up to ten vendors. Fordham Road in the Bronx features up to three sellers. Additionally, two regular vendors sell the books in Midtown on 33rd and 34th Streets between 6th and 7th Avenue, while downtown Manhattan has up to three street literature vendors selling on Fulton Street and on various Broadway corners.
8. Besides printed matter, works of art—including paintings, photographs, and sculptures as well as T-shirts and other items bearing political messages—are considered works of expression protected by the First Amendment and can therefore be sold without a license.
9. One observed exception is a mobile vendor who sells street literature out of a wheeled cart in Harlem, moving between local stores and restaurants. Also, a female vendor in downtown Brooklyn sells from a movable wooden cart that she sets up at a fixed location during vending hours.
10. The West African trading business is not limited to New York City but has numerous outposts all over the country, including cities like Atlanta, Boston,

Washington, Philadelphia, New Orleans, Houston, Chicago, and Los Angeles (Stoller 2002: 81). As Stoller points out, although many merchants can be found among West African immigrants, many also work in other occupations, including jobs such as stock clerks, security guards, and grocery store delivery men (7).

11. I use pseudonyms in place of the two vendors' real names, mainly to keep disapproving statements about the respective other vending group confidential.
12. Due to the study's limited time frame and focus on just two vendors, the material obtained offers only fragmentary insight into selling practices, vendor relations, and attitudes toward the business. It intends, however, to point out general tendencies and developments in New York City's outdoor street literature vending scene.
13. The latest U.S. Bureau of Labor statistics, from May 2015, show the unemployment rate of African Americans to be almost twice as high as that of the entire nation. (http://www.bls.gov/news.release/empsit.t02.htm; http://www.bls.gov/news.release/empsit.nr0.htm.)
14. The same conceptual understanding applies to terms like "Black business" and "African American self-employment."
15. The implementation of Affirmative Action opened public-sector contracting to African American–owned businesses, allowing them to begin serving a more general, nonminority market by the 1970s in areas like wholesaling, finance, insurance, and real estate, but to this day a large number of businesses are small retail firms in the personal service industry (Boston 1999: 74f.).
16. According to recent statistics from the United States Department of Labor, in 2011 only 3.8 percent of Blacks reported to be self-employed, in comparison to 7.2 percent of the white and 5.8 percent of the Hispanic population (http://www.dol.gov/_sec/media/reports/blacklaborforce).
17. Attempts to counter such negative images and stimulate ventures into self-employment can be found in (online) magazines such as *Black Entrepreneurship* and *Black Enterprise*.
18. Apart from the British-held Caribbean islands, Cuba, Panama, and Martinique, the countries of origin of foreign-born Blacks at the time also included West Africa and France (Watkins-Owens 1996: 45).
19. The term "bootstrapping" probably refers to the idea of lifting oneself up by one's own bootstraps. In a business context it refers to a successful entrepreneurial activity accomplished without any outside help. Self-publishing and self-distribution of books are not new phenomena in the African American literary scene (Reid and Abbott 2003: 25; Jacques 1997: 40, 1998: 34). E. Lynn Harris so successfully distributed his book *Invisible Life* on the streets that Doubleday eventually published it in 1992 (Jacques 1998: 37). However, no other genre of African American fiction has been self-published and distributed on the streets to the same degree as street literature.
20. Street literature novels are occasionally supplemented by titles on conspiracy theories and manipulative power strategies. The most common books on conspiracy theories include *Behold the Pale Horse* by William Cooper (1991), *Making of the Whiteman* by Paul Lawrence Guthrie (1992) and *The Willie Lynch*

Letter and The Destruction of Black Unity by Slave Chronicles (2004). Books dealing with strategies of control include Robert Greene's *The 48 Laws of Power* (1998), *The Art of Seduction* (2001), and *The 33 Strategies of War* (2006) as well as the ancient Chinese military treatise *The Art of War*, attributed to Sun Tzu.

21. The cover price refers to the price printed on the back cover of a book. It is usually $14.95 for softcover street literature titles and between $21.99 and $26.99 for hardcover novels, which are still rare on the market. Street vendors sell the novels tax-free, whereas indoor bookstores add tax to the cover price.
22. The term "overhead costs" refers to rent, taxes, and utilities. According to NYC governmental regulations, street vendors have to pay taxes for the products sold; however, to my knowledge the majority of vendors do not comply with this rule (http://www.nyc.gov/html/sbs/nycbiz/downloads/pdf/educational/sector_guides/street_vending.pdf; http://streetvendor.org/for-vendors/faq/).
23. Among the first novels Adeyemi sold are Sister Souljah's *The Coldest Winter Ever* (1999) *Flyy Girl* by Omar Tyree (1993), Eric Jerome Dickey's *Liars Game* (2001), and *Milk in My Coffee* (1999).
24. Street vendors and other distributors of street literature concurred that sales had begun to flatten by 2005 (McCune 2005).
25. This is not to say that street literature is exclusively read by women. Many buy books and send them to their boyfriends or husbands in prison. The high number of street literature readers behind bars, both male and female, is confirmed by authors, publishers, and bookstore staff who ship books to correctional facilities (Benjamin, personal communication, 24 June 2010; Hopkins, personal communication, 3 July 2010; Clark, personal communication, 15 December 2009).
26. Two are located on 125th Street between Frederick Douglass Boulevard and 7th Avenue; one is in Queens on 163rd Street and Jamaica Avenue; another is in downtown Brooklyn on Fulton Street; and two are in the Bronx, one at 149th Street and 3rd Avenue and the other at 168th Street and Grand Concourse.
27. One attempt to regulate this trade was made in 1979 by New York Mayor Ed Koch, who moved several of Harlem's outdoor vendors to Mart 125, an indoor market also located on 125th Street. However, efforts to prepare vendors to found their own indoor stores failed, mainly because the customer flow was too low and vendors could not afford the daily rent they had to pay for their indoor spots (Zukin 1995: 241; Benson 2006: 5f.).
28. In contrast to many other West African immigrants, Adeyemi came to stay in the United States, where he also remarried. However, he still sends remittances to his first wife and their children, who continue to reside in West Africa.
29. Street vending itself has contributed to the genre's commercialization, as editors from established presses, having realized the genre's profit potential, recruited authors based on the selection offered at bookstalls (Kilgannon 2006: 1).
30. His main vending location is in the South Bronx on 838 Westchester Avenue in front of a fish market. The second, on 225th Street in front of a Target department store, attracts residents from the entire borough.

31. According to the latest New York State Department of Labor statistics for April 2015, the borough's unemployment rate was 8.3 percent, in comparison to 5.2 in Manhattan, 6.4 in Brooklyn, and 5.4 percent in Queens (http://www.labor.ny.gov/stats/pressReleases/county_rates.pdf).
32. According to the self-published author Randy Kearse, with the current digital printing machines a print run of 2,000 copies costs approximately two dollars per book (Kearse, personal communication, 1 September 2006). Author and publisher Wahida Clark states that printing in China brings the unit price down to less than one dollar; however, it takes several weeks to ship the books to the United States (Clark, personal communication, 15 December 2009).
33. Jackson's main business partners include the African American independent press Augustus Publishing as well as authors like K'wan, Eric S. Grey, Treasure Blue, and Brother Inch, who all actively participate in the marketing of their books.
34. In March 2008, the New York City Council approved plans to rezone the area around 125th Street. The rezoning plan aims to transform Harlem's main business street into a major residential and commercial corridor, adding over 2,000 new condominium apartments and high-rise buildings up to twenty-nine floors high. The plan will not only push out many current residents, most of whom will not unable to afford the new type of housing; but most likely will also have severe effects on the community's street vendors, as indicated by the suggested "reduction of corridor density" and "enhancement of the pedestrian realm" in the Department of City Planning's proposal (http://www.nyc.gov/html/dcp/html/125th/index.shtml).

Bibliography

Alexander, Michelle. 2010. *The New Jim Crow: Mass Incarceration in the Age of Colorblindness*. New York: The New Press.

Austin, Regina. 1994. "'An Honest Living': Street Vendors, Municipal Regulation, and the Black Public Sphere." *Yale Law Journal* 103 (8): 2119–2131.

———. 1995. "'A Nation of Thieves': Consumption, Commerce, and the Black Public Sphere." *The Black Public Sphere: A Public Culture Book*, ed. The Black Public Sphere Collective. Chicago: University of Chicago Press.

Bates, Timothy. 1997. *Race, Self-Employment, and Upward Mobility: An Illusive American Dream*. Baltimore, MD: John Hopkins University Press.

Benson, Joshua. 2006. *Regulating Street Vendors in New York City: Case Studies*. Master's thesis, Columbia University.

Bluestone, Daniel. 1991. "'The Pushcart Evil': Peddlers, Merchants, and New York City's Streets, 1890–1940." *Journal of Urban History* 18 (1): 68–92.

Boston, Thomas. 1999. *Affirmative Action and Black Entrepreneurship*. New York: Routledge.

Chiles, Nick. 2006. "Their Eyes Were Reading Smut." *New York Times*, 4 January.

Dawkins, Wayne. 2005. "Street Smarts: Book Vendors Count on Foot Traffic, Marketing Instinct and the First Amendment in the Battle for Profits." *Black Issues Book Review* (July–August): 46–47.

Duneier, Mitchell. 1999. *Sidewalk*. New York: Farrar, Straus and Giroux.

Fairlie, Robert W. 1999. "The Absence of the African-American Owned Business: An Analysis of the Dynamics of Self-Employment." *Journal of Labor Economics* 17 (1): 80–108.

Fratoe, Frank. 1988. "Social Capital of Black Business Owners." *Review of Black Political Economy* 16 (4): 33–50.

Graaff, Kristina. 2010. "Reading Street Literature, Reading America's Prison System." *Pop Matters* (February). http://www.popmatters.com/feature/119786-reading-street-literature-reading-americas-prison-system/.

———. 2013. "Street Literature and the Mode of Spectacular Writing: Popular Fiction between Sensationalism, Education, Politics and Entertainment." In *Contemporary African American Literature: The Living Canon*, ed. Lovalerie King and Shirley Moody-Turner. Bloomington and Indianapolis: Indiana University Press.

———. 2015. *Street Literature: Black Popular Fiction in the Era of U.S. Mass Incarceration*. Heidelberg: Heidelberg University Press Winter.

Green, Shelley, and Paul Pryde. 1997. *Black Entrepreneurship in America*. New Brunswick, NJ: Transaction.

Jacques, Geoffrey. 1997. "More Than a Niche." *Publishers Weekly* 244 (50): 38–42.

———. 1998. "More Books, More Readers, More Sales." *Publishers Weekly* 245 (50): 34–39.

Jones, Vanessa. 2008. "The Real World: Teens Say They're Reading Urban Fiction because It Reflects Life in the City. Should Parents Be Concerned?" *Boston Globe*, 3 November.

Kilgannon, Corey. 2006. "Street Lit with Publishing Cred: From Prison to a Four-Book Deal." *New York Times*, 14 February.

McCune, Jenny. 2005. "The Rise of Urban Fiction." *The Independent Book Publishers Association*. http://www.ibpa-online.org/articles/shownews.aspx?id=2157.

New York City Council. 2013. "Legislation Details, §2-314 List of Street Restrictions." http://www.nyc.gov/html/dca/downloads/pdf/general_vendor_law_rules.pdf.

New York Department of Consumer Affairs. 2010. "Street Vending Fact Sheet." http://www.nyc.gov/html/sbs/nycbiz/downloads/pdf/educational/sector_guides/street_vending.pdf.

Reid, Calvin, and Charlotte Abbott. 2003. "Talkin' About Black Books." *Publishers Weekly* 250 (49): 24–30.

Rodriguez, Junius P. 2007. "Provision Grounds." In *Slavery in the United States: A Social, Political, and Historical Encyclopedia*, ed. Junius P. Rodriguez. Santa Barbara, CA: ABC Clio.

Sassen, Saskia. 1988. "New York City's Informal Economy." Conference on Comparative Ethnicity. ISSR Working Papers in the Social Sciences. Los Angeles, CA: Institute for Social Science Research.

Stoller, Paul. 2002. *Money Has No Smell: The Africanization of New York City*. Chicago: University of Chicago Press.

Sweeney, Megan. 2010. *Reading Is My Window: Books and the Art of Reading in Women's Prisons*. Chapel Hill: University of North Carolina Press.
Tabb, William K. 1970. *The Political Economy of the Black Ghetto: Why the Mass of Black Americans Has Been Forced to Accept Economic Deprivation in an Age of Prosperity*. New York: W. W. Norton.
Target Market News. 2010. *The Buying Power of Black America*. Chicago, IL: Target Market News.
Walker, Juliet E. K. 1997. "Slave Entrepreneurs." In *Dictionary of Afro-American Slavery*, ed. John David Smith Randall M. Miller. Westport, CT: Greenwood.
———. 2009. *The History of Black Business in America: Capitalism, Race, Entrepreneurship*, 2nd ed., vol. 1. Chapel Hill: University of North Carolina Press.
Watkins-Owens, Irma. 1996. *Blood Relations: Caribbean Immigrants and the Harlem Community, 1900–1930*. Bloomington and Indianapolis: Indiana University Press.
Weeks, Linton. 2004. "New Books in the Hood: Street Lit makes Inroads with Readers and Publishers." *Washington Post*, 31 July, C01.
Williams, Timothy. 2008. "In Plans for Vacant Harlem Market, City Envisions a Culture Base." *New York Times*, 2 September.
Young, Nicholas Maurice. 2007. "Toward a Rethinking of Race, Culture and the African American Entrepreneur." In *Handbook of Research on Ethnic Minority Entrepreneurship: A Co-Evolutionary View on Resource Management*, ed. Léo-Paul Dana. Northampton, MA: Edward Elgar.
Zukin, Sharon. 1995. *The Culture of Cities*. Malden, MA: Blackwell Publishers.

PART III

The Spatial Mobility of Urban Street Vending

CHAPTER 7

The Urbanism of Los Angeles Street Vending

Kenny Cupers

Street vending is an omnipresent feature of the urban landscape of Los Angeles. It takes place on the city's sidewalks, in parks, and at squares, but also at highway intersections, on parking lots, in leftover spaces, and in privately owned spaces like outdoor mall plazas.[1] Large-scale Latin American migration and the economic downturn of the 1980s led many poor, often undocumented immigrants to turn to street vending as a key means of economic survival. Since then, street vending has gained increasing visibility in the city. The majority of the roughly ten to fifteen thousand vendors in Los Angeles are Latina/o migrants selling freshly cut fruits and vegetables, homemade foods, and carbonated drinks on the street, carrying their wares in everything from back pockets and baskets to carts, cars, and trucks (see Figures 7.1, 7.2, 7.3, and 7.4).[2]

Despite the ubiquity of mobile vending, Los Angeles municipal legislation prohibits it.[3] It is one of the few major U.S. cities to impose an outright ban, in contrast to, for example, New York City, where street vending is regulated and half of the estimated twelve thousand vendors are licensed (Street Vendor Project of the Urban Justice Center 2006: 6). Over the past twenty-five years, this legislation and the accompanying police enforcement of the street vending ban have inspired various forms of protest and political mobilization, public debate, planning proposals, and an experimental program to legalize vending in particular neighborhoods of the city.

In the past, street vendors were often cast as part of a "traditional" or "backward" economy found in the so-called developing world but soon to disappear as labor moved toward full-time, stable, regulated employment in a modern industrialized context. In past decades, however, the persistence and growth of informal activities across the globe have contradicted such projections, not only in developing countries but also in "advanced" postindustrial cities like Los Angeles. Scholars have attributed this development to the relative decline of welfare state regulation and Fordist industrial production, and the emergence of new economic regimes escaping nationally organized regulation. These more flexible regimes are generated by globalizing capital flows, which themselves rely on the informalization and transnationalization of labor (Portes and Sassen 1987; Portes, Castells, and Benton 1989; Sassen 1991, 1998; Roy and Al Sayyad 2004).

Yet, as much as this political economic perspective explains the resurgence of street vending in cities like Los Angeles, it remains silent about its consequences on the ground. While some more recent scholarship has drawn attention to vendors' political mobilization (Cross 1998; Weber 2001) or creative entrepreneurship (Jones 1988; Balkin 1989; Waldinger, Aldrich, and Ward 1990; Kloosterman and Rath 2003; Cross and Morales 2007), the spatiality of street vending has only recently become a focus of research.[4] Coming closest to offering a theoretical framework for understanding street vending as a spatial rather than merely economic or cultural practice is the work of Margaret Crawford, John Kaliski, and John Cross (1999). They cast street vending as a key instance of what they call *everyday urbanism*.

This notion is fundamentally inspired by the work of French thinkers Henri Lefèbvre and Michel De Certeau. In the immediate postwar decades, Henri Lefèbvre was one of the first to rescue the realm of the everyday from theoretical neglect and dismissal.[5] While he acknowledged everyday life could be victim to the alienating forces of capitalism and bureaucracy, he also presented it as harboring the seeds of change and opening up to the meaningful and the authentic. The authors of *Everyday Urbanism* view this positive, liberating aspect of the everyday as holding crucial potential for the contemporary city (Crawford et al. 1999). Further borrowing Lefèbvre's concept of the "production of space," the authors understand street vending as creative intervention rather than spatial misuse. Street vendors produce new kinds of spaces for themselves and others in the city and in doing so broaden the definition of public space. The authors' second theoretical underpinning refers to Michel De Certeau's distinction between strategies (of the strong) and tactics (of the weak). Whereas strategies operate in space—by setting what is "proper" in the city's demarcated spaces—tactics operate in time. As such, temporary or ephemeral practices of everyday life like street vending offer a counterweight to the officially sanctioned uses of space.

Ultimately, everyday urbanism is a critique of the formalism that dominates the discipline of architecture and the reductive rationality of urban planning, and the kind of architectural and urban thinking that sustains it. Against both these dominant norms, Crawford et al. set the basic premise that lived experience is more important than physical form in defining the city. They use the term "urbanism" to loosen the ideological grip of these disciplines. Urbanism is not just the construction materials of bricks, concrete, and asphalt, the solid matter of building. It is also more than the knowledge and practice of architects, urban planners, or policy makers. Understood in very loose terms, urbanism is a field that encompasses not only the materiality of the built environment and the knowledge of experts but the multitude of practices, visions, and interventions that make up urban life itself.[6] Such an understanding brings into focus the tensions between the planned and the unplanned city—the realm of experts and the world of everyday practitioners. If, following the authors, we understand the purview of urbanism as framing life in the city in the broadest possible terms, we should also be able to take into account a far wider range of elements, including the temporal qualities of the urban environment and thus also those produced by street vending.

Despite the fruitfulness of these theoretical propositions, they raise as many questions as they try to answer. To what extent, then, is street vending a form of everyday urbanism? Is it so merely by virtue of its presence as an urban practice in the city? The notion of the everyday is hardly monolithic: what is everyday to some is not to others. So to whom are Los Angeles' street vendors *everyday*? And what makes them *urbanists*? How exactly does street vending in Los Angeles allow us to imagine a kind of urbanism that differs from the dominant one?

This chapter argues that the answers to these questions lie in the specific way street vendors create space in Los Angeles. More than in other U.S. and Latin American cities, street vendors in this "mobile city"—in which the prevailing urban form is expressive of car-based mobility—are also on the move. Unlike the street vending markets in Mexico City or the organized vending spots of New York City, street vending in Los Angeles is at once more precarious and more mobile. Due to law enforcement, and to the dynamics of urban space itself, the space of street vending in Los Angeles exists by virtue of movement. More than any other American city, Los Angeles can be seen as founded on individual (auto)mobility. Street vendors are not only inscribed within this culture but also transform it by offering alternative forms of mobility that remake urban space. What makes Los Angeles street vending understandable as a specific form of urbanism, rather than just one of many urban practices of contesting the streets in the contemporary city, is vendors' creativity and ability to move through the city—on foot with their goods, or by car, van, or truck. This kind of concrete urban mobility and the symbolic meanings it entails are the subject of this chapter. Though clearly distinct from vendors' transnational or socioeconomic mobility, their urban mobility relates directly to both why they are outlawed and how they creatively tackle the constraints of social class, foreignness, and racism.

My analysis is based on a combination of ethnographic fieldwork and historical analysis.[7] In the first part, based on interviews and participant observation, I focus on the street vendors themselves and reveal how they transform the city as they move. Tracing their movements by car and on foot, in and through urban neighborhoods of Los Angeles, particularly East Hollywood and downtown, at different times of the day and on different days of the week allowed me to map the dynamic geography of vending. Next, referring to local newspapers, government documents, the archives of nonprofit organizations, and interviews with government officials and activists, I discuss the regulation of vending and the symbolic meanings of mobility shaping debates about such regulation. These transcend the pragmatic register of ways to make the city work and cut to the core of its identity. Finally, using these same sources, I analyze the efforts to legalize street vending in Los Angeles since the mid 1980s. These efforts demonstrate how Los Angeles street vending became an object of urban planning and intervention.

The Mobile Space of Street Vending

Although predominantly of Central and Latin American origin, the vendors of Los Angeles share neither a single race or ethnicity, nor a similar background or social group. Some fled from problems in their home countries; others came to seek economic opportunity. Some arrived yesterday; others have been in the same neighborhood for decades. Some entered the United States officially; others came undocumented. Some have become permanent residents. Others have families waiting for them elsewhere, do not intend to stay, and aim to maintain a deliberate elusiveness: here today but not tomorrow, if things go according to plan. Regardless of effectively expecting to return to their home countries, they live to derive maximal profit from their stay and remain flexible in their personal lives. Still others might initially have been transnational migrants but have subsequently stayed or moved elsewhere within the United States. More than their contribution to a transnational economy through remittances (see Suro et al. 2001), their labor marshals both local and transnational networks of aid, skill, and culture (cf. Hannerz and Smith 2001:101–122). These networks result from concrete spatial strategies and mobile practices in the city.

Latino neighborhoods like Boyle Heights, parts of downtown, and East Hollywood have particularly high concentrations of street vendors. In such dense lower-income immigrant areas, car ownership is less common and the streets are more intensely used by pedestrians. Street vendors not only bank on the existing foot traffic, but also actively contribute to the liveliness of the streets by giving pedestrians a reason to pass by, stop, consume, or chat. Some bus and subway stops become open-air markets during rush hour, when commuters are enticed to buy cheap meals, snacks, and various knickknacks. Vendors in these neighborhoods often live close by and walk to work.

Daisy is one of them. She is a young Honduran woman who sells cut fruit on a busy street corner in the MacArthur Park neighborhood. She explained to me how she came to Los Angeles:

> I came illegally to the United States. I have four children in Honduras. I came here out of necessity. I have always been a street vendor. I was given the opportunity to work at this cart so I could make things better for my family, my children. ... I like business, and have always been in it since I was small. I worked in the market [in Honduras], and I think I am going to continue it because I like it. ... My plan is to build a house, a house in my own country. Then I will go back.

Her cousin, Gloria, who moved to Los Angeles twelve years ago, has helped Daisy by paying for her trip to the United States, offering her a room in her own house, and giving her this job working at least eight hours a day, six days a week. Gloria explained: "My husband had the initial idea to get the fruit cart, but the work and food preparation is hers. ... It helps us to live and pay the rent, that's it." Daisy receives a weekly paycheck from her cousin and regularly sends remittances home. Gloria was a food vendor herself for a long time, selling tacos in the same neighborhood. She and her husband recently purchased two stainless steel fruit carts, and besides her cousin she now employs an acquaintance from her church community to operate them. Every day except Sunday, the carts are moved to the same street corner in the MacArthur Park neighborhood. In the evenings her husband picks them up and moves them to a nearby commercially owned commissary where they are stored and cleaned following county health laws.

Although such vending spaces depend on daily rhythm, they seem relatively fixed. Fruit cart vendors like Daisy have reason to change location only when sales decrease, a chance at a better location arises, or police harassment forces them to move. Police enforcement, which consists of a hefty fine (up to one thousand dollars) and in some cases confiscation of goods or the cart itself, is haphazard. The regime of enforcement is thus a factor in the dynamics of street vending spaces (Muñoz 2008). When crackdowns in targeted areas subside, however, vendors tend to reappear in those very same areas—possibly even on the same spots, if not on the other side of the corner or less than a block away. In this sense, the role of police enforcement in the creation of vending spaces is less consequential than the economic logic of street vending itself.

Other types of vending in dense neighborhoods like those around MacArthur Park do not require a stationary spot at all: vendors simply stay on the move. Ice cream vendors, and all those who are able to carry their wares in bags, walk the sidewalks to maximize contacts with potential customers. Others combine walking with setting up shop, laying down their wares on a blanket. This allows them to relocate to wherever foot traffic is more intense at particular moments of the day, and also to disappear quickly when police show up (see Figure 7.2). Still others follow much the same procedure using shopping carts.

In most of Los Angeles, however, where sidewalk traffic tends to be rather sparse and the majority of potential customers are in cars, different kinds of vending spaces emerge. A "typical street" in Los Angeles may seem more dominated by cars than its New York City counterpart, but this has less to do with car traffic than with what happens alongside it: in Los Angeles, buildings are more often set back from the road and separated by parking lots, which takes animation from the street into the domain of mini-malls, gas stations, and the private realm of the store and the restaurant. In such an environment, where sidewalks are insignificant, street vendors can easily appropriate under-utilized zones and use carts, tables, blankets, and so on to turn them into more animated public spaces. Major road intersections and highway off-ramps, on the other hand, can seem more hostile to such appropriation. They tend to offer plenty of leftover spaces for vendors to occupy: a traffic island or a median strip often suffices to set up shop. Many vendors' informal employers, who might be relatives and often come from the same social network of immigrants, drop them off in these places. Equipped with bags and baskets of fruit or prepared foods, they find themselves at different intersections every day, trying to sell their wares to drivers stopped in front of traffic lights. They interpret the laws of traffic engineering to create business opportunities and turn transitional moments into spaces of impulse shopping. These spaces are ephemeral in the temporal sense too: vendors are sometimes there for less than an hour—just as long as it takes to sell all their wares. They are then picked up or drive to the next location.

The more fortunate vendors can use a car as infrastructure for their entrepreneurial practices. Some set up shop simply by opening their trunk in a parking spot close to a public park or other recreational area where they are guaranteed potential customers. A couple of basic placards listing the menu of the day can be used to entice passers-by (see Figure 7.5). This strategy, which requires intimate knowledge of the city's urban rhythms, can be very efficient: vendors can sell a lot in a short amount of time and organize their schedule around other work. They can also close their shop as quickly as it was set up in case of looming police presence. Evenings and nights facilitate yet another rhythm of street vending. Business parking lots offer a second city of abundant space after regular office hours. Vendors, who know the life of the lot and its surveillance, have ample space to set up shop—which can range from a simple grill to a veritable outdoor restaurant (see Figures 7.6 and 7.7). By simply setting up a few tables covered with tablecloths, taking up not more than a couple of empty parking spots, they advertise themselves to passing traffic and turn hostile space into familiar, homely, safer places.

Vendors like these creatively employ the spaces dedicated to the infrastructure of the "mobile city," subverting the historically defined logic of much of Los Angeles's public space (see Norton 2008). As such examples illustrate, street vending is not an ephemeral practice in an otherwise unaffected space but instead actively shapes the urban spaces of Los Angeles by generating new kinds of public spaces and producing meaningful cultural landscapes based on the inventive potential of memory (Rojas 1991; Crawford et al. 1999; Muñoz, 2008). Vendors are key agents in the refamiliarization and domestication of Los Angeles's car-dominated space. But how they do so is perhaps even more important. Street vendors transform urban space primarily by virtue of their mobility: perhaps paradoxically, it is only by being mobile that they are able to transform highway intersections into shops and parking lots into restaurants. They actively produce urban space—often against the unwritten "rules" inscribed in those spaces and under threat of law enforcement—and succeed in doing so because they remain constantly on the move.

In their efforts to gain a foothold in the city, spatially and economically, street vendors derive their individual agency from their urban mobility. The everyday movements of Dina, a food vendor and a single mother of four, aptly demonstrate this. During the period I interviewed her, Dina was selling tacos outside a nightclub on weekends and tamales in the evening peak hours on a busy street corner in Koreatown. She explained to me:

> A friend of mine works at another night club and she asked me if I wanted to help her make food. She gave me 40 dollars per night for it. Then the owners of that club proposed I work at their other club, independently. ... I have

been vending illegally in the street for about eleven years now. ... The truth is that when my children were smaller, it was much more difficult [to support my family]. That is how I got the idea to vend illegally, on the street. ... I worked in a factory before, but could not support my family because the little money I earned there, I had to spend, and there wasn't enough left to pay rent.

She now cooks her street foods at home and works three to four nights a week, when her children are asleep. Some of the female food vendors I spoke with were single mothers who preferred street vending over a regular job like factory work. The flexibility of street vending allows these women to combine child care responsibilities with a viable income (see also Tinker 1987 and the essay by Dunn in this volume).

Vendors thus tend to use their urban mobility strategically. This contrasts with what would seem intuitively germane to street vending and what De Certeau identified as tactical, namely, a second-order, reactive, ad hoc, short-term pursuit in the face of oppression (De Certeau 1980). It is true that most vendors respond flexibly to enforcement. But whereas some migrants might resort to vending in utter destitution and without a conscious plan, many more vendors engage in vending as a creative long-term strategy in organizing their livelihood. Unbounded by the opposition between liberating tactics and oppressive strategies, street vending creates a mobile geography in close relation to various other actors—customers, business owners, police officers, and so on. Vendors' strategies of moving through the city depend as much on the reigning norms of their environment as on their personal situation and skill set. Movement strategies often are also gendered: male vendors tend to be more mobile, usually carrying their goods in a large bag or selling out of a cart, whereas many women tend to install their wares, often because they sell homemade hot foods requiring quite complicated handling and transportation (compare Figures 7.2, 7.3, and 7.4) (cf. Cornejo 2005).

The capacity to move allows vendors to exploit the temporal rhythms of the city. At noon vendors flock to commercial and industrial areas like the downtown garment district, where low-paid workers need cheap lunch options. During the evening peak they can be found at subway stops and highway intersections where traffic jams form ideal concentrations of potential customers. At night, they work outside bars and nightclubs. And on weekends they cater to the city's park visitors. Most vendors go back and forth between these multiple sites at different times of the day or the week, trying to increase sales and escape police enforcement. Despite the seeming ephemerality of this practice, vendors cultivate their own patterns of mobility, negotiating between flexibility and routine. They frequent the same sites at specific times of day so that local residents and customers can get used to them and identify their location as a place to get street food. When sales decrease, or when repeated police harassment forces them to move, they seek out different spots. Such patterns of movement reveal the variety of creative strategies involved in the seemingly unplanned practice of street vending. This creative ability allows vendors not only to survive but to maintain a way of life with an (albeit often limited) range of choice. In this sense, urban mobility is the key means by which vendors shape their position—as migrants, laborers, and citizens—in the city.

Regulation and the Symbolic Meaning of Mobility

The regulation of street vending in Los Angeles is a complex matrix in which power is distributed over a variety of institutions—governmental, nonprofit and private—and administrative levels—city, county, and state (see Figure 7.8). Legislatively, the city government has the most immediate effect on street vending: the Los Angeles Municipal Code prohibits vending in all the city's public spaces.[8] The state of California legislates street vending insofar as it pertains to public health and safety. It also issues sales permits in order to levy taxes.[9] These do not permit selling on the street, though some vendors assume that it does. This legislative intricacy is only heightened by the complexity of enforcement. Four different governmental bodies are responsible for enforcing laws against illegal vending on public land.[10] In addition, the private security forces of Business Improvement Districts have the power to remove street vendors from both private and public property. The enforcement of anti-vending laws is legitimized in three main ways: street vendors are seen as competing unfairly with local merchants; their food raises health concerns; and they threaten to obstruct what is officially designated as public space.

Despite the seemingly pragmatic nature of these official concerns, the increasing prominence of street vending in Los Angeles from the late 1980s onward aroused public resistance to street commerce far exceeding these practical concerns. In the local press, public health and other concerns were constantly diverted into moral justification. Among government officials as well, wild stories about street foods being prepared in dirty bathrooms and taken out of trash cans continue to circulate and legitimize enforcement. Meanwhile, few studies have examined the concrete effects of street foods on public health, and the one known nutritional study conducted thus far did not report any serious health risks (Taylor et. al. 2000). A similar attitude characterizes the local merchants who, rather than monitoring the actual effect of street vending on their own profits, tend to focus on its "dirtiness" and the way this affects the desired image of their street. Such perceptions can be influenced by minute aesthetic details. In the small private vending program around subway stops,[11] local shopkeepers complained that the umbrellas of Latina/o food vendors around the subway station would tarnish the reputation of the area and demanded that the colorful "Latino-looking" umbrellas be replaced by evenly colored, more corporate-looking ones (see Figure 7.9).

These types of symbolic meanings of street vending have predominated in the often edgy debates reported in the local press over the past decades. Some opponents have considered street vending a sign of backwardness and an element of the so-called Third World, with which their city should have nothing in common. In an opinion piece about street vending, a high-level policy official contended that "some parts of the city are like a Third World country" and that street vending was a sign that "the quality of life is eroding at a rapid pace."[12] Many residents have perceived street vendors as dirty, not only because of the trash their customers leave behind but also because roaming vendors are seen to negatively affect the "neighborhood feel." Others have pointed out that street vendors, as strangers with improper cultural backgrounds, make a desirable civic order impossible: "We're getting to be a Third World country. It's nasty. It's not clean. ... They set up outside like a fruit market. They're selling pillows on a stick. They're going door-to-door selling tamales. It's disgusting."[13] This view of vendors as an invasive element is reflected in official discourse as well. Bureaucrats and police have often compared street vendors to a spreading disease: "We are approaching a crisis situation here, and like cancer, it spreads. If you don't eradicate it, it's going to consume you."[14]

Such negative public perception goes far beyond pragmatic concerns with public health, safety, or urban traffic. It also transcends the politico-economic view of taxation as based on landed property; thus both prejudice against vendors and the interests of shopkeepers derive from the same cause. Vendors' mobility is understood as an undesirable elusiveness, and discussion about street vending often reflects deep-seated anxiety about the clean and the unclean. White middle-class public perception tends to categorize street vending as dirty, unclean, and disorderly—in short, "out of place"—and align it with failure to establish a certain civic order.

As evinced by existing analyses of spatial mobility in the city (e.g., Walkowitz 1992), such an order implies the question of who can or is allowed to move. In this case, however, vendors' mobility refers to more than their physical movements. It also carries symbolic meanings. And these soon came to be related to the desired urban image for Los Angeles. Responding to the emerging debate about street vending in the early 1990s, one newspaper report expressed this relationship by evoking mobile vending as an essential part of the dynamism of street life, and because of this, as a logically contested issue in Los Angeles:

> Is the city destined to be an urban, polyglot capital of the Third World, nurturing a crazy quilt of hundreds of cultures bringing their habits to its streets? Or can it somehow again become a staunch bastion of suburban values, including the separation of house and mall—a haven from colder, more crowded cities?... The question, it seems, is whether Los Angeles is a city like any other, where people meet to buy and sell on the streets, or, rather, some kind of non-city, somehow different, somehow better.[15]

The report thus suggested that the dominant symbolic meanings attached to the practice of street vending in Los Angeles were anathema to suburban domesticity, security, and stability—in other words, to things in place.

Opponents of street vending thus cast it as "out of place" in Los Angeles. Nonetheless, rather than a self-evident sign of the "Latin Americanization" of the United States, as Davis (2000) sees it, or an element in the creation of tight Latino neighborhoods and communities, following Rojas (1991), street vending is neither a simply indigenous nor a purely "foreign" cultural practice. Some immigrant vendors, before arriving in the United States, were indeed lifelong street vendors, but many others in Los Angeles had no previous experience with it and become vendors on the streets of Los Angeles only through contact with other vendors. Rather than being "out of place," then, street vending in Los Angeles is perhaps foremost a local invention resulting from transnational and urban mobility.

Since its exponential growth at the beginning of the twentieth century, Los Angeles has sought to be portrayed as the sunny, clean alternative to the "problem cities" of the industrial northeast (Findlay 1992: 268–276; Hise 2004: 545–547). This desire has informed fiction as well as realities of Los Angeles, producing a particular liking of the suburban ideal and an anxiousness about urban density and associated problems. It also underlies the establishment in the 1930s of a particularly intolerant law, still valid today, against street vending, which is widely regarded as a visible sign of such undesired urbanity. In this way, Los Angeles—the symbolic endpoint of America's westward development, founded upon the myth of movement as progress and modernity—became the only major U.S. city to outlaw the mobile practice of street vending. Street vending has evoked intense public debate in Los Angeles around questions such as "should there be street vending in our city?" and "what kind of place is a city full of street vendors, and do we want to live in it?" Rather than pragmatic questions of governance, the prohibition of street vending revolves around the symbolic meanings of mobility and the very identity of the city.

Legalizing as Immobilizing

Over the past decades, vendors, activists, and government officials have attempted to legalize vending and provide alternatives to outright prohibition and continuing police enforcement. These efforts began in the mid 1980s, when the number of street vendors in Los Angeles rose dramatically. After local business owners complained that "the problem with vendors was getting totally out of hand,"[16] police began enforcing an existing 1930s law against street vending. Violent crackdowns and harsh citations led a group of vendors to found the nonprofit Asociación de Vendedores Ambulantes or Street Vendors Association in 1988. Through legal assistance and with the help of other nonprofits, this organization first worked to stop police harassment but soon broadened its political ambitions to legalize street vending everywhere in Los Angeles. After negotiations with the city government in 1989, the organization succeeded in getting an official task force appointed to study street vending.[17] Over the following year this task force developed a proposal for regulating vending in Los Angeles. Its basic principle was the confinement of vending into designated districts where street vending was prominent. This principle of confinement, so I argue, was central to its ultimate failure.

After several years of debate, activism, and official negotiation, the Los Angeles City Council approved what was called the Sidewalk Vending Ordinance on 4 January 1994.[18] This ordinance established a two-year pilot program aimed at legalizing street vending in eight "special vending districts."[19] A Sidewalk Vending Administration was designed to guide this process and to protect vendors against police enforcement of the ban during the transition toward legal vending. Vendors, however, continued to be harassed as police forces intensified their crackdowns in the period immediately following the passage of the new ordinance.[20] Meanwhile, a number of the program's key advocates who had been actively involved in the formation of the task force left the City Council, and city government support for street vending dwindled. Also at this time, an internal division tore apart the Street Vendors Association, resulting in multiple lawsuits and a painful period of confusion and inactivity within the vendors' ranks.[21] This combination of difficulties impeded the success of all but one proposal for a vending district—the one in the MacArthur Park area—whose establishment took another four years.

Finally, in June 1999, seventeen purpose-built carts rolled out on the streets facing MacArthur Park.[22] The district was funded by the city's Community Development Department and managed by an independent nonprofit organization, the Institute for Urban Research and Development (IURD). The Community Development Department, which had funded the initiative with a five-year grant, had envisioned the program as becoming self-sustaining. However, high maintenance and administration costs prevented the program from achieving this goal, and in 2005 the IURD was forced to put an end to Los Angeles's first legal vending district.[23] Since then, the participating vendors have been searching for alternative ways to make a living. Most have continued to vend on the city's streets, returning again to illegal status. Good intentions thus produced the most unfortunate results: because the 1994 Sidewalk Vending Ordinance endorsed a stricter enforcement of illegal vending outside the official districts, vendors today are subject to more harassment than ever before.

Why did legalization ultimately fail? Many possible reasons have been suggested: resistance from fixed-location business owners, the simple fact of an existing law that resolutely outlaws street vending, the division within the ranks of the vendors' political organization, the city government's short-lived political support for vending, and so on. Weber (2001) has pointed to the atypical structure of vendors' political mobilization, its lack of transparency and participatory decision-making, and the race/ethnicity and class tensions. Another explanation, suggested by the comparison with day laborers (Valenzuela 2001), is the simply competitive nature of street vending, which directs vendors against each other instead of collectively toward a common goal. Another argument arises in comparison with street vendors in Mexico City, who have very successfully organized politically (Cross 1998). Whereas the latter are legal citizens in Mexico City, many Latina/o vendors in Los Angeles are undocumented migrants whose position in the city is more precarious. Such differences could explain the absence of proposals for vending areas after the 1994 ordinance or the lack of funding for vending programs.

But the most compelling explanation for the eventual failure to legalize vending in Los Angeles may lie in the proposal's basic principle. The idea of solving the problems of the informal economy by formalizing it was translated spatially into a strategy of containment with the Sidewalk Vending Program, operated by assigning vendors to designated, controlled areas within the city. At MacArthur Park, the vending area was limited to a small section of the neighborhood. The vendors were stationed alongside two of the park's edges. They were not allowed to vend on other streets or in the park, once their predominant places of business. This was partly a matter of public land use. The Community Development Department, which actually ran the vending program, only had jurisdiction over the pavement adjacent to the park. The Department of Recreation and Parks managed the park itself and had proposed charging the vendors a fixed daily rate to use it. The Community Development Department rejected the proposal, forcing vendors to stay on the sidewalk, where they had a hard time attracting customers. This diminished not only the individual profits of the vendors but also the popularity and viability of the program as a whole. The curbing of the flexibility and mobility that characterize street vending was thus a central reason for the program's failure to become economically self-sustaining.

The real object of reform in the Sidewalk Vending Program was not street vending as an urban practice itself, but its symbolic meanings. The IURD related the vending program explicitly to its campaign to "clean up" MacArthur Park.[24] By casting Latina/o vending as a unique cultural experience for tourists and new visitors to the park, street vendors became instrumental in the effort to rid the park of crime. This campaign's success was proven by police reports of reduced rates of crime during the operation of the vending district. The program essentially aimed to radically invert the dominant cultural meanings associated with street vending: no longer dirty, disorderly, and themselves part of the perceived problem of urban criminality, street vendors now came to be seen as positive agents in removing the park from the city's mental geography of danger. They became positive forces of social control—what Jane Jacobs called "eyes on the street"—as well as cultural ambassadors displaying a selective otherness, a cultural image stripped of its connotations with backwardness and enriched by a sense of authenticity. Rather than the normative assumption that this kind of practice does not belong in a contemporary city, street vending could now be seen as a valuable cultural experience to be consumed in designated locales.

Although this strategy revalorized street vending, it did not increase vendors' agency in concrete ways. Planning efforts to legalize, regulate, or otherwise govern mobile vending have thus far been focused on restricting vendors' mobility, both concretely, by limiting their physical movements within a perimeter, and symbolically, by attaching them to a clearly defined place in the city as ambassadors of "local culture." Legalizing therefore ultimately meant immobilizing the vendors, thereby cutting short their ability to create economically successful vending spaces. Some vendors, like Dina, operated for a while in the legal vending district and enjoyed the safety it offered them, but they now have returned to illegality, vending in multiple locations all over the city. By aiming to settle a practice that is inherently mobile, the planning project that resulted from calls for legalization ultimately neglected its core quality, namely, the capacity to move freely.

Conclusion

Street vending allows for an alternative understanding of the city in which the primary rationale is neither urban identity nor place but rather urban mobility. Instead of simply introducing a mobile element into an otherwise defined urban landscape, Los Angeles's vendors demonstrate how practices of mobility actually shape urban space. Every day, street vendors transform Los Angeles's often car-dominated spaces into new worlds of taste and consumption. They do not just respond or simply adjust, but also actively contribute to the "mobile city." In often unassuming ways, they transform it by shifting its urban spaces away from car-dominated efficient movement and toward the bodily movements of street interaction. Street vending in Los Angeles is more than just one of many contested practices in the contemporary city. It amounts to a specific form of urbanism in which mobility constitutes the main source of agency and, consequently, the main "site" of contestation and intervention.

In helping to shape the identity of Los Angeles, street vending has posed questions about how the city ought to be. So far, the resultant planning efforts have led only to denial of the very logic of this urban practice. Vendors' creative ability to move in the city has produced a kind of space for which the conventional tools of architecture and urban planning are inadequate. Street vending in Los Angeles to date has been governed by unadapted preexisting legislation, haphazard techniques of control, and often harsh forms of enforcement. Attempts to regulate it have forced vendors into particular urban roles and been unsuccessful thus far. Because of this failure, street vending should be able to inspire a next generation of activists, planners, and community organizers to rethink their professional toolbox. More flexible and mobile scenarios need to be developed to give vendors their "right to mobility" by following the essential logic of street vending itself rather than trying to restrict it. Street vending in Los Angeles, more than in any other American city, challenges us to rethink not only the box of what constitutes urbanism, but also its toolbox.

This kind of innovation might already be at work in the surge of a new type of street vending in recent years. Young Los Angeles chefs have caught on to street vending as a way of reaching new customers and are flocking to social networking tools like Twitter to promote themselves. These vendors cater to an entirely different kind of public, often serving upscale treats—organic ice cream or fusions of Korean barbecue and Mexican tacos—but they might have the potential to change the negative perceptions of vending that currently predominate in Los Angeles. Likewise, the arrival of New York's Vendy Awards—a yearly awards event for street food—in Los Angeles in 2010 is another occasion promising to lift some of the stigma that tends to categorize Latino food vending as dirty or poor. Though some have argued that such upscaling of street vending threatens to push more precarious vendors out of the trade, the arrival of these trendy chefs will not likely outweigh the estimated ten thousand Latina/o vendors providing cheap meals to Los Angeles's low-income workforce. Instead of co-opting the low, these highbrow trends may well have the opposite effect: they could positively change the symbolic meanings of street vending by distancing it from associations with poverty or even crime. Whatever the outcome of these new trends—which is up for study in the years to come—street vending in Los Angeles may prompt not only a new way of thinking about the city, but also novel means to change it.

Images

Figure 7.1. Typical food vending cart in East Los Angeles. These carts often comply with county health regulations, and the vendors experience less harassment from police in comparison with those who sell from boxes or blankets. Because of the relatively large investment involved in owning and managing these carts, many of the vendors are informal wage laborers employed by the cart owners.

Figure 7.2. Female food vendor near an elementary school in the MacArthur Park neighborhood. Vendors like this woman tend to sell in very limited time slots according to the school timetable. Such vendors are able to complement their regular household tasks with these flexible mini-enterprises because they involve minimal preparation and investment.

Figure 7.3. *Paletero* or Popsicle vendor around MacArthur Park. Vendors like this one complement their regular income by renting carts from *paleteria*s (commercial Popsicle vending facilities) on weekends and holidays.

Figure 7.4. A cluster of female food vendors in Koreatown, selling homemade foods such as tamales, tacos, yucca, *pastels* (meat pies), and *atol de elote* (hot corn drink). Such vendors can be found in densely populated neighborhoods of Los Angeles, especially at peak commuting hours.

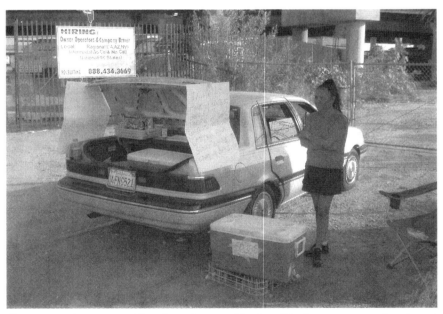

Figure 7.5. A women selling from her car. Vendors like her are most often found near the city's parks and recreation areas, where large crowds of potential customers gather on weekends.

Figure 7.6. A street food vending location before operation at the corner of Beaudry and Second Street, downtown Los Angeles.

Figure 7.7. The same corner at night, when vendors have transformed the desolate parking lot into an open-air restaurant.

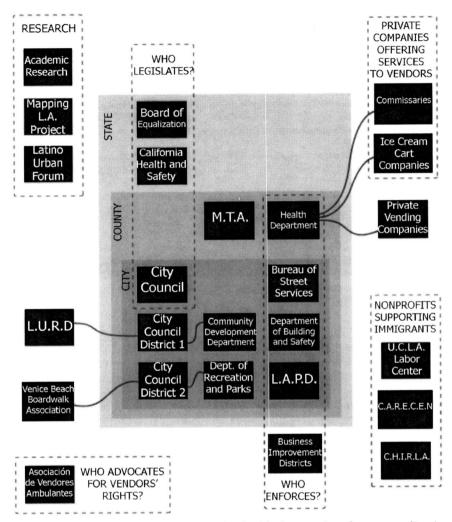

Figure 7.8. Map of the institutions involved with the practice of street vending in Los Angeles. The main levels of government are city, county, and state. Legislation, enforcement, and advocacy for street vendors are distributed among a variety of governmental, nonprofit, and private institutions.

Figure 7.9. Food vendor at the subway station at Santa Monica Avenue and Western Avenue. The Metropolitan Transportation Authority of Los Angeles has established a private program for vendors on its own property. Its vendors are carefully selected, pay monthly rent, and are subject to many additional requirements. Note the aesthetic and symbolic role of the green umbrellas, which contrast with those of many illegal vendors (e.g., those in Figure 7.4).

Kenny Cupers (PhD, Harvard University) is Associate Professor in the History and Theory of Architecture and Urbanism at the University of Basel. He specializes in nineteenth- and twentieth-century European architecture and urban history. His publications include *The Social Project: Housing Postwar France* (2014), *Use Matters: An Alternative History of Architecture* (2013), and *Spaces of Uncertainty* (2002).

Notes

1. The research for this chapter was in large part made possible by a research project under the direction of Margaret Crawford at Harvard University in 2005 and is very much indebted to her intellectual framework. I would like to thank Margaret and the many, often anonymous street vendors, who generously gave me their time for interviews and informal conversations. This essay was written in 2006–2007 and subsequently revised for this volume.

2. The exact number of vendors is unknown, and official documentation is lacking. Estimates range between 5,000 and 20,000 (*Los Angeles Times* Archives; La Asociación de Vendedores Ambulantes (Street Vendors Association) Records n.d.).
3. The Los Angeles municipal code (LAMC, 42.00 B) prohibits street vending except in very limited circumstances: on private property with the owner's permission and a conditional use permit; or in the case of motorized vehicles such as catering trucks, in conformance with legislation of the state of California. This municipal law was amended by the 1994 Sidewalk Vending Ordinance, as explained further in the chapter. First Amendment vending (which excludes food, drinks, and the other articles generally sold on the streets of Los Angeles) is theoretically exempt from this municipal legislation but rarely takes place outside of the officially designated zone on the boardwalk at Venice Beach.
4. An early exception was James Rojas's (1991) study of East Los Angeles, which included an analysis of the way street vendors occupied and created a "sense of place" in their neighborhoods. Lorena Muñoz's dissertation about street vending in Los Angeles (2008) uses a cultural landscape approach to examine how street vendors create a "sense of place" in particular neighborhoods of Los Angeles.
5. See Michel Trebitsch's preface in Lefèbvre (1991); see also Sheringham (2006).
6. This understanding of urbanism has a tradition of its own going back—at least in the American context—to intellectuals like Louis Wirth, Kevin Lynch, and Jane Jacobs.
7. My disciplinary background is in architectural history and urban studies. The main part of the fieldwork for this project took place in June–August 2005, with many additional but shorter visits in subsequent years. During this fieldwork period, my main methods were participant observation and interviews with both street vendors and spokespersons for the various institutions involved. I was able to interview most of the street vendors after building a relation of trust; others were selected through established contacts with nonprofit organizations such as the Institute for Urban Research and Development (Mama's Hot Tamales Café; Sandi Romero, director). The historical analysis is based on these interviews, the *Los Angeles Times* archive (period covered: 1985–2006), various other local newspapers, and the archive of the Street Vendors Association, which contains minutes, correspondence, flyers, testimony, reports, articles, clippings, and other materials created or collected by the Street Vendors Association during the 1980s and 1990s.
8. Its amendment, the 1994 Sidewalk Vending Ordinance, allows vending only in special districts yet to be established (see next section).
9. State legislation pertains to the California Health and Safety Code, which is enforced by Los Angeles County.
10. These are the Los Angeles Police Department; the Los Angeles County Health Department, which enforces the state health and safety rules; the City of Los Angeles Building and Safety Department; and finally the Street Use Department of the City of Los Angeles.

11. This program, explained further below, is run by the Metropolitan Transportation Authority.
12. "Platform," *Los Angeles Times*, 13 June 1994.
13. "Vendors Bring New Way of Life to Los Angeles Streets," *Los Angeles Times*, 25 December 1991.
14. Los Angeles Police Department supervisor quoted in "Street Vendors Eke Out a Living in Fear of Crackdown," *Los Angeles Times*, 21 July 1990.
15. "Vendors Bring New Way of Life to Los Angeles Streets," *Los Angeles Times*, 25 December 1991.
16. "Street Vendors Pay High Price for Unlicensed Trade in L.A.," *Los Angeles Times*, 26 October 1987.
17. See the Asociación's archives, and Weber (2001). See also "Group Alleges Harassment of Street Vendors," *Los Angeles Times*, 2 August 1988 and "Street Vendors—In Between a Rock and a Hard Place," *Los Angeles Times*, 23 December 1988; "Task Force Formed to Study Legalizing of Street Vendors," *Los Angeles Metro*, 8 July 1989; "Panel Urges Districts for Street Vendors Peddling," *Los Angeles Times*, 21 December 1990.
18. On its creation, see "Pushcart Power," *Los Angeles Times*, 25 July 1993; "Vendors Demand a Hearing at City Hall," *Los Angeles Times*, 1 August 1993; "Compromise to Legalize Street Vending Drafted," *Los Angeles Times*, 30 September 1993; "L.A. Looks for a Palatable Solution to Street Vending," *Los Angeles Times*, 9 December 1993.
19. Anyone would in principle be able to propose such a district, but it would have to be supported by a petition signed by 20 percent of the area's merchants and residents. Conversely, merchants and residents could veto the formation of such a district with a similar petition.
20. "Vendors Protest Against LAPD," *Los Angeles Times*, 2 August 1994.
21. See the Asociación's archives and Weber (2001).
22. "Street Vending District Opens on MacArthur Park," *Los Angeles Times*, 21 June 1999.
23. "With Funds Cut, Vendors Try to Cope—A Program that Let Food Be Sold from Street Carts Ended," *Los Angeles Times*, 28 July 2005.
24. See, e.g., "Sampling New Recipe for MacArthur Park," *Los Angeles Times*, 13 January 2002.

Bibliography

Balkin, Steven. 1989. *Self-Employment for Low-Income People*. New York: Praeger.
Cornejo, Jackelyn. 2005. *Street Vendors in the Westlake and Pico-Union Communities*. Undergraduate thesis, Occidental College, Los Angeles, CA.
Crawford, Margaret, John Kaliski, and John Cross. 1999. *Everyday Urbanism*. New York: Monacelli Press.
Cross, John C. 1998. *Informal Politics: Street Vendors and the State in Mexico City*. Stanford, CA: Stanford University Press.

Cross, John C., and Alfonso Morales, eds. 2007. *Street Entrepreneurs: People, Place and Politics in Local and Global Perspective.* London: Routledge.

Davis, Mike. 2000. *Magical Urbanism: Latinos Reinvent the U.S. City.* New York: Verso.

De Certeau, Michel. (1980) 1984. *The Practice of Everyday Life.* Trans. Steven F. Rendall. Berkeley: University of California Press.

Findlay, John M. 1992. *Magic Lands: Western Cityscapes and American Culture After 1940.* Berkeley, Los Angeles, and London: University of California Press.

Hise, Greg. 2004. "Border City: Race and Social Distance in Los Angeles." *American Quarterly* 56 (3): 545–558.

Jones, Yvonne. 1988. "Street Peddlers as Entrepreneurs: Economic Adaptation to an Urban Area." *Urban Anthropology* 17 (2–3): 143–170.

Kloosterman, Robert, and Jan Rath. 2003. *Immigrant Entrepreneurs: Venturing Abroad in the Age of Globalization.* New York: Berg.

La Asociación de Vendedores Ambulantes (Street Vendors Association) Records. N.d. Southern California Library for Social Studies and Research, Los Angeles CA.

Lefèbvre, Henri. (1974) 1991. *The Production of Space.* Trans. Donald Nicholson-Smith. Oxford: Blackwell.

Lefèbvre, Henri. 1991. *Critique of Everyday Life.* London and New York: Verso.

Los Angeles Municipal Code. Section 42.00. Los Angeles, CA.

Los Angeles Sidewalk Vending Ordinance. 1994. Nos. 169318, 169319, and 169320. Los Angeles, CA.

Los Angeles Times. 1985–2006 archive.

Muñoz, Lorena. 2008. "'Tamales… Elotes… Champurrado…' The Production of Latino Vending Landscapes in Los Angeles." PhD dissertation, University of Southern California.

Norton, Peter D. 2008. *Fighting Traffic: The Dawn of the Motor Age in the American City.* Cambridge, MA: MIT Press.

Portes, Alejandro, and Saskia Sassen. 1987. "Making It Underground: Comparative Material on the Informal Sector in Western Market Economies." *The American Journal of Sociology* 93 (1): 30–61.

Portes, Alejandro, Manuel Castells, and Lauren A. Benton, eds. 1989. *The Informal Economy: Studies in Advanced and Less Developed Countries.* Baltimore, MD: Johns Hopkins University Press.

Rojas, James. 1991. *The Enacted Environment: The Creation of "Place" by Mexicans and Mexican Americans in East Los Angeles.* Master's thesis, Massachusetts Institute of Technology.

Roy, Ananya, and Nezar Al Sayyad. 2004. *Urban Informality: Transnational Perspectives from the Middle East, Latin America and South Asia.* Lanham, MD: Lexington Books.

Sassen, Saskia. 1991. "The Informal Economy." In *Dual City: Restructuring New York,* ed. John Hull Mollenkopf and Manuel Castells. New York: Russell Sage Foundation.

———. 1998. *Globalization and Its Discontents.* New York: The New Press.

11. This program, explained further below, is run by the Metropolitan Transportation Authority.
12. "Platform," *Los Angeles Times*, 13 June 1994.
13. "Vendors Bring New Way of Life to Los Angeles Streets," *Los Angeles Times*, 25 December 1991.
14. Los Angeles Police Department supervisor quoted in "Street Vendors Eke Out a Living in Fear of Crackdown," *Los Angeles Times*, 21 July 1990.
15. "Vendors Bring New Way of Life to Los Angeles Streets," *Los Angeles Times*, 25 December 1991.
16. "Street Vendors Pay High Price for Unlicensed Trade in L.A.," *Los Angeles Times*, 26 October 1987.
17. See the Asociación's archives, and Weber (2001). See also "Group Alleges Harassment of Street Vendors," *Los Angeles Times*, 2 August 1988 and "Street Vendors—In Between a Rock and a Hard Place," *Los Angeles Times*, 23 December 1988; "Task Force Formed to Study Legalizing of Street Vendors," *Los Angeles Metro*, 8 July 1989; "Panel Urges Districts for Street Vendors Peddling," *Los Angeles Times*, 21 December 1990.
18. On its creation, see "Pushcart Power," *Los Angeles Times*, 25 July 1993; "Vendors Demand a Hearing at City Hall," *Los Angeles Times*, 1 August 1993; "Compromise to Legalize Street Vending Drafted," *Los Angeles Times*, 30 September 1993; "L.A. Looks for a Palatable Solution to Street Vending," *Los Angeles Times*, 9 December 1993.
19. Anyone would in principle be able to propose such a district, but it would have to be supported by a petition signed by 20 percent of the area's merchants and residents. Conversely, merchants and residents could veto the formation of such a district with a similar petition.
20. "Vendors Protest Against LAPD," *Los Angeles Times*, 2 August 1994.
21. See the Asociación's archives and Weber (2001).
22. "Street Vending District Opens on MacArthur Park," *Los Angeles Times*, 21 June 1999.
23. "With Funds Cut, Vendors Try to Cope—A Program that Let Food Be Sold from Street Carts Ended," *Los Angeles Times*, 28 July 2005.
24. See, e.g., "Sampling New Recipe for MacArthur Park," *Los Angeles Times*, 13 January 2002.

Bibliography

Balkin, Steven. 1989. *Self-Employment for Low-Income People*. New York: Praeger.
Cornejo, Jackelyn. 2005. *Street Vendors in the Westlake and Pico-Union Communities*. Undergraduate thesis, Occidental College, Los Angeles, CA.
Crawford, Margaret, John Kaliski, and John Cross. 1999. *Everyday Urbanism*. New York: Monacelli Press.
Cross, John C. 1998. *Informal Politics: Street Vendors and the State in Mexico City*. Stanford, CA: Stanford University Press.

Cross, John C., and Alfonso Morales, eds. 2007. *Street Entrepreneurs: People, Place and Politics in Local and Global Perspective*. London: Routledge.
Davis, Mike. 2000. *Magical Urbanism: Latinos Reinvent the U.S. City*. New York: Verso.
De Certeau, Michel. (1980) 1984. *The Practice of Everyday Life*. Trans. Steven F. Rendall. Berkeley: University of California Press.
Findlay, John M. 1992. *Magic Lands: Western Cityscapes and American Culture After 1940*. Berkeley, Los Angeles, and London: University of California Press.
Hise, Greg. 2004. "Border City: Race and Social Distance in Los Angeles." *American Quarterly* 56 (3): 545–558.
Jones, Yvonne. 1988. "Street Peddlers as Entrepreneurs: Economic Adaptation to an Urban Area." *Urban Anthropology* 17 (2–3): 143–170.
Kloosterman, Robert, and Jan Rath. 2003. *Immigrant Entrepreneurs: Venturing Abroad in the Age of Globalization*. New York: Berg.
La Asociación de Vendedores Ambulantes (Street Vendors Association) Records. N.d. Southern California Library for Social Studies and Research, Los Angeles CA.
Lefèbvre, Henri. (1974) 1991. *The Production of Space*. Trans. Donald Nicholson-Smith. Oxford: Blackwell.
Lefèbvre, Henri. 1991. *Critique of Everyday Life*. London and New York: Verso.
Los Angeles Municipal Code. Section 42.00. Los Angeles, CA.
Los Angeles Sidewalk Vending Ordinance. 1994. Nos. 169318, 169319, and 169320. Los Angeles, CA.
Los Angeles Times. 1985–2006 archive.
Muñoz, Lorena. 2008. "'Tamales… Elotes… Champurrado…' The Production of Latino Vending Landscapes in Los Angeles." PhD dissertation, University of Southern California.
Norton, Peter D. 2008. *Fighting Traffic: The Dawn of the Motor Age in the American City*. Cambridge, MA: MIT Press.
Portes, Alejandro, and Saskia Sassen. 1987. "Making It Underground: Comparative Material on the Informal Sector in Western Market Economies." *The American Journal of Sociology* 93 (1): 30–61.
Portes, Alejandro, Manuel Castells, and Lauren A. Benton, eds. 1989. *The Informal Economy: Studies in Advanced and Less Developed Countries*. Baltimore, MD: Johns Hopkins University Press.
Rojas, James. 1991. *The Enacted Environment: The Creation of "Place" by Mexicans and Mexican Americans in East Los Angeles*. Master's thesis, Massachusetts Institute of Technology.
Roy, Ananya, and Nezar Al Sayyad. 2004. *Urban Informality: Transnational Perspectives from the Middle East, Latin America and South Asia*. Lanham, MD: Lexington Books.
Sassen, Saskia. 1991. "The Informal Economy." In *Dual City: Restructuring New York*, ed. John Hull Mollenkopf and Manuel Castells. New York: Russell Sage Foundation.
———. 1998. *Globalization and Its Discontents*. New York: The New Press.

Sheringham, Michael. 2006. *Everyday Life: Theories and Practices from Surrealism to the Present*. Oxford: Oxford University Press.
Street Vendor Project of the Urban Justice Center. 2006. *Peddling Uphill: A Report on the Conditions of Street Vendors in New York City*. New York: Street Vendor Project of the Urban Justice Center.
Suro, Roberto, Sergio Bendixen, B. Lindsay Lowell, and Dulce C. Benavides. 2001. *Billions in Motion: Latino Immigrants, Remittances and Banking*. Southern California: Pew Hispanic Center and Multilateral Investment Fund.
Taylor, Denise S., Valerie K. Fishell, Jessica L. Derstine, Rebecca L. Hargrove, Natalie R. Patterson, Kristin W. Moriarty, Beverly A. Battista, Hope E. Ratcliffe, Amy E. Binkoski, and Penny M. Kris-Etherton. 2000. In *Street Foods in America: A True Melting Pot*, ed. R. V. Bhat and A. P. Simopoulos. Basel: Karger.
Tinker, Irene. 1987. *Street Foods: Testing Assumptions about Informal Sector Activity of Women and Men*. Monograph appearing as *Current Sociology* 35 (3).
Valenzuela, Abel. 2001. "Day Laborers as Entrepreneurs." *Journal of Ethnic and Migration Studies* 27 (2): 335–352.
Waldinger, Roger, Howard Aldrich, and Robin Ward. 1990. *Ethnic Entrepreneurs*. London: Sage.
Walkowitz, Judith. 1992. *City of Dreadful Delight: Narratives of Sexual Danger in Late-Victorian London*. Chicago: University of Chicago Press.
Weber, Clair M. 2001. "Latino Street Vendors in Los Angeles: Heterogeneous Alliances, Community-Based Activism, and the State." In *Asian and Latino Immigrants in a Restructuring Economy: The Metamorphosis of Southern California*, ed. Marta López-Garza. Stanford, CA: Stanford University Press.

CHAPTER 8

Selling in Insecurity, Living with Violence

Eviction Drives against
Street Food Vendors in Dhaka and
the Informal Politics of Exploitation

Benjamin Etzold

Walking through the busy streets of Dhaka, the capital of Bangladesh, one can witness the business practices of a very vivid trade. At every other street corner, small street food shops and mobile vendors sell myriad tasty snacks, full meals, sweets, fruits, and beverages at prices that even the urban poor can afford. The sale of prepared food in public space is not a marginal economic activity but an important employment opportunity, not only but particularly in the Global South (Tinker 1997). Street food vendors contribute crucially to urban food security (Keck and Etzold 2013) but are often confronted with harsh regulations, as they appropriate public space illegally. Whether street vending should be tolerated or "pushed back" is a controversial debate in many metropolises (see case studies in Brown 2006; Cross and Morales 2007; Bhowmik 2010; de Cassia Vieira Cardoso, Companion, and Marras 2014).

Sheringham, Michael. 2006. *Everyday Life: Theories and Practices from Surrealism to the Present*. Oxford: Oxford University Press.
Street Vendor Project of the Urban Justice Center. 2006. *Peddling Uphill: A Report on the Conditions of Street Vendors in New York City*. New York: Street Vendor Project of the Urban Justice Center.
Suro, Roberto, Sergio Bendixen, B. Lindsay Lowell, and Dulce C. Benavides. 2001. *Billions in Motion: Latino Immigrants, Remittances and Banking*. Southern California: Pew Hispanic Center and Multilateral Investment Fund.
Taylor, Denise S., Valerie K. Fishell, Jessica L. Derstine, Rebecca L. Hargrove, Natalie R. Patterson, Kristin W. Moriarty, Beverly A. Battista, Hope E. Ratcliffe, Amy E. Binkoski, and Penny M. Kris-Etherton. 2000. In *Street Foods in America: A True Melting Pot*, ed. R. V. Bhat and A. P. Simopoulos. Basel: Karger.
Tinker, Irene. 1987. *Street Foods: Testing Assumptions about Informal Sector Activity of Women and Men*. Monograph appearing as *Current Sociology* 35 (3).
Valenzuela, Abel. 2001. "Day Laborers as Entrepreneurs." *Journal of Ethnic and Migration Studies* 27 (2): 335–352.
Waldinger, Roger, Howard Aldrich, and Robin Ward. 1990. *Ethnic Entrepreneurs*. London: Sage.
Walkowitz, Judith. 1992. *City of Dreadful Delight: Narratives of Sexual Danger in Late-Victorian London*. Chicago: University of Chicago Press.
Weber, Clair M. 2001. "Latino Street Vendors in Los Angeles: Heterogeneous Alliances, Community-Based Activism, and the State." In *Asian and Latino Immigrants in a Restructuring Economy: The Metamorphosis of Southern California*, ed. Marta López-Garza. Stanford, CA: Stanford University Press.

CHAPTER 8

Selling in Insecurity, Living with Violence

Eviction Drives against Street Food Vendors in Dhaka and the Informal Politics of Exploitation

Benjamin Etzold

Walking through the busy streets of Dhaka, the capital of Bangladesh, one can witness the business practices of a very vivid trade. At every other street corner, small street food shops and mobile vendors sell myriad tasty snacks, full meals, sweets, fruits, and beverages at prices that even the urban poor can afford. The sale of prepared food in public space is not a marginal economic activity but an important employment opportunity, not only but particularly in the Global South (Tinker 1997). Street food vendors contribute crucially to urban food security (Keck and Etzold 2013) but are often confronted with harsh regulations, as they appropriate public space illegally. Whether street vending should be tolerated or "pushed back" is a controversial debate in many metropolises (see case studies in Brown 2006; Cross and Morales 2007; Bhowmik 2010; de Cassia Vieira Cardoso, Companion, and Marras 2014).

In Dhaka, the city authorities largely tolerated the unlicensed sale of food on the streets for decades. However, changing governance regimes; shifting public discourses around security, corruption, and hygiene; and increasing conflicts over public space led to the criminalization of the street trade, in particular during the reign of the so-called Caretaker Government of Bangladesh (2007–2008).[1] All street vendors in Dhaka are vulnerable to evictions from their vending site, destruction of their vending units, harassment by the police, or exploitation by local power brokers—forms of structural and direct violence that are, in turn, legitimized through the cultural violence of the hegemonic discourse. But instead of being mere victims of violence, street vendors do manage to navigate the violent arenas of street vending, employing multiple strategies to reduce their exposure to violence, cope with losses, weather periods of reduced income, and thereby secure their livelihoods.

This chapter debates the everyday violence inherent in the arenas of street food vending in Dhaka. It addresses three central questions. What role does street food vending play as a livelihood opportunity in Dhaka? How does violence manifest itself in the arenas of street vending? And how do the street food vendors act in the context of violence? In order to answer these questions, I follow a violence-vulnerability framework and draw on the insights of actor-oriented empirical research conducted in Dhaka over three years, from 2007 to 2010. I rely on information gathered in semi-structured interviews with street food vendors and other stakeholders, using participatory research tools (i.e., Venn diagrams)[2] and a quantitative survey ($N = 120$) of street food vendors at six characteristic vending sites within the area of Dhaka City Corporation.[3] On this basis, I show that the notion of "violence" helps to highlight the blatantly unjust conditions under which vulnerable actors seek to sustain their livelihoods. The chapter thereby questions the existing modes of urban governance in Dhaka and the relation between the state and its citizens.

Vulnerability and Violence in Contested Urban Arenas

How do people secure their livelihoods under the adverse conditions of natural disasters, war and conflict, economic crises, and everyday insecurities? This is the core questions of social vulnerability research, which is interested in the capabilities and adaptation strategies of individuals, households, and communities whose human security is jeopardized (Wisner et al. 2003; Birkmann 2006; Bohle 2007b). From this perspective, vulnerability is conceived as an aspect of social practices and human agency that is "embedded in social and environmental arenas, where human security, freedoms, and human rights are struggled for, negotiated, lost and won" (Bohle 2007b: 9). Violence is one of many stressors or shocks that contribute to the vulnerability of a person, household, or social group such as street vendors. Employing an actor-oriented approach, this chapter looks at the social vulnerability to everyday violence in Dhaka's contested arenas of street vending.

The renowned conflict and peace researcher Johan Galtung (1990: 295) has framed violence, in the broadest sense, as "needs-deprivation" and introduced a distinction between three types of violence (Galtung 1969, 1990, 2002) that has also influenced empirical research in development geography (Peluso and Watts 2001; Bohle 2007a; Fünfgeld 2007). To commit *direct violence* is "to harm and hurt someone, by physical and/or verbal means" (Bohle 2007a: 129). Manifestations of direct violence can be regarded as social events in which the involved actors are easily identifiable. In contrast, *structural violence* manifests itself in specific forms of injustice, exploitation, deprivation and marginalization that are imposed "on people through the strategic manipulation of the economic structures and power relations of a society" (Bohle and Fünfgeld 2007: 669). Structural violence is a continuous process rather than a singular event. The actors involved are often concealed because the violence occurs "below the surface of the social fabric" (Fünfgeld 2007: 22). Meanwhile, *cultural violence* refers to discourses and institutions that produce, maintain, and renew violent actions and processes and thus "legitimize direct and/or structural violence" (Galtung 2002: 11). The social legitimization and deep internalization of violence can result in the specific disposition to perceive violence as normal and a "natural" matter of fact (Fünfgeld 2007: 18ff.).

Regarding the vulnerability to violence, the "relative positions of vulnerable actors within the shifting fields of power that deeply influence their abilities to live with violence" (Bohle 2007a: 130) are particularly important. According to the French sociologist Pierre Bourdieu, these "fields of power" are on the one hand expressions of the social relations between different actors, for example, street vendors, policemen, or local criminals. The structure of these fields depends on these actors' respective capacities, that is, the economic, cultural, social and symbolic capital available to them, and on their habitus—their acquired dispositions to think and act in a particular way (Bourdieu and Wacquant 1992). But on the other hand, fields have spatial implications because their inherent social order becomes realized in distinct places through the spatial distribution of people, goods, and services. Bourdieu (2005: 120) calls this projection of social space onto the level of physical space *occupied* or *appropriated physical space.*

In the following, the term *arena* is used to denote the hybrid, contested character of public space, as both social fields and physical spaces lie at the core of social and indeed spatial struggles (Bohle 2007a; Etzold et al. 2009). I consider four crucial dimensions to the term, all of which relate to Bourdieu's theory of practice. The first dimension defines the arenas as social fields and the second as material spaces; the third dimension pertains to the social relations of the field as exemplified in these distinct physical spaces; and the fourth regards arenas as particularly contested sites of struggles (Etzold 2013). Streets are good examples of arenas, for they are distinct physical places where the agents at a place—for instance, food vendors at a street corner—know one another and recognize their common interests and identity. But streets are often also the places of contestations between hegemonic actors such as state and city authorities, and subaltern actors like street vendors. In cities of the Global South, such conflicts over the urban space can become violent when the needs of impoverished citizens are inadequately addressed, and when questions of citizenship and distributional justice are intentionally ignored (Bayat 1997; Holston and Appadurai 1999; Banks et al. 2011).

Against this background, the question of how vulnerable people actually act in the context of violence can be analytically divided into four sub-themes mirroring basic principles of vulnerability research: exposure, sensitivity, coping, and adaptation (Bohle 2007b). The first area of scrutiny asks whether the respective actors or groups are subject to violence in terms of their position in physical space (exposure to violence). The second sub-theme concerns how their respective positions of power, which relate to their capacities (or capital), social networks, and experiences, make them vulnerable to violence (sensitivity to violence). Third, the short-term responses that aim at overcoming adverse impacts of violence need to be looked at (coping with violence). Fourth is an assessment of long-term changes in behavior that help to reduce vulnerable people's exposure and sensitivity to violence and contribute to their livelihood security in the longer run (adapting to violence).

Selling in Insecurity: Contested Governance and Livelihoods of Street Food Vendors in Dhaka

In the year 2015, around eighteen million people live in the megacity of Dhaka (UN 2014). After the garment industry and rickshaw pulling, street vending is probably the third most important employment opportunity for the urban poor in Bangladesh (Salway et al. 2003; World Bank 2007). Roughly two million garment workers, 750,000 rickshaw pullers, and 300,000 street vendors live and work in Dhaka (Islam 2005; Siddiqui et

2010). Among world cities, Dhaka thus has one of the highest numbers of hawkers (Bhowmik 2010). On the basis of official labor statistics and my own surveys, I estimate that some 97,000 street vendors sell prepared food items, and around 425,000 people or 2.9 percent of Dhaka's total population depend on the income generated by street food vendors. As my own surveys indicate, each vendor serves 84 customers per day on average. This means that more than eight million people—in other words, more than half of the citizens—take some street food every day (Etzold 2013).[4]

Although the significance of street food for urban food security is beyond doubt, street food vending is illegal in Dhaka under the Pure Food Ordinance of 1959, Dhaka Metropolitan Police Ordinance of 1976, and Dhaka City Corporation Ordinance of 1983.[5] In fact, hawkers cannot obtain licenses to legally sell food in public space. As street food vending is a classical informal activity, what follows introduces Dhaka's street food trade in the light of some key attributes of the informal economy (ILO 1972; Chen 2005; Etzold et al. 2009).[6] First, the street vending business is easy to enter. Almost all the street food vendors are rural migrants to the city, but only 38 percent (in this survey) have migrated to Dhaka in the last ten years. Fairly little capital is needed to open a small food stall or sell snacks or fruits in a mobile manner. However, some money and a good social network are necessary to actually get access to a vending site. Second, most vendors (95 percent) own their vending units themselves, or else they belong to family members or friends who also help with small loans, needed for investment. Third, most of the vendors are self-employed and operate their business alone (69 percent), though some more permanent street food shops (30 percent) have one to three constant helpers. Many women help at home with the preparation and processing of the food sold on the street and thereby contribute significantly to the household income (8 percent said so), but they are underrepresented among the street food vendors themselves (only 5 percent).[7]

Fourth, despite having little formal education (45 percent of vendors are illiterate, and only 10 percent have more than five years of schooling), most vendors develop business skills on the streets that enable them to see opportunities and seize them. Fifth, despite vendors' hard-earned business skills, the street trade is marked by low incomes, absence of social security or state benefits, long working hours (fourteen hours daily, on average), and poor working conditions. Street vendors face particularly high exposure to extreme weather conditions as well as air, water, and noise pollution. Moreover, they are constantly at risk of harassment and eviction. Street food vending is thus a day-to-day business involving considerable risk and uncertainty for the vendors and their families. Sixth, the market for street food is highly competitive; each vendor has to find his or her specific economic niche. As a result, a broad variety of food items are sold on the streets of Dhaka (during fieldwork, more than one hundred different street food items were counted). Products range from full rice meals like rice curries to snacks like *fuchka,* samosas, or plain bread rolls; sweets like *jilapi* and biscuits; fruits including banana, papaya, and *amra;* drinks such as tea, coconut milk, or sugarcane juice; and ice cream and curd drinks like *matha*. The food items are prepared either directly on the street by the vendors (13 percent in the survey) or at home (12 percent); snacks, however, are often made by small food-processing factories in Dhaka and then distributed to and sold by hawkers (75 percent).

Accordingly, business models and mobility patterns of street food vendors vary broadly. The variety of vending styles includes mobile vending units, operated by vendors selling products alone by walking around with a basket, tray or flask (20 percent of vendors in the survey); semi-mobile vending units such as push-carts and rickshaws that are moved occasionally to reach consumers at different places at specific times (36 percent); semi-permanent vending units, like tables set up for the day at a particular site (13 percent); more permanent but not consolidated vending units, such as food stalls that are built illegally at a specific site (21 percent); and permanent consolidated huts, which are not considered street food vending units in this study.[8]

In Dhaka, street food vendors earn an average daily profit of around 284 Bangladeshi Taka (BDT) (~ $3.67 in U.S. dollars)—quite a substantial income compared to the wages of untrained employees in the garments industry, day laborers, and rickshaw-pullers (World Bank 2007). Nonetheless, two out of three street food vendors live below the poverty line for Dhaka (Etzold 2013). The hawkers' income varies substantially depending on the food products sold, the vending site, the number of customers, the hours they work, and the time of the year. The survey found that permanent vendors who sell from consolidated huts, are clearly better off than the other vendors: with an average of 781 BDT per day (adding up to a net monthly income of 24,000 BDT, ~ $309) and an overall monthly household income of more than 6,000 BDT per person living in the household. They can also afford to spend more than twice what the mobile vendors spend on food. Looking only at the criteria of housing, food expenditure, household income, and business profit, the survey results clearly show that the continuum of vending styles is also a continuum of vulnerability. Among all vendors, the mobile vendors profit least from their business (only 220 BDT vs. a total average of 338 BDT per day) and have the lowest monthly household income per person (2497 BDT vs. 3927 BDT). They also have to cope with the greatest food insecurity (with a monthly food expenditure per person of only 758 BDT vs. 886 BDT), and face the worst housing con-

Table 8.1. Types of Street Food Vending and Livelihood Characteristics of the Vendors

Street Food Vending Types	Share in sample	Shops run by women	Literacy rate	Living in bad housing	Food expenditure per person in household per month	Income per person in household per month	Business profit per day
Permanent shop consolidated	11%	0%	23%	0%	1553 BDT	6423 BDT	781 BDT
Permanent shop unconsolidated	21%	0%	40%	8%	906 BDT	3389 BDT	300 BDT
Semi-permanent	13%	20%	60%	13%	800 BDT	4648 BDT	291 BDT
Semi-mobile	36%	7%	37%	5%	772 BDT	4032 BDT	309 BDT
Truly mobile	20%	0%	54%	29%	758 BDT	2497 BDT	220 BDT
Mean	100%	5%	43%	11%	886 BDT	3927 BDT	338 BDT
Mean for street food vendors only	**89%**	**5.6%**	**45%**	**12%**	**804 BDT**	**3624 BDT**	**284 BDT**

Source: Field Survey 2009 (*N* = 120)

ditions (29 percent live in slums under bad housing conditions, or even on the street). However, there are exceptions to this general trend; for example, some semi-permanent vendors, 20 percent of whom are women, are also in a particularly vulnerable position as they are exposed more than others to evictions and harassment and regularly have to cope with confiscation of their equipment and exploitation. As further delineated below, the rights of access to public space are crucial livelihood assets of the urban poor (Brown 2006; Hackenbroch et al. 2009) and can largely explain the differences in the vulnerability outcomes of different types of street food vendors.

Living with Violence: Eviction Drives against Street Food Vendors in Dhaka

Street Vendors' Double Exposure to Evictions

In South Asia, about 40 percent of urban inhabitants live in slums under conditions of vulnerability and uncertainty, and many live under constant threat of eviction (Davis 2007; Bohle and Sakdapolrak 2008). In Dhaka, more than one-third of the population lives in one of the city's five thousand slum clusters (Centre for Urban Studies 2006). Along with crime and "ordinary" violence, slum dwellers also face structural violence in terms of denied basic needs and human rights violations. The primary source of insecurity among Dhaka's urban poor, besides their precarious economic situation, is their insecurity of tenancy (IGS 2008). Evictions and destruction of slum settlements are a recurring theme in Dhaka's history. A survey from 2003 found that 65 percent of slum dwellers fear eviction (Hackenbroch et al. 2008). In recent years, slums have been cleared mainly to make space for high-rise housing developments and infrastructure projects, in the process of reclamation of rivers and lakes, or for purposes of "city beautification" (ibid.). More than two-thirds of Dhaka's street food vendors live in slums. They risk losing their homes in slum eviction drives and losing their livelihood during police raids at their vending sites. Street vendors are therefore "doubly exposed" (O'Brien and Leichenko 2000) to evictions.

The authorities have largely tolerated vendors' appropriation of public space for many decades, but state actors are occasionally compelled to react to hawkers' informal appropriation of public space and evict them. For instance, on 19 January 2007—only eight days after the political turmoil around the takeover of political power by the "Caretaker Government"— the military-backed interim regime started eviction drives against street vendors in Dhaka in a campaign later extended to other cities. A representative from a hawkers' association[9] was quick to announce that eight million hawkers all over Bangladesh had lost their main source of income, which would affect 70 to 80 million people in Bangladesh. A journalist announced that the "life for 100,000 hawkers and street-vendors of the city has turned into a hellish nightmare" after the most radical "clean-up" drives ever to take place in Dhaka (A. Hossain 2007). In a personal interview almost a year later, the same journalist, who frequently reports on evictions in slums and at vending sites, noted that the authorities knew very well that their eviction drives against hawkers were ineffective and would not solve the problem of encroachment on public space. They were even aware that the destruction or disruption of the street economy would be detrimental to urban poverty alleviation. But still they meant to continue violent expulsions, because "the military thinks they can impress people with cosmetic measures, ... the vendors are used as cannon-fodder for political purposes" (interview with A. Hossain, journalist, December 2007). This observation is in line with James Scott's argument that it is important for the elites in power to symbolically defend their claims against the suppressed subalterns: "The decisive assertion of symbolic territory by public retribution discourages others from venturing public defiance … these acts are meant as public events for an audience of subordinates. They are intended as a kind of preemptive strike to nip in the bud any further challenges of the existing frontier" (Scott 1990: 197). In its first year, the Caretaker Government forcefully evicted more than 60,000 people from slums, making no effort to relocate them (interview with M. Q. Khan, president of the Coalition for the Urban Poor, January 2008), destroyed dozens of unauthorized wholesale and kitchen markets (Keck 2012), and repeatedly displaced thousands of street vendors from important public sites. The interim government's actions seemed to be meant as warnings and symbolic demonstrations of power at a time of political insecurity.

In an expression of cultural violence, the eviction drives against hawkers were legitimized before the public through powerful narratives delegitimizing the street economy. The city authorities, planners, and growing urban middle class generally claim that street food vending is obsolete, unhygienic, disorderly, and "in the way"; meanwhile, street vendors' contributions to food security and the urban economy are hardly acknowledged.[10] In their bid to demonstrate its political will and capacity to make change, the interim government used the same depreciative story lines to justify its violent actions against street vendors. The eviction campaign would contribute to fighting corruption, restoring law and order, improving public security, and clearing public space for a more fluid traffic flow and a more livable city (Etzold 2013). At politically critical times, the campaign showed that Dhaka's street vending sites were the arenas in which both conflicts over the political future of Bangladesh and contestations over the "appropriate use of space" (Cross and Karides 2007) would play out.

Manifestations of Violence in Daily Encounters between Street Vendors and the State

At the very local level, evictions in Dhaka are a "normal" part of the violent encounters between street vendors and the state. The interests of hawkers, who appropriate public space in order to sustain their livelihood and profit as much as possible, stand against those of the police, for example. On the one hand, police officers simply execute orders issued by superiors and try to maintain peace and public order. In doing so, they often commit acts of direct violence: they evict hawkers from their vending sites by order of high officials and resort to physical violence when vendors do not obey orders immediately; they occasionally destroy shops, confiscate vending equipment, and sometimes arrest street vendors; and they verbally harass hawkers. But on the other hand, many policemen also try to reap small benefits from their formal position of state power, for instance through the extortion of "security payments" or so-called *chanda*—an act of structural violence. But actors' social practices are not guided by the formal requirements of state representatives' roles or their personal rent-seeking alone, as the following examples illustrate.

In front of Dhaka's Medical College Hospital (DMCH), located at the verge of Old Dhaka, street food vendors, other hawkers, and pavement dwellers struggle over access to public space to secure their livelihoods. In this arena, the street food trade is regulated by shifts in demand for food—and by altering modes of governance, as the rigor with which formal rules are implemented changes regularly (Etzold et al. 2009). The director of this public hospital, who is the most relevant and powerful actor in this arena, wants to "eradicate this kind of profession [street food vending] in Dhaka, because unsafe food cannot be allowed in this age of civilization" (interview with director of DMCH, January 2008). The director deploys security guards whose main duties are to ensure security on the hospital premises; monitor the entrance of patients, their relatives, and medical personnel; and keep the entry gates of the hospital clear of street vendors. An interview with one of the gatemen revealed that only right in front of the hospital, when the director is present during the day, does he perform his duties attentively and forces vendors to leave the area. In the evening, when his superiors have left the scene, he asserts, the vendors do not create any problems, and he tolerates their vending activities right at the main gate. He legitimizes the deviation from his formal responsibilities by referring to street vendors as poor city dwellers who also need to sustain their livelihoods somehow. He therefore turns a blind eye to the hawkers whenever he can and refrains from acts of direct violence. As a public employee at the lower end of the hierarchy, he naturally chats and buys tea and snacks from them regularly—although he also enjoys the benefit of free drinks or cigarettes from them due to his relative position of power (interview with a security guard at DMCH, June 2010; see also Etzold et al. 2012).

Similarly, many policemen share the street vendors' lifeworld and reside in the same neighborhoods with them. Without bribes, a low-ranking police constable receives a regular monthly salary of only 5,000 BDT, significantly less than the 8,500 BDT a food hawker earns on average. Not infrequently, policemen are seen sitting at small street shops, having their lunch or a snack, drinking a cup of tea, or gossiping and joking with the hawkers (see Figures 8.1 and 8.2). According to a (higher-ranking) police sergeant, the police and street vendors maintain quite good relations. Normally, although the sale of prepared food on the street is "totally prohibited, because it is unhygienic," they will tolerate the vendors' illegal activities because both the vendors and many of their consumers, such as rickshaw pullers, are very poor and have no choice but these kinds of informal business. Nevertheless, if they see too many food hawkers at a particular site—which, in this policeman's opinion, impedes the flow of traffic—or upon receiving orders to enforce the ban from superiors, they will try to stop them. Then, several police officers team up to carry out a raid on a vending site. The extent of direct violence in these eviction drives depends on whether the vendors cooperate, the police sergeant said: if they quickly leave the vending sites, the vendors have nothing to fear. But if they hesitate, the police will confiscate vending equipment such as benches, tables, and stoves and take them to the police station. Meanwhile, if the vendors resist, the police have to resort to physical violence (interview with a police sergeant, January 2008). A commander in the special Anser police force, which the government deploys at times of political crises to ensure security and maintain discipline (in this example, at the hospital in mid-2009), admitted that when a street vendor starts arguing and does not want to leave after a warning, they "need to" slap him in the face and "have to" use their batons. By beating one, he said, they set an example for the others (interview with an Anser commander, June 2009).

Living with Violence: Livelihood Strategies of Street Vendors in Contested Arenas

Being in a clearly inferior position, most street vendors see the violence in their arenas as an inevitable, indisputable matter of course and align

Figure 8.1. A policeman taking some tea and snacks from a permanent (unconsolidated) street food shop.

their routines and interactions accordingly with these unjust "rules of the game." Most vendors fear the unpredictable brutality of policemen. Many hawkers have experienced beatings themselves during eviction drives and hardly any dare to argue with police officers directly. But still, instead of being mere victims of violence, street vendors do possess agency, and many manage to live with violence in the street vending arena. They

Figure 8.2. A group of policemen have called a mobile tea vendor to sell them some hot *cha*.

know, of course, that hawking without an official license is illegal. But as there are no licenses for street food vending in Dhaka[11] and access to formal employment is very restricted in Bangladesh, they assert that they have the right to street vending as their livelihood. Moreover, their personal life experience has accustomed them to the culture and politics of the street. Street vendors, therefore, perceive their appropriation of public space as legitimate and use multiple strategies to reduce their exposure to violence, cope with losses from evictions, and adapt their livelihoods in the long run.

Exposure and Sensitivity to the Direct Violence of Evictions

The aforementioned vending styles can be seen as different modes of appropriating public space, and the authorities react differently to each of them. Mobile vendors are largely tolerated because they do not threaten the state's monopoly on regulating public space. However, the more permanent vendors challenge the state's authority with their more comprehensive spatial appropriation and thus are more likely to be displaced. Overall, 58 percent of the vendors said that eviction drives by the police pose a problem to them. A third of the food vendors from consolidated permanent shops said they are often affected by evictions, but very few had lost any equipment or suffered greatly reduced income. None of them had ever been arrested during an eviction drive (see Table 2). Semi-permanent vendors are most severely affected by evictions because they set up their shop for the day—always at the same site—and cannot move their equipment and goods quickly when they need to. One-third of them are often affected by eviction, and one-quarter have lost equipment in recent evictions. Interestingly, the evictions did not cause serious financial damage in absolute terms. But the loss of their equipment and the longer periods without work and income can pose an even greater threat to their livelihood.

Coping with Violent Evictions

Police raids pose a challenge to all street vendors who encounter them and are thus forced to cope with the state's efforts to reclaim the streets. The vendors use different coping strategies to reduce business losses, continue vending as soon as possible, and secure their livelihoods in the longer run. Although 38 percent of the mobile vendors are regularly affected and 21 percent have lost some equipment, they incur smaller losses than do semi-mobile and semi-permanent vendors, mainly because of their greater flexibility. Following a particular regular route, they walk or cycle around and sell a fairly limited number of goods from a basket or tray, or tea from a flask. They spend less time at one site and are generally less embedded and less dependent on the local politics of their arena. When-

Table 8.2. Types of Street Food Vending and Exposure and Sensitivity to Police Evictions

Street Food Vending Types	Share of vendors often affected by evictions*	Share of vendors who lost goods or equipment in recent evictions	Losses due to eviction (last month)	Days without work after eviction	Share of vendors once arrested in evictions	Daily payment of security money ($n = 35$)**
Permanent shop consolidated	31%	0%	15 BDT	0.2	0%	100 BDT
Permanent shop unconsolidated	16%	4%	32 BDT	0.3	4%	91 BDT
Semi-permanent	33%	27%	300 BDT	4.4	0%	160 BDT
Semi-mobile	28%	14%	202 BDT	2.8	5%	105 BDT
Truly mobile	38%	21%	131 BDT	0.8	4%	42 BDT
Mean	28%	13%	145 BDT	1.8	3%	97 BDT
Mean for street food vendors only	**28%**	**15%**	**160 BDT**	**2.0**	**3%**	**97 BDT**

Source: Field Survey 2009 ($N = 120$)
* often = affected a few times a month, a few times a week, or daily by evictions
** Calculation only for those 30 percent of the respondents who admitted that they have to make daily security payments

ever a dispute arises with other, more permanent vendors, or when they perceive an upcoming eviction drive, they simply move away and thereby largely circumvent trouble. Another advantage of their high mobility is that even when more permanent vendors are made to leave a vending site, they are often allowed to stay because they occupy less space (see maps in Etzold et al. 2009; Etzold 2013). Semi-mobile hawkers follow the same strategy. Although they are slower, they can still move their pushcarts and rickshaws away from the eviction "hotspots" toward safer ground. Semi-permanent vendors, who use tables or bigger pushcarts for their daily business, can move only with considerable effort. In case of an eviction drive, they mostly try to store or hide their equipment and food at their site—some even hoist goods up into trees, where they are out of sight, and then go a safe distance away themselves. Permanent vendors, who have built little "huts" out of bamboo, wood, tin sheeting, or plastic, simply close their shops. But before reacting, most vendors carefully observe what is happening. Part of the informal deal between vendors and the police is that lower-ranking officers walk the streets before a raid is about to take place, warning the vendors by saying "Move away, move away, brother!" Actual eviction drives only happen when higher-ranking police sergeants, who are eager to see results, show up.

Figure 8.3. A popular street food vending site on Dhaka's University Campus before a police truck has stopped there. Two police officers are telling the vendors to leave the site. 3 December 2007, 9:30 A.M.

Figure 8.4. Half an hour later, most street vendors have cleared the footpath and stored their food items and equipment behind the fence. Two policemen are patrolling. 3 December 2007, 10:00 A.M.

After a "normal" raid that has not been carried out very violently, mobile and semi-mobile vendors reappear at their vending sites within minutes; meanwhile, more permanent vendors retrieve the goods they have hidden and reopen their shops. Within an hour the vendors have reclaimed their vending spots, and business is back to normal as if nothing had happened (see Figures 8.3–8.5). During large, more radical raids, by contrast, many shops are demolished, large amounts of food are spoiled, and the disruption of the vendors' livelihoods lasts longer. After the brutal eviction drives at the beginning of the interim government's rule in late January 2007, the vendors selling food in front of the university hospital, for instance, could not resume their business for more than a month because the police frequented the site more often and the local "patrons" did not grant their informal approval to return to vending. In such a crisis, vendors have to make substantial outlays to replace destroyed or confiscated equipment while also withstanding a longer period of income shortage and feeding their families in the absence of profits from street vending. At such times they draw on their savings or borrow money from family members, friends, or moneylenders. In a rapid succession of evic-

Figure 8.5. Once the police truck and officers have left, the vendors quickly return their equipment to the footpath and continue operating their street food shops as usual. December 3, 2007: 10:30 A.M.

tion drives such as those occurring during the two years of the Caretaker Government at certain highly contested public sites in Dhaka,[12] the situation can become critical, especially for semi-mobile and semi-permanent vendors. With every new raid they fall deeper into debt, further aggravating their already vulnerable situation (see case studies in Etzold 2013).

Adapting to Violent Arenas: The Informal Politics of Exploitation

In Dhaka, it is not formal laws that define the everyday practices of street vendors, but rather the informal arrangements between them and powerful agents at their vending sites. The social relations and institutions in operation in the local arenas explain the contradiction between "formal rigor" in terms of violent evictions and "informal tolerance" of street vending (Etzold et al. 2009; Etzold et al. 2012; Etzold 2013).

First, wholesale traders, street vendors, and slum dwellers are "protected" by personal relations, political affiliations, or "security payments" to representatives of city authorities, service providers, elected politicians, or police officers. Without this ambivalent protection, it is difficult, if not impossible, to succeed in business or simply organize everyday life in Dhaka (World Bank 2007; IGS 2008; Hossain 2011; Keck 2012). The structural violence of extracting money (so-called *chanda* payments) from street vendors is one facet of the informal operating rules in Dhaka's street vending arenas. Vending spots are allocated to individual vendors, and each spot has its specific price. Most street vendors pay between 10 and 500 BDT per day to so-called linesmen, who hand this money over to local *mastaan*s (musclemen), who are often also part of the formal system of political parties or trade unions (World Bank 2007). The bigger the shop and the higher its business volume, the more the vendor has to pay (payments average 97 BDT). The least successful mobile vendors pay less (42 BDT) than the semi-mobile (105 BDT) and then semi-permanent vendors (160 BDT). Notably, most of the permanent vendors (91 BDT) would not even admit to paying anything. Having received the payment, the *mastaan*s in turn allow vendors to sell at "their" usual spots, provide them with information about police evictions, and serve as middlemen in negotiations with more powerful actors, such as the police or local political leaders, who also get their share of the extracted money.[13]

Second, street vendors who are interested in securing their business in the long run are willing to accept the local "rules of the street" and invest in social capital. Monir, a semi-mobile vendor selling tea on Dhaka University campus, explained the obligatory rules for all vendors in front of the hospital as follows: they have to "maintain a close relationship with local powerful persons and political leaders" and "pay *chanda* to police officers for being allowed to continue vending," and they are also obliged to "build a strong community with other vendors so that we can help each other in difficult times" (interview with Monir, September 2008). Good social relations at a site and mutual support can pay off for hawkers. Immediately after eviction drives, some more established vendors, linesmen, *mastaan*s, local political leaders, and the police open negotiations about the duration of the vending ban, the return of confiscated equipment, or the temporarily arrested vendors' release from police custody. Thus the vendors' social capital is not only key to gaining access to specific vending sites but also crucial to their coping capacity in times of crises.

Regardless of whether or not the police carry out eviction drives brutally, whether or not equipment is confiscated, and whether strict street vending bans last an hour or a month, most food hawkers eventually re-appropriate "their" vending sites. Police raids, which resemble a cat-and-mouse game, do not seem intended to effectively discourage the street trade, but rather to demonstrate the power of the state and remind the vendors of the necessity of paying for their informal acclaimed "right" to do their business (Keck 2012). This structural violence of extortion merits criticism from a normative standpoint, as the subordinate actors are clearly exploited by those in power. But it also needs to be noted that bribes and "little favors" are culturally embedded in the everyday life of most cities of the Global South and can be seen as routinized social arrangements or informal institutions that benefit both parties (Illy 1986; Etzold et al. 2009). Although highly dependent on a few local patrons, street vendors have at least some limited security of tenure, which increases their resilience in face of disturbances such as evictions. Meanwhile, the substantial payments that the powerful—both formal state actors and informal power brokers—are able to extract from the street economy amount to the astonishing sum of 49 million U.S. dollars per year (my estimate).[14] According to the logic of the "politics of illegality" that Anjaria (2010) described for the case of street vendors in Mumbai, state actors are not interested in permanently resolving the contested hawkers' issue, for instance, by legalizing street vending or declaring special vending zones (Etzold 2014). They rather seek to criminalize street vending or keep the hawkers' "legal status in a constant state of flux" (Anjaria 2010: 82). It is no surprise then, that police raids in Dhaka do not succeed in driving hawkers off the streets permanently: the informal modes of governing street vending not only efficiently provide customers with cheap food but also create a capital surplus that reinforces hegemonic local power structures. An exploitative political economy is thereby consolidated.

Conclusion: Everyday Violence in Contested Arenas of Street Vending

As illustrated, there are multiple manifestations of violence in arenas of street vending in Dhaka. During eviction campaigns hawkers experience direct violence such as beatings, the destruction of vending equipment, and displacement from vending sites. They are thus impeded in meeting their needs for survival, well-being, and freedom. Both, harassment by police officers and exploitation in patron-client relations, are evidence of structural violence in the local arenas. This procedural violence contributes to constant fear, insecurity, and misery among vendors and also causes deep frustration and humiliating feelings of inferiority, helplessness, and powerlessness. Both forms of violence are legitimized by powerful discursive practices: vending practices are declared illegal, street food is labeled unhygienic, and eviction drives are extolled as serving order and public security. This "illegalization" of hawkers leads to their further marginalization and exploitation. Further, the perception of direct and structural violence as "normal" in Dhaka is an indicator of cultural violence. In turn, street vendors have internalized their seemingly inferior social position and experience insecurity, injustice, and vulnerability as real and, even worse, unchangeable.

Evictions are cat-and-mouse games that help to maintain the political and economic order in the local arenas. Although street vendors clearly suffer from repeated evictions, they do still possess agency. For them, selling under conditions of insecurity and living with violence means constantly trying to cope with shock, stress, and disturbances. They are forced to invest in exploitative informal arrangements such as paying security money, which nevertheless helps them gain access to vending sites, enables them to operate their business over the long term, and increases their resilience to evictions. Their agency, understood as the available space for action, depends on their position in informal networks of power, which determines their sensitivity to violence.

This chapter has demonstrated the multifaceted nature of violence in Dhaka. But from another angle, it illustrates the multidimensionality of human security. More than the absence of direct violence that is "freedom from fear," or the absence of structural violence that is "freedom from want and humiliation," human security emerges when cultural violence is absent too, allowing spaces of "freedom to live in dignity and self-determination" to open up (Ogata and Sen 2003; Bohle 2007b). Yet, as exemplified in this case study on street food vendors, human security is still more a vision than a reality in Dhaka, one of the biggest and most ambivalent megacities of the Global South.

Benjamin Etzold is a postdoctoral researcher and lecturer in the Geography Department at the University of Bonn. His PhD research on urban livelihoods, street vending and food security, and governance of public space in the megacity of Dhaka, Bangladesh, was published in 2013 as the book *The Politics of Street Food: Contested Governance and Vulnerabilities in Dhaka's Field of Street Vending* (Steiner Verlag). Results of his recent research projects have been published in the journals *Population, Space and Place, Climate and Development, Migration and Development, Geographica Helvetica, Erdkunde*, and *Die Erde*.

Notes

I greatly appreciate the cordiality and generosity of Dhaka's street food vendors, who not only gave me detailed information about their business but also allowed me to glimpse their life. I would like to thank the German Research Foundation (DFG), which funded this research as part of a project on the "Megaurban

Food System of Dhaka" (Grant No. BO 680/35-1/2) within the research program "Megacities—Megachallenge: Informal Dynamics of Global Change" (SPP 1233). I wish to thank Prof. Dr. Hans-Georg Bohle (University of Bonn/Germany, Geography Department), Dr. Wolfgang-Peter Zingel (University of Heidelberg/Germany, South Asia Institute), and Prof. Dr. Shafique uz-Zaman (Dhaka University/Bangladesh, Department of Economics) for their continuous support, and to my fellow researchers in the megacities program. I also wish to thank the research assistants, in particular Taufique Hassan, Sania Rahman, and Md. Ajfal Hosain, for their help in my empirical research. Last but not least, thanks are due the editors of this volume and the reviewers Patrick Sakdapolrak, Antje Schultheis, and Anna Zimmer.

1. The Caretaker Government was an interim government to prepare the national election in 2008.
2. I took an inductive approach that included hundreds of conversations, interviews, and group discussions with (mainly male) street vendors, aiming at understanding the vendors' interests and practices from their perspectives. However, it was not possible to take an *emic* perspective as a researcher, as my insufficient Bangla language skills clearly limited the research in that I had to rely on student assistants, who translated the qualitative interviews directly and facilitated two quantitative surveys.
3. The investigated study sites were publicly accessible places within the Dhaka City Corporation area, including two slum areas—one settlement illegally built in Dhaka's North where roughly 10,000 people live in poor housing conditions (Bishil Slum), and one consolidated but run-down settlement of 90,000 inhabitants near the center of Dhaka with a mix of residential and industrial use (Islambagh); two important transport hubs in the city from where passengers travel to all regions of Bangladesh—a ferry terminal (BIWTA at Sadar Ghat) and a bus terminal (Saidabad); one important traffic square in the city's elite quarter (the Gulshan One area); and one street in front of the city's second-biggest public hospital (Dhaka Medical College Hospital) in the immediate vicinity of Dhaka University.
4. The estimate of the number of street food vendors in Dhaka (Statistical Metropolitan Area) in 2010 and their economic impact is based on the latest available population data from the UN; the Bangladesh Government's Labour Force Survey 2001 and Population Census 2001; my own food consumption survey (N = 204), which was conducted in 2009 in nine slums; and my own street vendor survey (N = 120), conducted in 2009 at six study sites.
5. The Pure Food Ordinance dates back to 1959 and has not been changed since. It states that "no premises shall be used for ... the manufacture or sale of ice-cream or any pickled, potted, pressed or preserved food ... unless such premises have been registered by the occupier thereof" (Chap. 2, section 21). The Dhaka City Corporation Ordinance of 1983 stresses that "the Corporation may ... prohibit the manufacture, sale or preparation, or the exposure for sale, of any specified article of food or drink in any place or premises not licensed by the Corporation; ... prohibit the hawking of specified articles of food and drink in such parts of the City as may be specified" (Chap. 3, section 95). With regard to the access and use of public space in Dhaka, it says that "no person

shall make an encroachment, movable or immovable, on, over or under a street or a drain or any land, house-gully or building or park except under a licence granted by the Corporation and to the extent permitted by the licence" (Chap. 7, section 115). The law texts can be accessed online on the website "Laws of Bangladesh": http://bdlaws.minlaw.gov.bd/.
6. The "modern formal economy" is understood as the economic sector regulated by the institutions of modern nation-states and characterized by corporate levels of capitalist organization, whereas the "informal sector" refers to activities that are "largely ignored, rarely supported, often regulated and sometimes actively discouraged by the Government" (ILO 1972: 4). The classical characteristics of the informal sector—namely, ease of entry, reliance on indigenous resources, family ownership of enterprises, small size and scale of operation, low but labor-intensive productivity, self-employment, skills acquired outside the formal school system, and unregulated and competitive markets—are helpful for a first descriptive assessment of the street food trade.
7. In most countries of the Global South, the street food trade is largely in the hands of women (Tinker 1997, Brown 2006). In Bangladesh, in contrast, only a minor share of the street vendors are female. In my own survey only 6 out of 120 vendors (5 percent) were women. The main reason is the Islamic norm of *purdah*, which restricts the movements of women, and thus also their opportunities to work, in public space. Nonetheless, women play a crucial yet sometimes "invisible" role in the street food trade in Dhaka, as they are often involved in the home-based preparation of the food that the men sell on the street. Women at home may also cook lunches that are supplied in metal containers (*tiffins*) to workers at their workplaces, to shop owners in their shops, and to businessmen in their offices.
8. Tinker (1997: 17) defined "a street food business as one selling ready-to-eat foods from a place having more than three permanent walls." Vendors who sell from permanent and consolidated structures are therefore not considered as "real" street food vendors in this study, but rather serve as a comparison group.
9. In Bangladesh, only formally employed laborers such as factory workers or state employees are normally organized in highly politicized trade unions (cf. Siddiqui and Ahmed 2004; IGS 2008). Whereas many hawkers of clothes and other consumer products in Dhaka are organized in associations, only 3 percent of the interviewed street food vendors (all of them permanent) were members of a hawkers' association. Unlike in India, where local advocacy coalitions effectively influenced the National Policy on Street Vending (cf. Bhowmik 2010), in Bangladesh the street vendors do not have a recognized political voice (Etzold 2014).
10. Ten major discursive "story lines" were identifiable in interviews with experts and state representatives and a media analysis of 210 articles from the *Daily Star* newspaper (from 2003 to 2009). Three rather positive narratives revolving around the themes "urban poverty and livelihoods," "the utility of street vending," and the "local food culture" addressed street food vending as a necessary, vital, and even important aspect of urban life. In contrast, six narra-

tives set street vending in a negative light, addressing it as illegal, illegitimate, inappropriate, and threatening to public order. These latter story lines can be labeled "a functional city", "modernity and development", "food safety and hygiene", "public security", "corruption and extortion", and "illegality" (see Etzold 2013).
11. Only vendors who sold prepared food from consolidated structures—they are by definition then not *street* food vendors—had some kind of license from the city authorities (four of 120 interviewed vendors).
12. Whereas evictions are carried out regularly at some highly contested vending sites, the police are not present at all at other places. Each vending site has a specific "value" according to its location in the city, socioeconomic environment, and unique local history. In general, street vending in slums is little contested because it is a basic feature in the slum economy and the local politics of power: policemen are uninterested in fulfilling their duties in slums, or are discouraged from doing so by local musclemen. Of the vendors at one of the slum sites, only 15 percent said they were often affected by evictions, only 5 percent of them had ever lost any equipment or had to close their shop for a day; and nobody had ever been arrested. In stark contrast, the street in front of the public hospital, for instance, is highly contested. Due to the hospital director's engagement in drives against crime, indiscipline, and unhygienic conditions, the hawkers there are subject to frequent evictions and harassment by the police (30 percent said so). Thirty-five percent had lost equipment and food items in the past and spent, on average, four days without work after a police raid. Fifteen percent of them have been arrested—many several times. The vendors at the ferry and the bus terminal face similar conditions, but their goods are confiscated less often and their total losses are lower (Etzold 2013).
13. Only 70 percent of the vendors in this survey admitted to paying *chanda*. But the in-depth interviews are proof of the existence of these payments, and of the general trend regarding the daily amount each group of vendors has to pay. In a local newspaper, a journalist explained how the eviction drives against hawkers at the very beginning of the Caretaker Governments' rule had affected "a section of the law enforcers, local unit political leaders, Dhaka City Corporation (DCC) staff and the organized criminals [among whom were many lower-ranking leaders of the then ruling Bangladesh Nationalist Party] that collect tolls from the illegal street vendors. ... Each street vendor had to pay a daily toll ranging from Tk 30 to Tk 200 to these elements and they would be driven out otherwise. ... Around 50 percent of the tolls go to local political kingpins' pockets, 15 percent to party activists, 15 percent to police and the rest to the 'linemen'– the ones employed to collect the tolls for their bosses." ("City Walkways Freed from Hawkers," *The Daily Star*, 19 January 2007; for similar accounts see also "Hawker Eviction: Why Drive Fails Again and Again," *The Daily Star*, 5 February 2007).
14. Taking my own estimate of 97,000 street food vendors in Dhaka and this survey's results (showing that vendors on average pay *chanda* of 97 taka daily) are taken as a base, it can be assumed that 9.5 million taka are extorted from Dhaka's street food vendors every day. That amounts to a yearly sum of 3.43

billion taka (48.9 million U.S. dollars, at the prevailing exchange rate at the time of the survey in December 2009) illegally collected from street food vendors alone, that is, not including hawkers of other goods.

Bibliography

Anjaria, Jonathan S. 2010. "The Politics of Illegality: Mumbai Hawkers, Public Space and the Everyday Life of the Law." In *Street Vendors in the Global Urban Economy*, ed. Sharit K. Bhowmik. New Delhi and Abingdon: Routledge.

Banks, Nicola, et al. 2011. "Neglecting the Urban Poor in Bangladesh: Research, Policy and Action in the Context of Climate Change." *Environment and Urbanization* 23 (2): 487–502.

Bayat, Asef. 1997. *Street Politics: Poor People's Movements in Iran*. New York: Columbia University Press.

Bhowmik, Sharit K., ed. 2010. *Street Vendors in the Global Urban Economy*. New Delhi and Abingdon: Routledge.

Birkmann, Jörn, ed. 2006. *Measuring Vulnerability to Natural Hazards: Towards Disaster Resilient Societies*. Tokyo, New York, and Paris: United Nations University Press.

Bohle, Hans-Georg. 2007a. "Geographies of Violence and Vulnerability: An Actor-Oriented Analysis of the Civil War in Sri Lanka." *Erdkunde* 61 (2): 129–146.

———. 2007b. *Living with Vulnerability: Livelihoods and Human Security*. Bonn: United Nations University, Institute for Environment and Human Security.

Bohle, Hans-Georg, and Hartmut Fünfgeld. 2007. "The Political Ecology of Violence in Eastern Sri Lanka." *Development and Change* 38 (4): 665–687.

Bohle, Hans-Georg, and Patrick Sakdapolrak. 2008: "Leben mit der Krise. Vertreibung von Slumbewohnern in der Megastadt Chennai." *Geographische Rundschau* 60 (4): 12–21.

Bourdieu, Pierre 2005. "Ortseffekte." In *Das Elend der Welt*, ed. Pierre Bourdieu et al. Konstanz: UVK.

Bourdieu, Pierre, and Loïc Wacquant. 1992. "The Purpose of Reflexive Sociology (The Chicago Workshop)." In *An Invitation to Reflexive Sociology*, ed. Pierre Bourdieu and Loïc Wacquant. Chicago and London: University of Chicago Press.

Brown, Alison, ed. 2006. *Contested Space: Street Trading, Public Space, and Livelihoods in Developing Cities*. Rugby: ITDG.

Chen, Martha A. 2005. *Rethinking the Informal Economy: Linkages with the Formal Economy and the Formal Regulatory Environment*. Research Paper No. 2005/10. United Nations University, World Institute for Development Economics.

Cross, John, and Marina Karides. 2007. "Capitalism, Modernity, and the "Appropriate" Use of Space." In *Street Entrepreneurs: People, Place and Politics in Local and Global Perspective*, ed. John Cross and Alfonso Morales. London and New York: Routledge.

Cross, John, and Alfonso Morales, eds. 2007. *Street Entrepreneurs: People, Place and Politics in Local and Global Perspective*. London and New York: Routledge.

Centre for Urban Studies. 2006. *Slums of Urban Bangladesh: Mapping and Census, 2005.* Dhaka: Centre for Urban Studies (CUS).
Davis, Mike, 2007. *Planet of Slums.* London and New York: Verso.
de Cassia Vieira Cardoso, Ryzia, Michele Companion, and Stefano Marras, eds. 2014. *Street Food Governance: Between Culture, Economy, and Health.* New York: Routledge.
Etzold, Benjamin. 2013. *The Politics of Street Food: Contested Governance and Vulnerabilities in Dhaka's Field of Street Vending.* Stuttgart: Franz Steiner Verlag.
———. 2014. "Towards Fair Street Food Governance in Dhaka: Moving from Exploitation and Eviction to Social Recognition and Support." In *Street Food Governance: Between Culture, Economy, and Health,* ed. Ryzia de Cassia Vieira Cardoso, Michele Companion, and Stefano Marras. New York: Routledge.
Etzold, Benjamin, et al. 2009. "Informality as Agency: Negotiating Food Security in Dhaka." *Die Erde* 140 (1): 3–24.
Etzold, Benjamin, et al. 2012. "Doing Institutions: A Dialectic Reading of Institutions and Social Practices and Its Relevance for Development Geography." *Erdkunde* 66 (3): 185–195.
Fünfgeld, Hartmut. 2007. *Fishing in Muddy Waters: Socio-Environmental Relations under the Impact of Violence in Eastern Sri Lanka.* Saarbrücken: Verlag für Entwicklungspolitik.
Galtung, Johan. 1969. "Violence, Peace, and Peace Research." *Journal of Peace Research* 6 (3): 167–191.
———. 1990. "Cultural Violence." *Journal of Peace Research* 27 (3): 291–305.
———. 2002. *Rethinking Conflict: The Cultural Approach.* Strasbourg: Council of Europe.
Hackenbroch, Kerstin, et al. 2008. "Coping with Forced Evictions: Adaptation Processes of Evicted Slum Dwellers in Dhaka." *TRIALOG* 98: 17–23.
Hackenbroch, Kerstin, et al. 2009. "Spatiality of Livelihoods: Urban Public Space and the Urban Poor in Dhaka." *Die Erde* 140 (1): 47–68.
Holston, John, and Arjun Appadurai. 1999. "Cities and Citizenship." In *Cities and Citizenship,* ed. John Holston. Durham, NC, and London: Duke University Press.
Hossain, Ahmede. 2007. "Facing an Uncertain Future." *The Daily Star Forum,* 2 February.
Hossain, Shahadat. 2011. "Informal Dynamics of a Public Utility: Rationality of the Scene behind a Screen." *Habitat International* 35 (2): 275–285.
IGS (Institute of Governance Studies). 2008. *The State of Governance in Bangladesh 2007: Expectations, Commitments, Challenges.* Dhaka: BRAC University, IGS.
Illy, Hans F. 1986. "Regulation and Evasion: Street Vendors in Manila." *Policy Science* 19 (1): 61–81.
ILO (International Labour Office). 1972. *Employment, Incomes and Equality: A Strategy for Increasing Productive Employment in Kenya.* Geneva: ILO.
Islam, Nazrul. 2005. *Dhaka Now: Contemporary Urban Development.* Dhaka: Bangladesh Geographical Society.
Keck, Markus. 2012. "Informality as Borrowed Security: Contested Food Markets in Dhaka, Bangladesh." In *Urban Informalities: Reflections on the Formal and Informal,* ed. Michael Waibel and Colin McFarlane. London: Ashgate.

Keck, Markus, and Benjamin Etzold. 2013. "Resilience Refused: Wasted Potentials for Improving Food Security in Dhaka." *Erdkunde* 67 (1): 75–91.

O'Brien, Karen, and Robin Leichenko. 2000. "Double Exposure: Assessing the Impacts of Climate Change Within the Context of Economic Globalization." *Global Environmental Change* 10 (3): 221–232.

Ogata, Sadako, and Amartya Sen, eds. 2003. *Human Security Now.* New York: United Nations Commission on Human Security.

Peluso, Nancy L., and Michael Watts, eds. 2001. *Violent Environments.* Ithaca, NY, and London: Cornell University Press.

Salway, Sarah, et al. 2003. "A Profile of Women's Work Participation among the Urban Poor of Dhaka." *World Development* 31 (5): 881–901.

Scott, James C. 1990. *Domination and the Arts of Resistance: Hidden Transcripts.* New Haven, CT, and London: Yale University Press.

Siddiqui, Kamal, and Jamshed Ahmed, 2004. Dhaka. In: Siddiqui, Kamal, et al., eds. *Megacity Governance in South Asia. A Comparative Study.* Dhaka: The University Press Limited.

Siddiqui, Kamal, et al. 2010. *Social Formation in Dhaka, 1985–2005: A Longitudinal Study of Society in a Third World Megacity.* Surrey: Ashgate.

Tinker, Irene. 1997. *Street Foods: Urban Food and Employment in Developing Countries.* New York and Oxford: Oxford University Press.

UN (United Nations). 2014. *World Urbanization Prospects: The 2014 Revision.* New York: United Nations Department of Economic and Social Affairs, Population Division.

Wisner, Ben, et al. 2003. *At Risk: Natural Hazards, People's Vulnerability, and Disasters.* London: Routledge.

World Bank. 2007. *Dhaka: Improving Living Conditions for the Urban Poor.* Dhaka: The World Bank Office.

CHAPTER 9

The Street Vendors Act and Pedestrianism in India
A Reading of the Archival Politics of the Calcutta Hawker Sangram Committee

Ritajyoti Bandyopadhyay

This essay makes an attempt to comment on the politics of street vending in Calcutta, going beyond the optic of the "informal economy."[1] As a preliminary exercise to generate an alternative academic vocabulary of street vending, it explores three issues, namely, "pedestrianism," "archiving," and "judicialization" of the street vendors' mobilization. This move is necessary for two reasons.

First, in order to say that street vending existed even before its "discovery" by the experts of the informal economy in many "third world cities" in the early 1970s, one needs to question the "naturalized" connection between the informal economy as a conceptual apparatus translating and ordering data into information on poverty, unemployment, and entrepreneurship, and street vending as its empirical site—a "case study." This uncoupling enables us to rescue street vending from the case study mode of academic enquiry. It seems rather important instead to study the discovery of street vending as a new archival moment that created a vocabulary of development. Subsequently, certain influential terms such as "low-circuit economy," "service sector," and so on seeped from this literature into the language of popular activism and became registers along which the archive was shaped.

Second, several recent micro and macro studies of the informal economy have demonstrated a clear trend of what can be called uninformalization at the heart of the informal economy. They observe that the need to survive in the globally competitive market has led to moves to standardize labor relations and commodity chains within the informal economy. For instance, scholars have noticed both a dramatic slowing of the growth of casual employment since the beginning of the new century, and a corresponding growth in the number of regular workers and self-employed within the informal sector (Kundu and Mohanan 2009). In addition, organizational activities *outside* the scope of official trade unions in both the formal and the informal sectors have increased significantly, calling for a reconceptualization of the formal economy/informal economy binary. Scholars have reported two kinds of unionization: (a) extension of the already registered trade unions accommodating workers in the informal economy or providing affiliation for new unions in the informal economy; and (b) unions organized by informal workers themselves outside the fold of the existing legal trade union complex. Both types of unions have combined the issues of labor rights and representation with the concerns of economic and business development (Bonner and Spooner 2010). In short, the three major attributes of informal economy—namely, the existence of a casual labor force, paralegality, and lack of organization—are now put in question.

"Hawkers," as we call various petty traders on city streets and footpaths (also known as pavements and sidewalks), or "street vendors," as we call hawkers in the more formalized world of urban policy, received much media attention in India in the first half of 2014. This was part of the dual effect of the enactment of the Street Vendors (Protection of Livelihood and Regulation of Street Vending) Bill and the celebration of the exceptional career of Prime Minister Narendra Modi, who began as a humble *chaiwalah* (tea vendor)—the ordinary urban everyman. Modi's Bharatiya Janata Party (BJP) led a successful campaign connecting hundreds of tea stalls across the country through digital media. Modi interacted with the wider public across the country at the interface of digital media and the "traditional" tea stall—India's much-touted "informal" platform for political opinion formation. The entire campaign was also given the brand name *Chai pe Charcha* (conversation over tea). While initiating this interface in his home state Gujarat, Modi said that a "tea stall is like a footpath Parliament; all topics under the sun are discussed."[2]

Certainly, the Street Vendors (Protection of Livelihood and Regulation of Street Vending) Act (henceforth SVA) promises some amount of certainty to the tenuous existence of one segment of the lower rung of the petty bourgeoisie in the Indian urban scene, ironically through spatial zoning. In his campaign, on the other hand, Modi introduced a new political figure—the hawker/street vendor—through autobiographical reckoning: "I have myself learnt a lot while selling the tea. Sometimes there were insults also. It was a very special experience."[3] Interestingly, the hawkers/street vendors with whom India's prime minister identifies himself are not the peasantry or the working class or even the middle class of the twentieth century; they are a new "national category" and speak for a mass phenomenon associated with the street of the twenty-first century's fast-urbanizing India.

Setting the Agenda for an Alternative Framework

This essay is primarily concerned with the governmental rationalities involved in the SVA. I argue that the two preexisting powerful discourses of informality and pedestrianism intersect to promote mandates to ensure street vendors' livelihood while also spatially constraining street vending through stringent zoning norms. I also show how the SVA has existed as a justiciable idea since the early 2000s, long before it was formalized as a national act. What does it tell us about the life of law and activism in a postcolonial democracy?

More than a decade ago, in a relatively under-cited essay, Ray Bromley (2000) invited the scholars to rethink the connection between informal economy and street vending. He refused to regard street vending as just a segment of the informal economy and invited scholars to develop new analytical tools to describe the phenomenon. Since then, we have progressed very little. Critical scholarship on the subject, if it advanced at all, remained within its established field from the economics to the politics of informal economies, with prevailing and emergent forms of contestation over the meaning of the urban public space being the dominant academic orthodoxy (Anjaria 2008). Put differently, since the 1970s, when a typical researcher of the informal economy tended to focus on the "trade aspect" of street vending in the context of unemployment in the "Third World" cities (McGee 1973) the focus has gradually shifted to the spatial and performative aspects of street vending.

This essay goes further to explore whether the politics of street vending can be conceptualized in relation to the stated purpose of the footpath as the pedestrian's right of passage. In this connection, I propose a reading of the SVA that shows how the prevailing traditions of organized mobilization of hawkers and the SVA are in complex conversation with each other.

The Salient Features of the Street Vendors Act

The deliberations over the Street Vendors Act formally started in 2001, when the Ministry of Urban Development and Poverty Alleviation formed a national task force comprising members of the government of India, state governments, municipal bodies, street vendors' unions, and experts. The twelve years between the formation of the task force and the enactment of the Street Vendors Bill witnessed the consolidation of hawkers' demands for the end of a bribe-seeking "predatory state" through a central legislative act that would "empower" them to withstand the "everyday experience of vulnerability" to the state, the corporate economy, and middle-class activist civic bodies in many Indian cities. During the bill's passage, both the National Alliance of Street Vendors (NASVI)[4] and the National Hawker Federation (NHF)[5]—the two major bodies of street hawkers—began to claim credit for it, congratulating the United Progressive Alliance (UPA) government and UPA Chairperson Sonia Gandhi for enabling the hawkers to defend their rightful claims to the urban economy. Leaders from both bodies published solidarity pictures with Sonia Gandhi and Rahul Gandhi on their websites and on social media.

The SVA introduces four important regulations with long-term implications:

1) It divides the entire public space of the city into two zones—the vending zone and the non-vending zone—with a clause of "public purpose" under which a vending zone can be made a non-vending zone for the "greater public good."
2) It articulates the basic framework of the "participatory" management of street vending in the vending zones. The participatory body, called the Town Vending Committee (TVC), is supposed to mediate between the local state and civil society. Containing representatives of the government, street vendors, banking and welfare organizations, NGOs, and civil society, it is required to recruit 40 percent of its members from among the street vendors themselves, and these registered street vendors have the right to elect their representatives. Thus, the street vendors have voting rights to elect only a section of the TVC's members that does not even constitute a majority of the members of this crucial decision-making body. Once again, the term "participation," as in all other instances of "participatory democracy," conceals more than it reveals.

3) The demarcation of the vending zone and the non-vending zone is envisioned as micro-managed by the TVC. According to the law, each TVC is to come up with city-specific zoning norms based on a discussion among stakeholders. In demarcating vending zones, the TVCs must maintain a proper balance between the usable space and the number of vendors without compromising issues of traffic, public health, and the environment. If the government wishes to make changes to this balance, the law requires it to consult the concerned TVC. In the vending zone, registered vendors both stationary and mobile can vend with legitimacy. Needless to say, the exercise of their rights is subject to compliance with sanitation and public health codes. They are also liable to pay periodic fees for use of public resources.
4) The SVA requires that municipal governments undertake a periodic census of street vendors in their respective jurisdictions, and that street vendors be registered based on these surveys. Registered street vendors are allowed to vend in designated locations in the vending zone. Municipal governments are to conduct all censuses and registrations with the help of the street vendors' associations and unions, which prompts one of the oldest questions in labor studies: What happens to those who do not belong to any association or union that represents the voice of the worker in the government? What if the associations and unions decide to restrict the incoming flow of aspiring street vendors by pushing them out via a cumbersome bureaucratic process of enumeration and registration as per the norms of the SVA? What happens to existing street vendors every five years, when the government identifies a reserve army of street vendors on the city's doorstep waiting to get registered? If the available city space is finite (which indeed it is in all cities) then such a situation will bring the rent-seeking, predatory state back onto the scene, and the existing vendors will have to bribe the police and municipal authorities to retain their stalls. This means that the existing ranks of registered vendors can be regulated by database, by the availability of land, and by deployment of the classic mechanism of the threat of loss of employment in a case of putative excess. The TVC thus maintains a sort of employment bank, and the use of the law not only codifies the street vendor but also creates a regulated surplus of street vendors.

To summarize, the SVA blends the association of street vendors with zoning principles under the umbrella supervision of the TVC, where a balance in the representation of often conflictual social and political interests is maintained under bureaucratic executive leadership (Government of India 2014: 7–8). The decade-long deliberations on the SVA have left at least four significant legacies that will continue to shape the politics of street hawking in the era since the act's passage. First, the SVA signals a concerted effort by the Indian state to govern the informal economy in general and to integrate the street vendors question with concerns regarding urban spatial planning.[6] Second, it has stepped up the pace of association formation among street hawkers. My findings point to the formation of social group–specific unions within the NHF in line with the SVA's requirement that women,[7] Scheduled Castes, and Scheduled Tribes be represented. The NHF, as a federal body of several associations and unions of street vendors, can easily accommodate the micro-fragmentation of its member organizations. This also suggests that the vocabulary of the association might undergo some changes in the course of actual implementation of the SVA. Third, the promulgation of "public sector"–type quotas for managing the hawkers' representation in the TVC and the treatment of street hawking as a transitory employment bank seem to suggest an expanded government role in structuring street hawking. Fourth, the SVA seeks to resolves a central paradox associated with any kind of formal recognition of "stationary" street vendors.

The paradox lies in the question of how it is possible to formally recognize the privatization of public space. The footpath is primarily for the pedestrian, who does not loiter around but moves continuously from one point to the other. Any kind of formal legal recognition of stationary street vendors violates the very foundation of the bourgeois notion of property distributed neatly between private and public domains. Then what is so formal about the legal recognition of street vendors? I argue that the SVA permits street vending in limited and restricted space by considering it an acceptable exception to the rule of property. Unlike the rights of the abstract pedestrian, which are fundamental to the law of public space in a bourgeois city, the street vendor's right is founded on a series of exceptions and contingent legality. That is why the SVA is so invested in articulating the conditions under which the rights of the street vendor are realizable.

The position of the SVA is not unique. In a series of verdicts between the 1980s and 2000s, different high courts and the Supreme Court of India remained fairly consistent in their opinion regarding street vending.[8] Members of the public can rightfully use walkways, and their right is balanced and checked by fact that the other members of the public enjoy the same right. The government, as the public administrator, has to protect all such public rights by imposing constraints on every user of the street. What is the rationale behind allowing the hawker to occupy space on streets in violation of the basic "public purpose" of it? Arguably, it is the spatial aspect, not the trade aspect, of street hawking that comes under *general state regulation*. The Street Vendors Act is thus much more concerned with sedentary hawkers than with nomads and ensures that the sedentary hawker does not develop a long-term legal claim to a vending space by erecting any kind of permanent or semipermanent structure. Now, with the legalization of street vending, the associations have to change their posture in relation to law and property. When street vending was illegal, the associations justified street vendors' stake in the public space in the language of the collective moral claim of the poorer social groups to the city (Chatterjee 2004). The SVA introduces a new channel of relationship between the government, the street vendors, and the rest of the society. The association now has become a law-implementing agency.

I hold that the SVA has to be read as part of a long-term process of institutionalization of what can be called a "state-union complex" engaged in the rational management of both human and nonhuman elements, subjects and objects, bodies and spaces. I contend that the time is ripe to develop an alternative framework that goes beyond the overworked optic of the informal economy that so long has thrived around the formal/informal binary, to understand the dynamics of the state-union complex in connection with the current moment of urbanization in Indian cities.

The Indian Judiciary and Street Vending

This section considers how the Indian judiciary normally conceptualizes street vending on public space.[9] The first example comes from Justice Y. Chandrachud's verdict of 3 July 1985 in the Bombay High Court.[10] The Bombay Hawkers' Union filed a case to settle scores with the Bombay Municipal Corporation, pushing for the creation of hawking zones and issuance of sufficient hawking licenses. The judgment above all upholds the universal meaning of the public street and posits street vending as a potential threat to the public interest, specifically the pedestrian's *right of passage*:

> Public Streets, by their very nomenclature and definition, are meant for the use of the general public. They are not laid to facilitate the carrying on of private trade or business. If hawkers were to be conceded the right claimed by them, they could hold the society to ransom by squatting on the centre of busy thoroughfares, thereby paralysing all civic life. Indeed, that is what some of them have done in some parts of the city. They have made it impossible for the pedestrians to walk on footpaths or even the streets properly so called.

Nevertheless, the verdict refrains from asking the municipal corporation to launch any drastic eviction drive, considering that "encroachment" on public property for livelihood is a mass phenomenon in India. It proposes to apply the discretion of the municipal corporation to "tolerate" street hawking in less thronged footpaths. The opinion thus concludes:

> We should, therefore, decide that within the constraints of our resources, we would concentrate on the removal of such obstructions/projections on certain streets and public places where the pedestrians or vehicular traffic is most intense and where any obstruction/projection on the street or pavement is likely to cause great harm to public interest and cause nuisance. For example, the roads leading from suburban Railway Stations to the residential areas in the Suburbs or roads in the Central Business District in South Bombay connecting the Suburban Railway Stations with the offices and other places of work as also certain arterial roads on which major goods and public transport vehicles move, could be considered as important roads and pavements where no hawkers should be allowed to do their business.

Time and again, judges have asked municipal corporations to stop encroachment whenever such an attempt is made. Otherwise, in the long run, the encroachers tend to make ethico-moral claims to public space that often compel the government to decide on a series of exceptions to the rule of public property. In the case of the footpath, the law of public property ensures the right of passage of the pedestrian—a classless, nameless, abstract individual who by virtue of mobility is distinguishable from any static being on the way, be it a tree, a potentially dangerous manhole, a hawker with a stall, or a lamppost. As potential obstructions to pedestrians' mobility, static elements have to be legally *equalized* and zoned out.

This notion is absolutely central to any modern law governing public spaces in any national context. A further example comes from Section 372 of the Calcutta Municipal Act, 1980 (Government of West Bengal 1980: 759–760). This section empowers the municipal commissioner to "remove anything erected, deposited and hawked" in contravention of the act:

> *The Municipal Commissioner may, without notice, cause to be removed:*
> 1. *Any wall, fence, rail, post, step, booth, or other structure or fixture which may be erected or set up in or upon any street, footpath, or upon or over any open channel, drain, well or tank contrary to the provision of this Act;*
> 2. *Any stall, chair, bench, box, ladder, bale, board or shelf, or any other thing whatsoever placed, deposited, projected, attached, or suspended in, upon, from or to any place in contravention of this Act;*
> 3. *Any article whatsoever hawked or exposed for sale in any public place or in any public street and footpath in contravention of the provision of this Act, and any vehicle, package, boxboard, shelf or any other thing in or on which such article is placed or kept for purpose of sale, display, or otherwise.*

The SVA maintains a clear distinction between static objects (like a booth, "structure or fixture," vehicle, or "article whatsoever hawked and exposed") on the one hand, and bodies and the nodes of circulation (like the street, footpath, and drain) on the other. All static objects are viewed with equal suspicion of obstructing the free circulation of pedestrians, air, and water. The street vendor is nothing more than "an urban object, legitimate only insofar as she is static or in motion" (Blomley 2011: 87).

It is evident that the court orders, municipal by-laws, and SVA converge in envisioning the city as essentially a space of circulation. The role of the police, town planners, civil engineers, architects, and lawyers is to ensure circulation "in such a way that the inherent dangers of circulation are cancelled out" (Foucault 2007: 93). How do the custodians of circulation manage the sedentary (i.e., stationary) and peripatetic (i.e., mobile) elements on the street? The SVA suggests that to achieve the best possible circulation, the city must first of all de-sedentarize the potentially sedentarizing vending practices. This can be accomplished in two ways: (a) by ensuring that the material structure of stalls uniformly consists of collapsible elements such as folding tables and metal and plastic chairs, rather than the traditional wooden *chwukis* (low wooden seats to display merchandise); pushcarts and umbrellas, rather than bamboo structures and tarpaulin covers; removable plastic clothing racks, shelves, and cardboard boxes of various sizes; and (b) by setting softer regulation standards for peripatetic vendors. In many Indian cities, eviction operations were conducted precisely to change the material structure of the vending stalls. In Calcutta, for instance, the municipal corporation, along with the state government, implemented a prolonged drive codenamed "Operation Sunshine" to evict hawkers in 1996–97, deploying bulldozers to destroy semipermanent brick and concrete structures on the footpath. No wonder such a program of demolition was associated with the romanticization of the figure of the *pheriwala* (the peripatetic vendor). The SVA puts considerable emphasis on the general features of vending stalls and insists that the city adopt a uniform aesthetic approach to regulate the size of the stalls. The uniformity in the material structure of the stalls and the uniform use of particular colors in the stalls are expected to reflect the identity of a city. Meanwhile, the size of the stalls and the extent of regulation of street vending have to be consistent with the primary function of the footpath: the pedestrian's right of passage.

The Pedestrian's Right of Passage

Legal sociologist Nicholas Blomley calls the everyday assertion of the pedestrian's right of passage "pedestrianism"—a modern governmental rationality that does not focus only on the humans and appears to be an "obvious and uncontested goal for urban governments" (Blomley 2011: 8). The interest of pedestrianism is functional, in the sense that it seeks to arrange bodies and things in a finite place to ensure navigation. Pedestrianism, to quote Blomley, understands the sidewalk as a finite public resource that is always threatened by multiple, competing interests and uses. The role of authorities, using law as needed, is to arrange these bodies and objects to ensure that the primary function of the sidewalk is sustained: that being the orderly movement of pedestrians from point a to point b. (2011: 3)

Pedestrianism's primary means of classification is zoning. In this sense, the SVA is primarily intended to optimally arrange street vending, not to rescue the street vendor. Whereas "street vendor" refers to a human with a particular social location, the act of "vending" is nothing but the relationship among the street vendor, the stall, and the pedestrian as the potential customer. The switch from street vendors to street vending happens right in the title of the act: "Street *Vendors* (Protection of Livelihood and Regulation of Street *Vending*) Act, 2014."

Pedestrianism focuses on functional concerns such as flow, placement and circulation. In that sense, Blomley explains, "pedestrianism can treat" the *human subject* as essentially "an *object* [emphasis is mine], either in motion or at rest" (2011: 9). How then is it possible to resist pedestrianism that "structures the ways in which state agents think about and act upon the spaces of the city" (106)? Blomley is convinced that the opposition cannot come from the humanist, rights-based perspective so long upheld by activists and academicians who treat "public space as a space, first and foremost, of people" (8). In other words, Blomley opines, the "civic humanist" perspective of human rights is always already superseded by the apparently banal post-humanist perspective of pedestrianism. The alternative should then emerge from *"within* pedestrianism" (111, italics in the original). However, Blomley remains vague about the content of this alternative, internal to pedestrianism. Further, it is unclear whether one can consistently resist pedestrianism when the mobility of the pedestrian is compromised to facilitate private automobile traffic. It appears to be the gradation of speed that distinguishes the pedestrian from the sedentary hawker and also from users of automobiles. Interestingly, the rise of the use of private automobiles can only add to the official celebration of the pedestrian as deserving of rescue and preservation to keep the city more inclusive and democratic.

Consider a recent instance from Pune, a major Indian city in the state of Maharashtra. On 22 April 2012, the prominent local civic activist Gita Vir was hit by a motorcycle as she crossed the road by her apartment house. She fell on the footpath and died of her injuries. Vir was a founding member of the National Society for Clean Cities (NSCC), which started its journey in Bombay with the goal of inculcating good civic behavior in slum children, in part by teaching them to "respect the property of the others, particularly public property." On 21 April 2013, the Pune branch of the NSCC commemorated Vir's life and work by launching the Gita Vir Mission for Pedestrians' Safety to take up road safety issues with the Pune Municipal Corporation.[11] The case of the NSCC shows how state and society feed each other in pedestrianism. The fact that the city loses moral legitimacy if pedestrianism is not officially upheld is precisely the power of this rationale.

Pedestrianism as a Governmental Technique

I have so far argued that Blomley's notion of pedestrianism might offer an alternative optic to conceptualize the hawkers question by taking us to the very root of it. Where and how does the hawkers question emerge? The historiography of the informal economy only allows us to integrate the hawkers question into the larger issues of poverty, unemployment, and the right of the poor to *use* public space, as the society at large is indebted to the labor of the poor. All my examples have come from Indian cities, but to this point my claims are consistent with Blomley's perspective. This convergence indicates nothing less than the global reach of pedestrianism. How then are we to historicize and specify the contingencies of pedestrianism?

This essay studies how the hawker, from *within* pedestrianism, constructs a story of interpersonal obligation in which the engagement with objects is far from incidental. The clear binary between the "civic humanism" (Blomley's term) of the protester, academic, activist, and hawker, and the post-human pedestrianism of the planner, bureaucrat, and lawyer does not explain why pedestrianism in the SVA needs at all to use the rhetoric of care: "protection of livelihood of street vendors." Therefore it is necessary to study how pedestrianism works in specific historical contexts.[12] This normative understanding lacks a critical appreciation of how the perspective of the activist hawker becomes internal to the very logic of pedestrianism and emerges from *within* as a viable alternative. In the case of Calcutta, as I show in the remaining sections of the essay, this has happened through an active politicization of the archive and judiciary. My examples come from Calcutta, where I have studied the politics of footpath hawking for about a decade. Before focusing on my examples, I introduce some of the specific features of Calcutta's footpath hawkers in the next two sections, a detour that will prove productive as we proceed.

Footpath Hawkers of Calcutta

In the colonial archive of Calcutta, the term hawker appears alongside other, similar terms such as pavement seller, footpath seller, and *pheriwala*.

The hawker became part of Calcutta's vernacular in the post-partition era, when the state government initiated economic rehabilitation projects for refugees by building a number of "refugee hawker corners" in the city. Much of the city's retail expansion in refugee-dominated areas followed the establishment and stabilization of these hawkers' corners. These retail corners came under the Markets Regulation Act, so shop owners got trade licenses. Names like Klalighat Refugee Hawker's Corner still recall these spots' specific history. But even so, those who knew Calcutta between the 1950s and 1970s will verify that hawker or even *pheriwala* (*pheriweali*, for female vendor) was not yet a common term for a trader on a footpath, though these terms have been in use in the official government circuit since at least the late nineteenth century. The hawkers' popular appellations rather concerned their activity and the services they offered—thus, *phalwala* (fruit seller), *basanwala* (utensils seller), *machwala* (fishmonger), and so on. Each of these specific terms had a double meaning. A *phalwala*, for instance, could be sedentary, sitting regularly at a particular location, or nomadic, traversing a particular route at a regular interval.

Unlike in other industrial cities, where members of the former industrial working class are a substantial segment of the street hawkers, the majority of the hawkers in Calcutta, except in a few places, are migrants and refugees with agricultural and artisanal backgrounds. Following the geographical reshuffle brought by partition, older social ties, rural connections, and the spatial and legal redefinition of communities influenced the hawkers' modes of articulating claims to the city. Many of the skilled artisanal communities settled in different refugee camps in West Bengal and bordering districts. In Gariahaat, for example, refugee traders had kinship, village, and other social ties with these artisanal groups. Through artisanal connections forged across dispersed refugee settlements, Gariahaat emerged in the 1960s as a destination for a number of inter-district retail networks. By the late 1960s, hawkers had successfully erected semipermanent structures on footpaths and also occupied the now vanished Gariahaat Boulevard. They also entered the local economies of power through several neighborhood clubs and social and cultural events. The Youth Congress leaders of the 1970s, such as Subrata Mukherjee in Gariahaat, Somen Mitra in Sealdah, and their allies in other places, played a crucial role in forging links between Congress-sponsored clubs and the street economies. Gradually, a bond developed between the householders and the hawkers. These connections periodically helped the hawkers to withstand state violence in subsequent decades. The evicted hawkers were often seen to return with baskets of goods claiming that they had the moral support of the residents, the traders, and everyday visitors to the locality.

A Brief Account of the Hawkers' Movement in Calcutta

In a recent article I have identified some broad trends in the hawkers' movement in Calcutta (Bandyopadhyay 2015). Without going into detail, I will point out some important moments relevant to the framing of my argument in the rest of the essay. Two leftist political parties, the Communist Party of India (CPI) and the Forward Bloc, were the first to realize the need to unionize the hawkers in the early 1950s. By the late 1960s all the major and minor political parties, including the Congress Party, had hawkers' unions. This long history of unionization and labor militancy has kept the level of unionization in Calcutta relatively high compared to other important Indian cities. Second, until the formation of a citywide umbrella federation of hawkers' unions called the Hawker Sangram Committee (HSC) in 1996, the unions' spheres of activity were confined to particular streets and neighborhoods. Many of the unions still bear the name of the exact street where they have visibility. Third, until the late 1990s, eviction operations were confined to particular areas and responded to conflicts of business interests in those areas. Some ethnic and trade patterns are clear in the areas that remained prone to frequent localized eviction operations from the 1950s through the 1980s. Fourth, the new era of hawkers' mobilization started in 1996–97 when the state government, along with the city corporation and the city police, undertook "Operation Sunshine" which changed the earlier texture of footpath hawking in many ways, although the hawkers gradually reclaimed their position in the leadership of the HSC. Having emerged from the crucible of Operation Sunshine as a federation of several small-scale unions scattered all over the city, the HSC proved extremely successful in keeping hawkers united in dealing with both the state and the market. When organized retailers mount challenges, the HSC has recourse to the state, reminding it of its duty to take care of its dispossessed citizens. When the challenge comes from the state, the HSC resorts to the logic of entrepreneurial citizenship, which depicts hawkers as self-employed micro-entrepreneurs who need certain legal safeguards to contribute to the nation's development.

Pedestrianism of the Hawkers

In this section, I show how the HSC imagines an interactive world of pedestrianism to counter the pedestrianism of the experts. I call this encounter "archive," highlighting its traces in the framing of law and policy.

In March 2009 the HSC leadership decided to "sensitize" hawkers to the organization's basic code of conduct, which they were expected to respect while serving people on the street. The HSC formed a team that visited hawkers' stalls and interacted with the hawkers and pedestrians to try to form a public opinion against a sustained media campaign against hawkers. The basic idea was to reaffirm the hawker's intimate connection with rest of the society and establish the fact that hawking was not the primary cause of congestion, accidents, or pedestrian immobility. As a member of that team, I was asked in particular to demonstrate that the notion of a conflict of interest between pedestrians and hawkers was premised on factually wrong assumptions. The investigating team, comprised of hawkers and activists, visited as many as twenty busy street intersections of the city, observing transactions and talking to whoever was willing to talk to them. The list included shop owners, traffic cops, shopping mall employees, transport sector workers, office goers, pavement dwellers, hospital visitors, and daily commuters (in a particular rail-station area). Our observation and survey continued for two months. We asked hawkers about pedestrians and vice versa, but we spent more time observing how the pedestrians and the hawkers engage with each other and how the street apparatus—benches, traffic barriers, bollards, streetlamps, traffic lights and signs, bus and tram stops, taxi and auto rickshaw stands, public lavatories, municipal water taps, tree protectors, memorials, public sculptures, waste receptacles, and so on—framed and mediated human relations on the street.

Generally, the hawkers set up their stalls either in front of buildings, using the walls facing the footpath; or in the reverse position on the curbside edge of the footpath, facing the shops or buildings and keeping a corridor in the middle for pedestrian traffic. Food hawkers identify the midpoint between the municipal water tap and the drain at the curbside of the footpath as the ideal site for a food stall. Access to certain utilities by the footpath and proximity to congested transit places improve the chances of transaction. Strategically lucrative stall spaces are also traded and rented out. Shopkeepers often compete with each other to make agreements with the hawkers and thereby extend their shop interiors to the footpath. Such agreements are prevalent in the garment sector. Hawkers often sell the shopkeepers' merchandise at a lower price to access a different consumer base. In return, the shopkeepers allow the hawkers to keep their wares at the shops when the market closes. The hawkers also access electricity from the shops. Meanwhile, established retailers in the food, vegetable, and fruit sectors usually view hawkers providing similar services as potentially encroaching upon their consumer base. In these cases the authorities usually regard hawkers as usurping rate-payers' privileges. This antagonism often leads to small-scale eviction of hawkers in the vicinity of the marketplaces where they usually cluster.

Our evidence enabled the HSC to frame its official position regarding pedestrianism of the expert. Subsequently, the HSC organized a road show of photographs demonstrating how hawkers and pedestrians inhabit a world of networks in which categories continuously exceed their labels. The pedestrian breaks down into other figures (a stranger, a regular visitor, an office worker, etc.); the hawker becomes a pedestrian and a customer; the tree protector and lamppost turn out to be ideal supports for a tarpaulin cover. Many of our pedestrian respondents pointed out that in congested hawking areas like those in Shyambazaar and Gariahaat, the long continuum of tarpaulin roofs protected them from sunburn and rain. Some mentioned how in the late evenings the city was illuminated thanks to the abundance of electricity hookups at hawkers' stalls.

The more one observes these arrangements, the more one understands how the destiny of an object acquires infinite diversions in *association* with other objects, blurring the duality between the "acting subjects" and the "acted-upon objects" (Latour 1996).[13] In a number of street demonstrations, the HSC pointed out how the demolition of one stall in a particular area could lead to the destruction of a network of the small economies that kept the city habitable. Further, the demonstrations showed how at a busy street intersection, the pedestrian's right of passage was usually hampered by the presence of a range of other establishments: illegal extensions of shops; potholes; intermittent enclosures related to work being done on roads, drainage systems, and telephone and power lines (requiring enclosure and diversion of traffic for indefinite periods of time); legal as well as illegal parking spaces; illegal shrines on streets and footpaths, and so on. In explaining to the public that there are many causes of pedestrians' flight from footpaths, the HSC demonstrations included hawkers' stalls in the list of potential impediments to pedestrian mobility to assert that they are just one of many contributing factors to pedestrian immobility, and that their "encroachment" merits a grant of immunity, as hawkers contribute to the country's economy by providing the poorer social classes with "services" at a remarkably low cost. As one of the HSC leaders said, "We keep the city affordable and accessible to the poor. We are here as poor pedestrians require us to be here. We are also here to create the pedestrian." At this precise moment, the HSC invented an entire cosmos where the hawker's claim to space became a claim to enter the society's structures of obligation.

The HSC leader's comment encapsulates the political economy of street vending in cities like Calcutta. The leader reminds the rest of the city that hawkers also survive via circulation (the hallmark of pedestrianism) of commodities, money, and bodies. One needs to go beyond the apparent conflict of interest between the "mobile" pedestrian and the "immobile" hawker to appreciate much deeper structural connections among diverse elements of the street that implicate each other in mutual creation, often exceeding their intended utility.

The HSC intervenes in the larger public discourses on the "rightful" use of the footpath in such a way that the understanding of circulation in pedestrianism acquires polyvalence. However, this intervention discursively produces the footpath as a site of negotiation between the pedestrian (the formal legal-ideological subject) and the hawker (the entrepreneurial subject) at the cost of several other possibilities entailed by, for instance, the inclusion of pavement dwellers (those who live and sleep on the footpath) in this negotiation. Thus a study of the footpath becomes a study of the hawker and the pedestrian (Bandyopadhyay 2011).

A Definition Originating in an Archive: The New Term "Hawker Economy"

In considering the HSC's archival function, I bear three issues in mind: (1) the hawkers' ability to resist the ethnographer as the "Other" and control the flow of information from below, (2) the HSC's understanding of the political nature of records, and (3) its ability to produce governmental information, use records in what I call the state-union complex, and regulate *what can be said* about footpath hawking. This regulated discourse eventually redefined the footpath as a site of passage and enterprise.

In December 2005, the Calcutta Municipal Corporation decided to "identify and quantify" the hawkers of the streets and footpaths of the Calcutta municipal area, setting 1977 as a cutoff date so as to evict hawkers who joined the trade after 1977, when the Left Front came to form the government in the state of West Bengal. The 2005 survey was undertaken after the draft National Policy on Urban Street Vendors was promulgated for public scrutiny. The municipal corporation's proactive Left Front mayor's decision to enumerate the hawkers of Calcutta was in compliance with the mandate in the draft National Policy on Urban Street Vendors (2004) to create a full database of hawkers in every city. Initially, the HSC was a bit hostile to the very idea of a census, fearing that the government survey would misrepresent its voice. Later, the mayor came to understand that the municipal corporation's surveyors could not carry out the job without the active cooperation and partnership of the HSC.

The HSC's initial move was to intervene in two ways. First, its members began to follow the municipal corporation surveyors around and eventually to challenge the accuracy of their assessments. If, for example, a stall was vacant and the surveyor was on the verge of omitting it from the survey register, HSC workers related who the owner of the stall was and how long he or she had been trading there. The surveyor had to rely on the local knowledge or else accept a heightened administrative burden in conducting the survey. Second, the HSC undertook a self-organized counter-survey, including a sample of 2,350 hawkers distributed among twenty-one intersections. This pilot survey was the seed of all the subsequent surveys of hawkers in Calcutta. It coined a term—"hawker economy"—to refer to the complex network of human and commodity chains that links non-corporate players and provides livelihoods for millions in rural and urban India. The Calcutta Municipal Corporation accepted this survey as a basis for broader state-union collaboration. In 2007, the corporation undertook another survey of the hawkers. This time, it contracted a Calcutta-based, activist knowledge NGO that was once on very good terms with the HSC leadership.

Functions of Archives

In 2005, the mayor of the Calcutta Municipal Corporation formed a municipal consultative committee in which the HSC was a participating organization. Between 2005 and 2009, the committee met five times at the mayor's office. On each occasion, I found the leader, Saktiman Ghosh, attending the meeting with files and papers containing some sort of database of hawkers, the earliest court orders in favor of hawkers as well as the latest court order, and paper documents that he claimed were obtained from the office of an important government official in New Delhi or even a cabinet minister. Though suspicious of the government, he never forgot to mention his intimacy with upper-echelon functionaries who often updated him with new government secrets.

When the municipal corporation, in collaboration with the city police, decided to evict hawkers from Park Street, Saktiman presented a map showing the exact location of the HSC's affiliate hawkers in the Park Street area and claimed his clients had been operating in that area since the early 1970s. He presented past eviction records attested by the corporation, and records of police raids and confiscation of hawkers' wares. A police official told me the police department keeps records of confiscations, releases, and "minor crimes" for five years and then destroys them. The counterfoils the HSC held of the old records gave it a counterargument. Government functionaries could not produce those documents but could not ignore them either, as they bore official signatures. To the best of my knowledge, neither the municipal corporation nor the police department has ever created any centralized documentation of each and every operation and raid. But individual hawkers preserve what they receive from the government, be it an eviction certificate or a release order for confiscated goods. The papers feature dates, signatures of officials, and stamps. Often these records change hands along with the vending site, which suggests that the HSC's archive is not a frozen entity awaiting a historian but rather an archive in constant circulation enabling the HSC to function well in governmental space. The HSC's archival function enables it to convert the record of *transgression* to the record of *legitimation*.

Inner Contradictions of Archives

In April 2005, I visited the office of the HSC at College Street for the first time. Murad Hussain, then in charge of the office, assured me partial access to their archive, adding that some sensitive records would remain secret as otherwise they would reveal the "internal contradictions of the Committee." Those documents, Murad said, could be made public only if the HSC resolved to document its own history in the future. Acutely aware of the public nature of the act of writing history, Murad was not willing to allow me authorship of the HSC story. His ability to mark the border between secrets and revelation sparked my imagination in terms of the meaning of secrecy in the life of the record. The HSC's secret archive can be constructed to stand beside state archives or even compete with them, but it can also be a hiding space in which subversive memories are stored and preserved for possible future disclosure. Notably, when Murad denied my request to see the secret archive, he revealed a tension, or discomfort, with those records (note the Marxist term "inner contradiction" in Murad's statement). That is, Murad knew that those documents might contradict the official position of the HSC. This secret archive thus is not only a strength of the HSC but also a constant source of discomfort, if not threat. Therefore, the HSC preserves the right to write its autobiography and to disclose its own "secrets."

Archive as Law

In my early work, I refused to regard the HSC archive as just a missing parcel of the state archive, or as entirely analogous to the latter's logic. Instead I showed how the HSC archive is expressive of an essential incommensurability that is not reducible to the formal logic of the state archive. In researching the terms and tenures of the autonomy of what I called "archiving from below," I deliberately juxtaposed the problematic of the archive with the processes of everyday survival of forms of informality. A significant paradox distinguishes the case of the HSC from the archival

purpose of the state. In the informal economy, most mobilizations that make demands on the state are founded on a sidestepping, suspension, or violation of the law.[14] And yet, as Foucault (1989) says, archive is law—the law of what can and cannot be said. It is the place from which orders are issued to pasts and presents—where, as Derrida (1996) says, men and gods command; where violence institutionalizes itself as law. It represents a principle that, in Derrida's words, is "in the order of commencement as well as in the order of commandment" (1996: 2).

The HSC's archival intervention certainly does not come from outside the premises of pedestrianism, for it has to acknowledge that the footpath is primarily for the use of pedestrians. At every step hawkers have to profess readiness to shift from their existing location, should the government provide them with a viable alternative livelihood. Certainly the HSC fights for a law to protect hawkers' livelihoods while claiming to ensure pedestrian traffic via the footpath. To the HSC, pedestrians can be people who need to buy things from hawkers. Whenever the pedestrian stops, he or she appears to transgress the legal limits of being a pedestrian.

The Judicialization of Politics and the Politicization of the Court

In the last two decades there has been a steady "judicialization"[15] of the politics of street hawkers in many major Indian cities. They have taken refuge in the courts while continuing their anti-eviction struggle on the ground. In most rulings, as we have already seen, both the high courts and the Supreme Court have bolstered the cause of livelihood while restricting the radical spatial claims of the street hawkers. The HSC maintains strong connections with activist and progressive lawyers' collectives in India, such as the Human Rights Law Network (HRLN) and the Alternative Law Forum (ALF). When an eviction happens, the HSC lawyers process hundreds of petitions by the hawkers and file them all at once in the court, making it difficult for officials to maintain the court's everyday routine. To bolster the case of evicted vendors, HSC members clog the entrance of the court to make the judges aware of their moral and numerical strength.[16] In this way the judicialization of the HSC's politics politicizes the physical space of the court and disrupts its normal operation. There is no denying that by supporting the basic tenets of the Street Vendors Act, the HSC has succumbed to the bourgeois logic of spatial order.

The battle does not end here. We are yet to see how the SVA opens new possibilities of subversion when it is taken to the court and the street. The hawkers' success will depend on how well they are able to bring other poor social groups (shopkeepers, pavement dwellers, domestic workers, etc.) into the fold of their movement, and also on how they come to terms with the *bhadralok* (genteel class) of the city. It might be simplistic to think that state agencies—with strong moral support from the *bhadralok*—have been aggressively evicting hawkers only since the liberalization of the economy in the 1990s, yet this is how Operation Sunshine has so far been narrated in activist circles. Such a view fails to appreciate the complex relationship between the middle class and the poor in a city. In several cases, the *bhadralok* has patronized certain kinds of hawking in certain places and urged the government to preserve them as part of the city's great heritage. No doubt, the heritage parts of the famous College Street have restricted certain display practices of the book hawkers, but the heritage city nonetheless has sought to preserve the street's "bibliophilic" character. While launching an initiative for "model food vending zones" in some of the touristy parts of the city, Saktiman Ghosh opined that "if properly regulated" (state functionaries use this exact phrase) and "trained," the hawkers of Calcutta can become a tourist attraction: "The world-class city needs the world-class hawker." A dialectical reading of this statement reveals its two sides: not only can hawking become a spectacle of consumption in the sanitized, well-preserved world-class city, but the aspiring world-class city has accumulated enormous debt to the hawker. Thus, the hawker has the right to use the city space. This essay is an invitation to rethink the hawkers' question in Calcutta—which, I expect, will lead us to rethink the 'politics of the poor' in the global South.

The Politics of the "Urban Poor"

The last two decades have seen substantial additions to the literature on everyday negotiations between population groups and the state in postcolonial societies. Partha Chatterjee, for example, in a series of articles (2004, 2011), propounds the notion of "political society" as both a conceptual and an empirical space between the state and civil society in which various population groups negotiate with the governmental state for everyday entitlements of livelihood, often sidestepping the bourgeois law of property by taking recourse to a number of techniques, such as encroachment on public infrastructure, limited civil disobedience, and regulated violence. Chatterjee suggests that in the mid 1990s, members of India's urban middle class began to powerfully assert their desire to sanitize city space for "proper citizens." Still estranged from the arena of electoral politics, the middle class of the 1990s and 2000s resorted to influencing the decisions of enlightened despotic institutions such as the higher-level judiciary and the bureaucracy. Chatterjee seems to suggest that if civil society, peopled by the middle class, embraces the activist judiciary to reclaim space, then popular politics (i.e., political society) holds sway over the legislature.

Chatterjee confirms that in contemporary rural West Bengal, the "party's" ubiquitous presence in managing life and labor signals the dominant "social preference" *not* to resort to formal institutions like police and the court to resolve disputes. Such institutions, Chatterjee explains, are generally seen as "expensive, time-consuming, corrupt and insensitive to the specific demands of fairness in a particular case that only those intimately familiar with local histories and peculiarities could be expected to know" (Chatterjee 2009: 43). Overall, Chatterjee's findings confirm South Asian historiography's long-standing dominant trend of viewing the relationship between subaltern politics and legal institutions as marked by apathy, apprehension, distance, and exclusion.[17] This essay has discussed the changing articulations of hawkers' associations and unions, which have embraced the judiciary and politicized the courts. I have shown how the hawkers accomplished this task by pushing the boundaries of pedestrianism forward.

This perspective could lend itself to a critique of another impressive corpus of literature on law in the Global South. The usual routes taken by this literature (Devlin 2010) are (1) studying the hiatus between the formal law and its spatial manifestation, and (2) observing how various actors invest meaning in law according to their social exigencies.[18] As Devlin (2010) perceptively observes, this literature does not regard law as one of the many factors operating to produce urban space.

Conclusion

Our journey began with a call to go beyond the overworked optic of the informal economy to understand the politics of street vending. My readers may have reason to dispute my proposal. Indeed, one may argue that there is no singular optic of the informal economy, as it embodies an intensely heterogeneous world of economic and social activities outside of "normal labor relations", a world that refers to the primacy of free wage labor (the industrial worker) "over the entirety of dependent labor" (Mezzadra and Neilson 2013: 91). But undoing the concept of the informal economy would also obscure how this norm established itself in the Global North precisely during the so-called Fordist revolution. My answer to these critics is that I am not asking that the concept be withdrawn altogether, but rather that we suspend it and remember it strategically to allow the formation of a new vocabulary. The alternative vocabulary of pedestrianism, archive, and judicialization presents a case of Calcutta's street vendors navigating a changing world and engaging with the governmental state. More research is needed in different areas and domains to take this project forward.

I end with a note of caution. I do not wish to conflate the hawkers' voice with the HSC's official position. This essay is much more concerned with the latter. The HSC and the NHF are organizations of stall owners, who are often too apathetic to bring their employees or even family members who work with them into the fold of the association.

Ritajyoti Bandyopadhyay teaches history at the Centre for Studies in Social Sciences, Calcutta. He studies histories of mass political formation, urban space, and political modernity in late colonial and postcolonial Calcutta. He has published in various international journals and edited volumes, and is currently finishing his first book project commissioned by the Cambridge University Press.

Notes

1. Some of the research materials in this essay have been used in one of my recent articles (Bandyopadhyay 2015) to arrive at a separate thesis.
2. *Economic Times,* 12 February 2014. http://articles.economictimes.indiatimes.com/2014-02-12/news/47270106_1_chai-pe-charcha-campaign-narendra-modi-tea-stall.
3 "Narendra Modi Kicks Off BJP's Chai Pe Charcha Campaign; Says Tea Stalls Are Like Footpath Parliament," *The Economic Times,* 12 February 2014. bit.ly/chaipecharcha. Accessed 26 September 2014.
4. A national-level consolidation of street vendors' unions, cooperatives, associations and community-based organizations, NGOs, and individuals like academics, doctors, and lawyers who have a record of working with street vendors. For details of NASVI's membership policy, see http://nasvinet.org/newsite/nasvi-membership-policy-2/.
5. A national federation of more than 500 street vendors' unions/associations with roots in the Calcutta-based Hawker Sangram Committee. The NHF is connected to the National Alliance of People's Movement.
6. This is not to deny the existence of zoning norms in many cities in colonial and postcolonial times. In 1935, for instance, the Bombay Municipal Corporation imposed a ban on "hawker nuisance" on certain important streets. For details, see the elaborate report in the *Times of India,* 5 January 1935. Having said this, I should mention that such norms were often city-specific and there was hardly any correspondence among cities.
7. The Women Hawkers Adhikar Sangram Committee was founded in Calcutta in 2012.

8. See Sodan Singh, Etc. Etc. v. New Delhi Municipal Committee & ... on August 30, 1989 (AIR 1988, 1989 SCR (3)1038).
9. For a good summary of the views of various Indian courts on street vending, see Supreme Court of India, Maharashtra Ekta Hawkwers Union & ... v. Municipal Corporation, Greater ... on September 9, 2013. Author: G. Singhvi, Bench: G. S. Singhvi, V. Gopala Gowda.
10. Bombay Hawkers' Union And Ors v. Bombay Municipal Corporation And ... on July 3, 1985, Author: Y Chandrachud, Bench: Chandrachud, Y.V. (Cj).
11. *Times of India*, 20 April 2013. http://timesofindia.indiatimes.com/city/pune/Pedestrian-safety-mission-to-commemorate-civic-activist/articleshow/19641840.cms.
12. I am not, however, suggesting that such a study needs to be historically nuanced by constructing a story of difference between the street cultures in cities of the South and the North. In fact, Blomley's whole explication of pedestrianism stands above such historical relativism. Here, it would not be out of place to say that our entire generation grew up with the discourse of the Indian street as marked by registers of "difference" that taught us how our vernacular genius continuously mediates our import of the bourgeois categories *public* and *private*. Ironically, this is also the rationale behind colonial planners' construction of footpaths in Indian cities. Back in 1914, Patrick Geddes argued before the members of the Calcutta Improvement Trust that footpaths in Indian cities needed to be wider than their European counterparts, or else the fear of pollution through physical contact would dissuade Indians from using them (Geddes 1914). For a crisp, concise review of literature about the Indian street, see Jonathan Anjaria (2012).
13. I am thankful to my student Biboswan Bose for encouraging me to think about the politics of the HSC in this line.
14. Here the hawkers question becomes an instance of "political society"—a space of negotiation between the state and the civil society peopled by groups who exist by collectively sidestepping the bourgeois law of property (Chatterjee 2004).
15. For a general discussion of the meaning of "judicialization" see Domingo (2004), Comaroff and Comaroff (2007), and Randeria (2007). For a discussion of the judicialization of politics in contemporary West Bengal, see Nielsen (2009).
16. In this regard the HSC's mode of operation differs markedly from that of its predecessors in 1970s.
17. For illustration of this point see, e.g., the anthropological work of Bernard Cohn (1965) and M. N. Srinivas (1959) in the 1950s and 1960s, the historical work of Ranajit Guha (1999) and the Subaltern Studies collective in the 1980s, and modernist novels such as Satinath Bhaduri's *Dhoraicharitmanas* (1973). Also see Nielsen (2009) who provides a critique of this literature and a comprehensive account of judicialization of political mobilization in contemporary West Bengal.
18. See, e.g., the perceptive contribution by Jonathan Anjaria (2010, especially the section on the "everyday life of law"), which is one of the earliest contributions to the SVA literature.

Bibliography

Anjaria, Jonathan S. 2008. "Unruly Streets: Everyday Practices and Promises of Globality in Mumbai." PhD dissertation, University of California, Santa Cruz.
———. 2010. "The Politics of Illegality: Mumbai Hawkers, Public Space and the Everyday Life of the Law." In *Street Vendors in the Global Urban Economy*, ed. S. K. Bhowmik. New Delhi: Routledge.
———. 2012. "Is there a Culture of the Indian Street?" *Seminar,* 636. http://www.india-seminar.com/2012/636/636_jonathan_s_anjaria.htm
Bandyopadhyay, Ritajyoti. 2011. "Politics of Archiving: Hawkers and Pavement dwellers in Calcutta." *Dialectical Anthropology* 35 (3): 295-316.
Bandyopadhyay, Ritajyoti. 2015. "Institutionalizing Informality: The Hawkers' Question in Post-colonial Calcutta." *Modern Asian Studies,* DOI:http://dx.doi.org/10.1017/S0026749X1400064X (About DOI).
Bhaduri, Satinath. (1949, 1951) 1973. *Dhoraicharitmanas* (vol. 1, 1949; vol. 2, 1951). In *Satinathgranthabali,* vol. 2, ed. Sankha Ghosh and Nirmalya Acharya. Calcutta: Signet.
Blomley, Nicholas. 2011. *Rights of Passage: Sidewalks and the Regulation of Public Flow.* New York: Routledge.
Bonner, Christine, and Dave Spooner. 2010. "Organising Labour in the Informal Economy – Forms of Organization and Relationships", WIEGO, paper presented to XVII World Congress of Sociology (Research Committee 44: Labor Movements), July 2010, Gothenburg http://library.fes.de/pdf-files/ipg/2011-2/08_a_bonner.pdf.
Bromley, Ray. 2000. "Street Vending and Public Policy: A Global Review." *International Journal of Sociology and Social Policy* 20 (1/2): 1–28.
Chatterjee, Partha. 2004. *The Politics of the Governed: Reflexions of Popular Politics in Most of the World.* Ranikhet: Permanent Black.
———. 2008. "Democracy and Economic Transformation in India." *Economic and Political Weekly* 43 (16): 53–62.
———. 2009. "The Coming Crisis in West Bengal." *Economic and Political Weekly* 44 (9): 42–45.
———. 2011. *Lineages of Political Society: Studies in Postcolonial Democracy.* Ranikhet: Permanent Black.
Cohn, Bernard S. 1965. "Anthropological Notes on Disputes and Law in India." In *American Anthropologist,* n.s., 67 (6, part 2): 82–122.
Comaroff, Jean, and John Comaroff. 2007. "Law and Disorder in the Postcolony." *Social Anthropology* 15 (2): 133–152.
Derrida, Jacques. 1996. *Archive Fever: A Freudian Impression.* Trans. Eric Prenowitz. Chicago: University of Chicago Press.
Devlin, Ryan. 2010. "Informal Urbanism: Legal Ambiguity, Uncertainty, and the Management of Street Vending in New York City." PhD dissertation, University of California, Berkeley.
Domingo, Pilar. 2004. "Judicialization of Politics or Politicization of the Judiciary? Recent Trends in Latin America." *Democratization* 11 (1): 104–126.

Foucault, Michel. 1989. *The Archaeology of Knowledge*. London and New York: Routledge.
Foucault, Michel. 2007. *Security, Territory, Population: Lectures at the College de France, 1977–78*. Trans. Graham Burchell. Houndsmill: Palgrave Macmillan.
Geddes, Patrick. 1914. Note by Prof. Geddes on the Great South Road, Calcutta, in the Proceedings of the Meeting of the Land Committee of the Calcutta Improvement Trust (CIT), 27 November.
Government of India. 2007. *Annual Report of the Ministry of Housing and Urban Poverty Alleviation, Government of India, 2006–2007*. http://mhupa.gov.in/pdf/annual-reports/ar0607eng.pdf.
Government of India. 2014. *Street Vendors (Protection of Livelihood and Regulation of Street Vending) Act, 2014*. http://www.indiacode.nic.in/acts2014/7%20of%202014.pdf.
Government of West Bengal. 1980. *Calcutta Municipal Corporation Act* (West Bengal Act LIX of 1980). Part VI: Town Planning, Land and Land Use Control, Chapter XXI: Streets and Public Places, Section 372.
Guha, Ranajit. 1999. *Elementary Aspects of Peasant Insurgency in Colonial India*. Durham, NC, and London: Duke University Press.
Kundu, Amitabh, and P. C. Mohanan. 2009. "Employment and Inequality Outcomes in India." Paper presented for the OECD Seminar on Employment and Inequality Outcomes: New Evidence, Links and Policy Responses in Brazil, China and India, April, Paris.
Lahiri, Saumitra. 1997. *Operation Sunshine* (in Bengali). Kolkata: Bishwakosh Parishad.
Latour, Bruno. 1996. "On Actor-Network Theory: A Few Clarifications." *Soziale Welt* 47 (4): 369–381.
McGee, T. G. 1973. *Hawkers in Hong Kong: A Study of Planning and Policy in a Third World City*. Hong Kong: University of Hong Kong.
Mezzadra, Sandro, and Brett Neilson. 2013. *Border as Method, Or, The Multiplication of Labor*. Durham and London: Duke University Press.
Nielsen, K. B. 2009. "Farmers' Use of the Courts in an Anti-Land Acquisition Movement in India's West Bengal." *Journal of Legal Pluralism and Unofficial Law* 59: 121–144.
Randeria, Shalini. 2007. "De-Politicization of Democracy and Judicialization of Politics." *Theory, Culture and Society* 24 (4): 38–44.
Srinivas, M. N. 1959. "The Dominant Caste in Rampura." *American Anthropologist*, n.s., 61 (1): 1–16.

PART IV

Historical Accounts of Street Vending

CHAPTER 10

Street Vending, Political Activism, and Community Building in African American History
The Case of Harlem

Mark Naison

[Marcus] Garvey voiced the marvelous nature of his own rise when he asked ... "how come this New Negro? How comes this stunned awakening?" The ground had been prepared for him by such outspoken voices as those of Hubert H. Harrison, A. Philip Randolph, Chandler Owen, and W.A. Domingo. These and other stepladder orators—who began speaking along Lenox Avenue with the arrival of warm weather in 1916 and whose number rapidly grew with each succeeding summer—were the persons, who along with Garvey, converted the black community of Harlem into a parliament of the people during the years of World War I and after. (Hill and Bair 1987: xix)

Professor Robert Hill's comment on how street orators transformed Harlem into a "parliament of the people" during and after World War I is an excellent starting point for any effort to understand the place of street vending within the broad sweep of urban African American history. Though Black neighborhoods today may seem more politically quiescent than they were during the Depression or the 1960s, there may be more continuities than contrasts between political organizers who once promoted radical ideas on the streets of Harlem or the South Side of Chicago, and street vendors of today who sell books, incense, umbrellas, and sunglasses, or distribute religious literature. The radicals of the past were not just disinterested purveyors of ideas—they sold pamphlets and newspapers from the same platforms they used to make speeches. And street vendors of today, both indirectly and directly, are on the front lines of community struggles to resist gentrification and corporate penetration of Black and Latino urban neighborhoods.

In the context of global urban centers like New York, Chicago, San Francisco, or Los Angeles, street vending represents more than an unstable, sometimes dangerous strategy for income generation chosen by disfranchised and marginalized people: it can also be a site of resistance to neoliberal economic policies that have thus far—but not necessarily permanently—undermined more direct forms of protest against impoverishment, police violence, and deterioration of public services in urban Black and Latino neighborhoods. For the last thirty years, a combination of intrusive policing and mass incarceration, regressive taxation, market-oriented community development strategies, and attacks on unions have significantly undermined mass protest activity by people of color in U.S. urban centers (Thompson 2010). In cities from Baltimore to Buffalo, Detroit, Cleveland, and Newark, and in historic Black and Latino neighborhoods throughout New York City, the results are there for all to see—a reduction in the visibility and power of Black and Latino grassroots activism, intensified class and income segregation, the growth of the prison industrial complex, and, in a growing number of urban neighborhoods, gentrification and demographic inversion as capital reclaims once decayed neighborhoods for the upper middle class (Smith 1996; Davis 2002; Hyra 2008; Ehrenhalt 2008). For Black and Latino working-class youth, random police searches, metal detectors in schools, and the drug economy remain a reality untouched by the developers and middle-class newcomers penetrating their "hoods." The rapper Tupac Shakur (1992) provides a brilliant portrait of this dynamic in ghettos throughout the United States in the chilling song "Trapped":

They got me trapped
Can barely walk tha city streets
Without a cop harrassing me, searching me
Then asking my identity
Hands up, throw me up against tha wall

Didn't do a thing at all
I'm tellen you one day these suckers gotta fall

Even schools in Black and Latino neighborhoods, once centers of activism, have been deformed by the smothering weight of police surveillance and the drug economy, as reflected in the rapper Dead Prez's "They Schools" (2000):

I got my diploma in a school called Rickers
Full of teenage mothers and drug dealing niggas
In the hallway the popo was always present
Searchin' through niggas possessions, looking for dope and weapons

So depoliticized is the lived experience and mental universe of young people growing up in such conditions, that they cannot even imagine a time when Black neighborhoods were filled with orators expounding their political philosophies from soapboxes and stepladders, and hawkers sold radical and nationalist newspapers in virtually every business district serving Black communities (Anderson 2008). The pages that follow will put those experiences front and center. The goal is not only to remind the current generation of a time between the onset of World War I and the early 1970s when the streets in Black communities were filled with orators and street vendors promoting a wide variety of radical philosophies, but also to urge that this tradition of radical street speaking and political education be reinvented and restored. As the historical narrative that follows will point out, this tradition of street speaking and the accompanying sale of print material encouraged learning and discussion among working-class people and led directly to confrontational political activism, ranging from hunger marches and protests against eviction, to boycotts of neighborhood business that refused to hire Blacks, to commodity riots and protests against police brutality (Naison 1983).

Historicizing Street Vending in Harlem

The street vendors of today, who can still be found on the streets of Harlem and in some Black and Latino Sections of the Bronx, Brooklyn, and Queens (there are no remaining white working-class enclaves in New York City where street vending flourishes), represent an important potential link to this tradition of political activism. Some of these vendors sell books that promote an oppositional consciousness, be they street literature, Black self-help literature, or books and pamphlets promoting Black nationalism. Moreover, some of these community-based entrepreneurs, especially in Harlem, have been involved in protests against zoning laws and police practices designed to make communities more attractive to chain stores and market-level residential development (Tucker 2008; Zukin 2009).

Perhaps the most impassioned defense of street vending as a form of resistance to gentrification and oppressive police practices has come from the legal scholar Regina Austin. In her 1994 *Yale Law Journal* article "An Honest Living: Street Vending, Municipal Regulation, and the Black Public Sphere," Austin argues:

> Many blacks rightly understand that the line between the legal and the illegal in the area of economic activity is ephemeral and that the determination of the precise point at which the line is drawn is a matter of political struggle. Accordingly, blacks need to be in the thick of the battle, fighting for their interests. This means condoning, abetting and sometimes even engaging in illegal activity. (1994: 2119f.)

In urban Black communities, Austin argues, laws and police practices that bar income-producing activities by working-class people must be viewed with extreme suspicion by community residents. She advocates supporting the right of street vendors to sell their goods even when they lack the proper licenses.

Racialized Policing of Immigrant Street Vendors

In June of 2009 in the Bronx, the movement-building opportunities that can arise when activists follow Austin's advice were dramatized by an incident involving two members of the revolutionary hip-hop group Rebel Diaz. Rodrigo and Gonzalo Venegas, the MC and DJ of Rebel Diaz, were taking a friend on a tour of the Hunts Point neighborhood, where they lived, when they came upon police and Health Department officials confiscating the fruit of a Mexican street vendor who was selling without a license. When the Venegas brothers interceded on the vendor's behalf—first to translate the police's commands into Spanish, then to persuade the authorities to allow the vendor to keep his fruit—the officers at the scene cursed at and threatened them. When they asked for the officers' badge numbers, they were thrown to the ground, beaten, and arrested. This entire episode, captured by the Venegas brothers' friend on his cell phone, was sent out as a video to members of the Rebel Diaz artistic and political network, and in less than two hours nearly one hundred demonstrators were picketing the police precinct where the brothers were being held, demanding their release. Many participants in this demonstration were amazed that the captain of the precinct refused to release the brothers, despite damning visual evidence of police misconduct and mounting signs that this incident would be a rallying point for activists around the city.

The imperative to maintain police authority through intimidation and illegal force in this immigrant and working-class neighborhood was so powerful that neither the district attorney nor local elected officials were willing to try to get the charges dismissed. A year and a half later, a judge dismissed all charges against the Venegas brothers, actually congratulating them for all the work they did to empower young people in the South Bronx. Nonetheless, the extended time in which the charges remained is a telling reminder of how little standing street vendors and black and brown youth have in the calculations and governance strategy of many of those making and enforcing the law (Noor 2009).

In the light of this heavy-handed application of state power against immigrants exercising the right to make a living, and of activists exercising the right of free speech, it is instructive to recall a time in New York history when Black activists and their allies claimed Harlem street corners as a space to expound radical political philosophies from soapboxes and stepladders, sell newspapers and pamphlets on the streets, and organize rallies and marches aimed at local injustices. This is particularly significant at this current historical moment, when the city's social fabric is severely strained by a recession, and organizations like Picture the Homeless, the Harlem Tenants Council, and the Movement for Justice in El Barrio (the widely used Spanish term for East Harlem) are beginning to employ confrontational tactics to fight for the right to shelter, health care, and income—including the right to sell goods on the streets (Case 2009; Moynihan 2009; Ohrstrom 2008).

Staging Harlem: From Street Speaking to Street Vending

Here I revisit the long and illustrious Harlem tradition of street speaking, street organizing, and street commerce from which activists today can draw inspiration, beginning with a rousing passage from Irma Watkins-Owens's book *Blood Relations, Caribbean Immigrants and the Harlem Community, 1900–1930*:

> From World War I through the 1930's, the unclaimed territory of the Harlem street corner became the testing ground for a range of political ideologies and forum for intellectual inquiry and debate. The open-air arena claimed other adherents as well—barefoot prophets, musicians, healers and traders—competing for the souls and pocketbooks of the urban masses ... but on any day of the week, including Sunday, homebound Harlemites emerging from the subway at 135th Street and Lenox Avenue would most likely encounter congested sidewalks and the well toned voice of the street orator, often of African Caribbean descent, positioned atop a stepladder and surrounded by crowds of listeners. (1996: 92)

As Watkins-Owens's account makes clear, Harlem's stepladder orators shared the street with various people engaged in commercial ventures. These included numbers runners, evangelists, and street vendors selling products ranging from Southern delicacies (e.g., ribs, sweet potatoes, and pigs' feet) to clothing to "dream books" for the numbers trade. In an oppressed community, street politics and street economics were, in effect, two sides of the same coin. The population of Harlem, coming from the West Indies and the Spanish Caribbean as well as the American South, not only welcomed speakers calling for an end to racism, white supremacy, and colonial rule, but also used the streets of their neighborhood to launch a wide variety of income-producing activities, legal and illegal, that could compensate for their exclusion from nearly every important sector of New York's labor market.

Because discrimination in the mainstream economy was so fierce, some of Harlem's best known and most brilliant street speakers used their oratory as an income-producing activity, making the line between street speaking and street vending even more porous. The great Harlem socialist and nationalist Hubert Harrison, widely recognized as the founder of Harlem's "Street University," supported himself by collecting pennies, nickels, and dimes from the audiences at his street corner lectures, which lasted for hours and touched on subjects ranging from religion to Greek philosophy, women's suffrage, and the leadership strategy of Booker T. Washington (Perry 2009). As Harrison's biographer Jeffrey Perry points out, Harrison decided to support himself as a Harlem street speaker only after he was pushed out of his job at the post office by Booker T. Washington after criticizing the Tuskegee leader, and fired from his position as a lecturer for the Socialist Party for supporting the Industrial Workers of the World. Harrison always lived on the edge of poverty but made enough money from street speaking to pay his rent in a community that was hungry for leadership and hungry for enlightenment. He was also part street vendor, selling books and oils at his lectures.

Harrison's success, both in attracting audiences and in raising funds, was not lost on an ambitious young West Indian immigrant named Marcus Garvey. Garvey believed that people of African descent were on the bottom rung of every society they lived in, be it in Africa or the Western hemisphere, and wanted to build an organization that would unite Blacks to redeem Africa from European rule and take pride in their African ancestry. Coming at a time when the self-determination of nations and an end to colonial rule were a possible outcome of the world war, Garvey's message electrified audiences on the streets of Harlem, who contributed their energies and funds to the organization Garvey created, the Universal Negro Improvement Association (UNIA). With the funds Garvey raised from his

street speaking, he rented a headquarters in Harlem that he called Liberty Hall, founded the newspaper *The Negro World,* and started forming chapters wherever his ideas captured Black people's imaginations. By the early 1920s, the UNIA had become the largest Black organization ever created, with hundreds of thousands of members all over the United States and in more than forty different countries. Garvey's organization eventually foundered due to internal conflicts, financial difficulties, and prosecution of its leader for mail fraud by the U.S. Department of Justice, but the power of a message of Black pride and African redemption to move the masses of Black people left a powerful impression on Harlem and would spawn numerous offshoots preaching some variety of Black nationalism to the people of Harlem and other urban Black communities (Hill and Bair 1987; James 1998).

During the Depression, these small nationalist organizations, along with the Harlem section of the Communist Party USA, would give this emerging tradition of street oratory a more activist, confrontational dimension. As unemployment in Harlem rose to over 60 percent and large numbers of families faced eviction from their homes, local radicals, using soapboxes and stepladders as platforms and selling movement newspapers to enhance their visibility, promoted militant action to ease the economic distress of Harlem's hard-pressed residents. Street vending was almost as important a part of this strategy as street oratory. Every Communist Party member was given a quota of the party's tabloid-style newspaper, *The Daily Worker,* to sell in the neighborhood they were assigned to, not just to raise funds but to create a public presence on the streets that local residents could not ignore. This combination of street speaking and street vending, along with Depression conditions, helped the American Communist Party—the most thoroughly interracial organization on the American Left—become an integral part of a Harlem community that was initially quite suspicious of its message. By the beginning of 1932, Harlemites had become accustomed to the sight of Black and white teams of Communists putting the furniture of evicted families back in apartments and besieging charitable organizations to supply aid to starving families, and were even joining such actions themselves in sizable numbers, along with demonstrations to free "the Scottsboro Boys": nine Black teenagers accused of rape in the state of Alabama, in highly suspicious circumstances (Naison 1983). Meanwhile, local Black nationalist groups, suspicious of the Communist message of black-white unity, used their street corners to launch an entirely different movement, a "Don't Buy Where You Can't Work" campaign, to force Harlem businesses, most of them owned by whites, to hire Blacks as salespeople. Concentrating on the large department stores on 125th Street, this campaign spread like wildfire and ultimately forced major concessions from Harlem employers, though not without controversy about the nationalists' allegedly anti-white and anti-Semitic rhetoric.

By the mid 1930s the combination of Communist and nationalist agitation taking place daily on scores of Harlem street corners had created an aroused, informed community ready to rise up in protest of any manifestation of racism, whether local, national, or international. Street vending was an integral part of this community upsurge (McKay 1940). *Daily Worker* salesmen were visible on almost every Harlem street corner, and nationalist organizations were selling newspapers of their own, creating a vibrant contentious atmosphere that affected what people read as well as what they heard. "Virtually every block of Harlem was up for grabs," Peniel Joseph writes, "nationalists exhorting on one corner, while Socialists and others set up their headquarters fifty yards away. Pamphlets on class struggle, Pan-Africanism and trade unionism compressed decades of social history into easily digestible prose. Walking through parts of Harlem, you risked being bombarded by pamphleteers selling … propaganda that recounted the history of Negro oppression" (Joseph 2006: 3).

In 1935, this politically aroused community exploded following the arrest and alleged beating of a Black teenager in a Harlem department store, looting stores and fighting police in a two-day uprising, the first of its kind in modern African American history. No longer would a "race riot" consist of mobs of whites invading and attacking Black neighborhoods. Now Blacks, aroused by street oratory, marches, and picket lines, would rise up against the outsiders who controlled their neighborhoods politically or exploited it economically (Greenberg 1991).

This street-spawned atmosphere of militancy even spilled over into electoral politics. A new breed of activist politician rose to power in the late 1930s, symbolized by the election to the City Council and then to Congress of Reverend Adam Clayton Powell Jr. A leader of the "Don't Buy Where You Can't Work" drive and Communist campaigns against lynching and the Italian invasion of Ethiopia, Powell raised support for his campaign with street corner oratory as much as through the organizational machine he built in his church. His successor on the City Council, Harlem Communist leader Benjamin Davis Jr., who was elected in 1943, followed a similar strategy, using a powerful street team to mobilize support for his candidacy headed by the redoubtable Audley Moore—later famous as a Black nationalist under the name Queen Mother Moore (Horne 1994). Interestingly enough, the year of Davis's election was the year of the second Harlem Riot, provoked by an incident of police violence involving Black servicemen. Street sales of newspapers remained one of the most important ways for Communists to keep the Harlem community mobilized and aroused, even in wartime. "Negro and white canvassers sidled up alongside you," Malcolm X recalled, talking fast as they tried to get you to buy a copy of the *Daily Worker*: "This paper's trying to keep your rent controlled ... Make that greedy landlord kill them rats in your apartment" (Haley and Malcolm X, 1965: 76).

This extraordinary tradition of street-based activism came under fierce attack in the postwar years as anti-Communism became the dominant ideology throughout American society. Between 1947 and 1956, Communists in Harlem, like their counterparts around the nation, were arrested, deported, called before investigating committees, and forced out of their jobs in the school system, the welfare department, universities, and the media. The most famous Harlem Communist of all, Paul Robeson, became a virtual exile in his own land, deprived of his passport, barred from radio, TV, and movies, and prevented from singing for pay in most major concert halls. Rank-and-file Communists, harassed and followed by the FBI, fared even worse—by the late 1950s, Communist street speakers and *Daily Worker* sellers had virtually disappeared from Harlem neighborhoods where they once had been a respected presence (Biondi 2003; Duberman 1989).

But thanks to African American nationalists, many of them in small, obscure organizations, the tradition of Harlem street oratory and street vending survived, especially along its main thoroughfare, 125th Street. There, the message of black unity, Black pride, and African redemption was kept alive by leaders like Carlos Cooks of the African Nationalist Pioneer Movement, Charles Kenyatta of the Mau Mau Society, and ex-Communists Richard Moore and Audley Moore, who advocated elimination of the word "Negro" and affirmed the necessity of reparations for people of African descent. Malcolm X, when he first came to Harlem in the early 1950s, was amazed by the "many voices of black discontent on every busy Harlem corner ... dozens of their stepladder orators were trying to increase their following" (Joseph 2006: 13). Foremost among these leaders was a Dominican-born nationalist intellectual named Carlos Cooks, who headed an organization called the African Nationalist Pioneer Movement. Cooks got his ideas across to the community through stepladder lectures, the sale of newspapers and magazines (such as *The Street Speaker, Cavalcade Africana,* and *The Black Challenge*), a "Buy Black Campaign," and "Natural Beauty" pageants (Harris, Harris, and Harris 1992; Gumbs 2003).

But the most important presence on Harlem streets was a minister of a small Black nationalist religious group that called itself the Nation of Islam. It preached that white domination of the world was coming to an end and that Blacks should separate themselves from the "devil white man" before it was too late. That minister, Malcolm X, electrified Harlem crowds with his attacks on Christianity, mainstream civil rights organizations, and the idea that America could become an integrated society. Malcolm told his audiences that America was so poisoned by racism that it never could reform, and that Blacks had to separate themselves from white influences—and white people—to achieve self-determination and self-respect. Using the street corner as his pulpit, he recruited thousands of members to the Nation of Islam in Harlem and around the nation, and became Harlem's most feared—and respected—street orator (Haley and Malcolm X 1965).

All of these Harlem nationalists, it should be emphasized, sold more than ideas—they also hawked books, pamphlets, or their organization's newspaper. The Nation of Islam in particular excelled at street commerce, moving thousands of copies of its newspaper *Muhammed Speaks,* launched by Malcolm X, on the streets of Harlem each week and selling Nation of Islam–produced food products on the street—Shabazz Bean Pies—to signal that its members practiced what they preached. Street corner selling of *Muhammed Speaks,* which eventually reached a weekly circulation of over 500,000 became the Nation of Islam's most effective strategy for communicating with Black America. "*Muhammed Speaks,*" Peniel Joseph writes, "provided coverage of local and national civil rights struggles, black militancy and corresponding white resistance and African and Third World revolution.... The newspaper that Malcolm had established ... became the Nation of Islam's key to harnessing the militant passions that gripped the Black movement" (Joseph 2006: 25).

However, as the national civil rights movement made major gains and the war in Vietnam began to escalate, Harlem nationalists starting meeting competition from the Left. By the mid 1960s more radical organizations, some with a Marxist tinge, began competing with local nationalists for the ear of Harlem residents, and a new culture of radical opposition began to rise in the community. "From the mid 60's on," Haywood Burns wrote, "Northern cities were the scene of direct group action concerned with the basic needs of the community, rent strikes, picketing, sit ins, chain ins (sit ins where people chained themselves together) all represented the community's attempt to deal with its ills" (Burns 1971: xv). Massive riots, which some called ghetto rebellions, accompanied this political upsurge. In the summer of 1964, the police murder of a Black high school student triggered another Harlem Riot, larger and more damaging than the ones in 1935 and 1943. Yet another Harlem Riot took place following the murder of Rev. Martin Luther King Jr. in 1968.

New organizations, the most important of which was the Black Panther Party (BPP), arose out of this political upheaval. With its advocacy of armed self-defense and open espousal of a Marxists analysis of society, the BPP differed markedly from Black nationalist predecessors like the Nation of Islam and the African Nationalist Pioneer Movement. But in its emphasis on street oratory and sales of a movement newspaper, it was squarely in the same tradition (Foner 1970). The *Black Panther,* the BPP's newspaper, became as visible a presence on the streets of New York as *Muhammed Speaks* and emerged as the BPP's major vehicle for community organizing. As one New York Panther leader from Harlem recalled: "The day came when I met a man selling *The Black Panther,* the paper. I went wild in my pad reading that. The brother I bought the paper from told me to come to the meeting that night at 2025 Seventh Avenue, and I really dug that" (Burns 1971: xv).

However, the very features that made the Black Panther Party and its Latino counterpart, the Young Lords Party, stand out—armed struggle and Marxist politics—helped set in motion a level of government repression every bit as ferocious as what had greeted the Communist Party in the late 1940s and 1950s. By the mid 1970s, both of those organizations were a shadow of their former selves, decimated by arrests, splits, and the disillusionment of key cadres who went back to school or sought outlets for their social consciousness in media, education, or helping professions. Nationalist groups also suffered a decline, and the Nation of Islam split between those led by Wallace Muhammed, who wanted the organization to embrace Sunni Islam, and those led by Louis Farrakhan, who wanted to stay true to the Black Supremacist philosophy of the Nation of Islam's founder Elijah Muhammed (Van Deburg 1992). By the time the New York City fiscal crisis hit in 1975, Harlem had seen the last gasp of a radical political culture that depended on street oratory, street demonstrations, and the selling of radical newspapers and pamphlets to disseminate oppositional ideologies and inspire vigilance against control of Harlem by forces outside the community (Joseph 2006).

The collapse of that oppositional culture left Harlem relatively helpless in the face of an array of tragedies that beset that community from the early 1970s to the mid 1990s: an arson and abandonment cycle that destroyed much local housing; a city fiscal crisis that radically cut social services, especially fire, sanitation, and youth programs; and finally a crack epidemic that destroyed families and eroded the neighborhoods' sense of safety even as it made fortunes for a small number of high-level dealers (Holden 1994; Szalavitz 1999). By the time the crack epidemic had run its course in the mid 1990s, the community had become so politically demobilized that it was unable to resist the mass incarceration of large numbers of its youth or develop a viable opposition to the Giuliani administration's plan to redevelop Harlem as a potential site of middle-class settlement amidst scarce Manhattan real estate (Freeman 2006; Maurasse 2006).

Negotiating Space: Racialized Struggles Before and Beyond

To list the setbacks in Harlem is not to say that the community offered no street-level resistance to strategies of elite control and development plans that displaced its residents. Street entrepreneurship of various kinds, often pioneered by African immigrants, continued to flourish even in the face of local merchants' opposition; hip-hop jams commanded space in parks and playgrounds even without permits, taking their electricity from the bottom of light poles (Interview with LA Sunshine 2006); and Al Sharpton and other leaders kept the community vigilant in the face of incidents of police brutality in Black neighborhoods and mob attacks on Black people in neighborhoods like Bensonhurst and Howard Beach. The Black nationalist tradition lived on in portions of hip-hop and in movements like Louis Farrakhan's Million Man March (Zukin 2009; Freeman 2001; Joseph 2006).

However, the tradition of street oratory that had sustained Harlemites' daily vigilance about racial and economic injustice was gone for good. There were no more Hubert Harrisons, Marcus Garveys, Audley Moores, Carlos Cooks, or Malcom Xs. There were no Communist street speakers demanding that the furniture of evicted families be moved back into vacant apartments, no nationalist orators demanding that Black-owned business be given preference over Burger King and Starbucks, no marches on police precincts to protest police brutality. Thus, when the city's economy revived, a community battered by disinvestment, drug epidemics, mass incarceration, and the collapse of social services suddenly found itself becoming a hot new neighborhood for the upper middle class, filled with condos, chain stores, and chic cafés (Hyra 2006; Zukin 2009).

As working-class Harlemites find themselves increasingly powerless, doubled up in apartments or forced to move to the Bronx because of rising rents, we need to ask: Is a community without street speakers and protest meetings—one in which street vendors, no longer connected to political movements, are constantly on the defensive—a better place, and if so, better for whom? Some traditions are not missed when they are gone, but if working-class New Yorkers are going to have the power to gain access to jobs, affordable housing, and quality public services, then street speaking and street agitation, accompanied by street vending by economically motivated immigrants and politically motivated activists, represent traditions that need to be revived.

Mark Naison is a professor of African and African American Studies at Fordham University and the founder and principal investigator of the Bronx African American History Project. He is the author of five books and over one hundred articles on African American history, labor history, sports, and popular culture. His book *White Boy: A Memoir* was the subject of feature programs on BET and the Tavis Smiley Show, and was reviewed in the *New York Times, The Crisis,* and black newspapers throughout the nation. He is currently working with Robert Gumbs on a book of Bronx oral histories for Fordham University Press entitled "Before the Fires: An Oral History of African American Life in the Bronx from the 1930s to the 1960s."

Bibliography

Anderson, Elijah, ed. 2008. *Against the Wall: Poor, Young, Black and Male.* Philadelphia: University of Pennsylvania Press.

Austin, Regina. 1994. "An Honest Living: Street Vendors, Municipal Regulation, and the Black Public Sphere." *Yale Law Journal* 103 (8): 2119–2131.

Biondi, Martha. 2003. *To Stand and Fight: The Struggle for Civil Rights in Postwar New York City.* Cambridge, MA: Harvard University Press.

Burns, Haywood. 1971. "Introduction." In *Look for Me in the Whirlwind: The Collective Autobiography of the New York 21.* New York: Random House 21 vii–xv.

Case, Ken. 2009. "New York City Cracks Down on Homeless 'Tent City' in Harlem." *Newsroom New Jersey,* August 3.

Davis, Mike. 2002. *Dead Cities.* New York: W. W. Norton.

Duberman, Martin Bauml. 1989. *Paul Robeson.* New York: Alfred A. Knopf.

Ehrenhalt, Alan. 2008. "Trading Places: The Demographic Inversion of the American City." *The New Republic,* August 13.

Foner, Phillip, ed. 1970. *The Black Panthers Speak.* Philadelphia: J.B. Lippincott.

Freeman, Joshua B. 2001. *Working-Class New York: Life and Labor Since World War Two.* New York: The New Press.

Freeman, Lance. 2006. *There Goes the Hood: Views of Gentrification from the Ground Up.* Philadelphia: Temple University Press.

Greenberg, Cheryl Lynn. 1991. *Or Does It Explode? Black Harlem during the Great Depression.* New York: Oxford University Press.

Gumbs, Robert. 2003. "Interview with Bronx African American History Project." Bronx County Historical Society Archives.

Haley, Alex, and Malcolm X. 1965. *The Autobiography of Malcolm X.* New York: Ballantine Books.

Harris, Robert, Nyota Harris, and Grandassa Harris. 1992. *Carlos Cooks and Black Nationalism From Garvey to Malcolm.* Dover, DE: The Majority Press.

Hill, Robert A., and Barbara Bair. 1987. *Marcus Garvey: Life and Lessons.* Berkeley: University of California Press.

Holden, Constance. 1994. "Crack Use on the Wane in New York." *Science,* June 3.

Horne, Gerald. 1994. *Black Liberation/Red Scare: Ben Davis and the Communist Party.* Dover: University of Delaware Press.

Hyra, Derek S. 2008. *The New Urban Renewal: The Economic Transformation of Harlem and Bronzeville.* Chicago: University of Chicago Press.

James, Winston. 1998. *Holding Aloft the Banner of Ethiopia: Caribbean Radicalism in Early Twentieth-Century America.* New York: Verso.

Joseph, Peniel E. 2006. *Waiting 'Til The Midnight Hour: A Narrative History of Black Power in America.* New York: Henry Holt.

LA Sunshine. 2006. "Interview with the Bronx African American History Project." In the Bronx County Historical Society Archives.

Maurasse, David. 2006. *Listening to Harlem: Gentrification, Community and Business.* New York: Routledge.

McKay, Claude. 1940. *Harlem: Negro Metropolis.* New York: E.P. Dutton.

Moynihan, Colin. 2009. "Activists Arrested After Occupying East Harlem Lot." *New York Times,* July 23.

Naison, Mark. 1983. *Communists in Harlem during the Depression.* Urbana: University of Illinois Press.

Noor, Jaisal. 2009. "Judge Dismisses Case Against Rebel Diaz, Says 'Keep Up the Good Work.'" *The Indypendent,* June 22.

Ohrstrom, Lysandra. 2008. "'Hands Across 125th Street': Rezoning Foes Plan River to River Protest." *New York Observer,* April 7.

Perry, Jeffrey B. .2009. *Hubert Harrison: The Voice of Harlem Radicalism, 1883–1918.* New York: Columbia University Press.

Shakur, Tupac. 1992. "Trapped." *2Pacalypse.* Interscope Records.

Smith, Neil. 1996. *The New Urban Frontier: Gentrification and the Revanchist City.* New York: Routledge.

Szalavitz, Maia.1999. "Cracked Up." *Salon,* May 11.

Thompson, Heather. 2010. "Why Mass Incarceration Matters: Rethinking Crisis, Decline and Transformation in Postwar American History." *Journal of American History* 97 (7), 703–234.

Tucker, Marie Luisa. 2008. "Harlem Vendors Protest 125th Street Rezoning." *Village Voice,* April 15.

Van DeBurg, William L. 1992. *New Day in Babylon: Black Power and American Culture, 1965–1975.* Chicago: University of Chicago Press.

Watkins-Owens, Irma. 1996. *Blood Relations: Caribbean Immigrants and the Harlem Community, 1900–1930.* Bloomington: Indiana University Press.

Zukin, Sharon. 2009. *Naked City: The Death and Life of Authentic Urban Places.* New York: Oxford University Press.

CHAPTER 11

The Roots of Street Commerce Regulation in the Urban Slave Society of Rio de Janeiro, Brazil

Patricia Acerbi

Today, urban street commerce in Rio de Janeiro (hereafter Rio) is a widespread practice rooted in the city's colonial and slave past and consisting of activities such as fixed or mobile individual peddling as well as vending in outdoor markets. In the sixteenth century, Portuguese settlers of the Atlantic trading post participated in street selling, which was later incorporated into urban slave society and mainly carried out by slaves. By the nineteenth century, Rio was an entrenched Atlantic port city that became the seat of the Portuguese crown and empire in 1808 and the capital of the Brazilian Empire in 1822. This governmental presence and the profits of Atlantic slavery shaped the fabric of Rio's urban slave society. The slave trade in particular led to the steady availability of African-descended laborers throughout most of the nineteenth century. This essay seeks to understand the development of street commerce in an urban slave society and addresses the relationship between enslaved and free labor, and certain diasporic experiences, that comprised street vending in the city of Rio.

For most of the eighteenth and nineteenth centuries, Portuguese slave owners and African slaves shaped nearly all master-slave relations involved in street selling practices, while free people of color increasingly became a notable presence in the urban economy. With the gradual reduction of slavery in the second half of the nineteenth century and its final abolition in 1888, immigrants mainly from Italy, Spain, and Portugal entered the city's urban market relations and transformed the world of street commerce that had developed in the earlier period. In this urban slave society, street commerce was regulated through the system of *ganho*, an urban institution that simultaneously managed enslaved and free street vendors. The structural and experiential connections between street commerce and slavery did not disappear when an individual ceased to be a slave or when slavery was finally abolished in 1888. The system of *ganho*, by administering both enslaved and free vendors and regulating street commerce according to the needs of the urban slave society, transformed vending into a liminal space where participants, even if free, were subject to relations of patronage shaped by the slave society. By the turn of the century, the diasporic experiences of displacement had converged with urban renewal's marginalizing effects on Rio's street commerce. The practice and administration of urban street vending during the transition from slavery to free labor sheds light on the later, uneven development of street commerce in the twentieth century. Primarily, this chapter examines the role of the system of *ganho* in regulating ethnically diverse (slave and free) street vendors in order to understand the shifts that transformed street commerce into an ambiguous urban practice linking the formal with the informal economy.

Street commerce in nineteenth-century Rio was connected to the development of Atlantic modernity. By the nineteenth century, the triangular system of Atlantic slavery between Africa, the Americas, and Europe had produced technical, economic, and racial organizations, creating the conditions for modern industry and modern subjectivities rooted in experiences of dislocation and alienation (Blackburn 1997; Gilroy 1993). The displacement of enslaved Africans and subsequent (mostly Southern European) migration were constitutive of the diasporic practices and spaces that came to characterize street commerce in Rio. Urban slaves selling on the streets tended to be African-born and developed vending practices rooted in African cultures, including head-carrying and the occupation of street corners and plazas in ways that reflected social networks created among the African diaspora. In turn, the Southern European immigrants who entered the vending landscape as slavery declined introduced their own customs, such as ethnic particularity in street cries, vending locations, and products. They also adopted existing practices such as head-carrying (Chalhoub 1986; Ferrez 1989).

Because the Atlantic political economy of slavery and the ensuing shift to free labor depended on compulsory and voluntary migration to Rio, both African and European uprooting became part of a shared history of slavery and migration, of enslaved and free labor, of slavery and modernity. Certainly ontological differences distinguished an enslaved worker from a free, poor immigrant, but both were bound to the same Atlantic political economy and neither was a product of a linear pre-modern/modern dichotomy. Enslaved and free laborers were equally part of the modern project and coexisted alongside each other in street commercial practices, factory work, and several of the city's artisanal trades (Gomes and Negro 2006; Badaró Mattos 2004).

Nineteenth-Century Urban Slave Society and the System of Ganho

Fleeing Napoleonic invasion in 1807, Portugal's Prince Regent João and a royal court of fifteen thousand members took up residence in the colonial port city of Rio, where more than a third of the population was enslaved. The transfer of the Portuguese royal court from Lisbon to Rio profoundly altered urban slave society. As a major port of entry in the transatlantic slave trade between the African continent and Brazil, Rio was the destination of approximately ten thousand enslaved men and women from West-Central Africa every year (Schultz 2001). Most of these enslaved men, women, and children were sold to work on plantations, but many of them became urban slaves in the growing imperial capital, working as servants, artisans, peddlers, factory workers, and gardeners, among other occupations (Karasch 1987). Urban slaves who participated in street selling enjoyed greater freedom of movement than plantations slaves but were still subject to the brutalities of enslavement.

The state had greater regulatory authority over slave labor in the city than in the countryside, where master-slave relations were perceived as matters of the private sphere. In the city, the police took on the role of overseer, and as urban slave society and the presence of slaves working on the street expanded, so did policing and surveillance practices (Algranti 1988; Holloway 1993). To handle the increasing numbers of convicted slaves, a *calabouço* (slave dungeon) where corporal punishment officially took place was constructed in 1808, though imprisoned slaves were also held in military facilities throughout the city. As the city grew along with its free and freeborn population, the rationale of discipline and punishment changed, and so did the prison system. Official attempts to transition from a system of corporal punishment to a modern disciplinary society resulted in the closing of the allegedly outdated *calabouço* in 1874, the development of the military police, and the planned, rationalized expansion of the House of Correction and the House of Detention in the latter half of the century (Holloway 1993; Bretas 1996).

The 1807 relocation of the Portuguese royal court to Rio occurred under British escort once the Portuguese crown had agreed to open its ports to British trade. Following this loosening of trade barriers, a royal decree of 1810 suspended a previous rule prohibiting petty commerce in private homes and on the streets of Rio (Kessel and Worcman 2003). In a new colonial legal culture of loosened free trade and state control, increasing numbers of street peddlers took up the sale of grains, fowl, vegetables, drinks, sweets, cloth, and other goods. Owners of slaves and shopkeepers who employed peddlers were also responding to the consumer demands of a rapidly growing urban population. Traditionally, Portuguese men had handled the transactions of door-to-door vending while slaves or servants carried the merchandise. By the early nineteenth century, however, most slave owners preferred to instruct enslaved people of African descent in the duties of peddling, and door-to-door vending became a task performed by male and female slaves of all ages and physical ability (Gorberg and Fridman 2003). As depicted in many paintings and engravings of the early nineteenth century, enslaved Africans selling on streets, corners, and plazas were a common sight in the Portuguese imperial capital (Debret 1989; Gorberg and Fridman 2003). Independence from Portugal was gained in 1822, and in 1830 Rio's municipal council passed a specific code to regulate *ganho* labor and thus vending through formal licensing.[1]

The *ganho* system of selling on the street applied formal labor arrangements to the informal practice of vending in the urban slave economy. A set of municipal regulations and practices were instituted to administer *ganho* labor, which included street work performed by slaves, such as vending, transportation of goods, public works, garbage collection, and street lighting. In the sphere of street commerce, enslaved men and women, mostly of African origin, worked on the street as *ganhadores* ("wage-earning" slaves), which allowed them to establish social and economic networks with other enslaved and free workers. Also known as *escravos ao ganho*, *ganhadores* labored for masters and mistresses who lived in the city and profited from the "wages" their slaves earned on the street (Karasch 1987; Silva 1988; L. C. Soares 1988). After the first *ganho* labor code appeared in 1830, subsequent codes throughout the century tightened the regulation and policing of unlicensed *ganhadores*.[2] After 1830, slave owners planning to send their slaves to sell on the street *ao ganho* had to first register them with the municipality and pay for a *ganhador* license.

Formal licensing required slaves to wear a metal plaque exposing an engraved registration number that corresponded to the paper license. Any slave found vending without the pin was to be imprisoned and released upon his or her master's payment of incurred fines. The system of *ganho* thus positioned the municipality hierarchically above and often times in between urban slave owners and their slaves, as state interference in the "private" affairs of master-slave relations was generally unwelcome in Brazilian slave society. Because vending was an activity mainly carried out in public urban spaces, such as streets and market squares (and not on private plantations), the system of *ganho* delineated the order of public and private power. It was thus the municipality that licensed *ganhadores*, the police that regulated *ganho* labor on the street, and the master who profited from the earnings of slaves, as public regulation ultimately aimed to safeguard slave owners' private profits. But by the 1880s, state surveillance of *ganho* labor had shifted, and the police, rather than the municipality, came to solely administer the licensing of *ganhadores*—a practice that continued after its final abolition in 1888 and into the early twentieth century.[3] The increased policing of vendors and marginalization of street commerce after the abolition of slavery reflected the end of state protection of slave owners' property and profits.

In the first half of the nineteenth century, enslaved peddlers often sold goods that were produced in the master's household and urban garden (e.g., wax candles and foodstuffs), whereas valuable goods such as silk and silver continued to be sold by European vendors. African slave labor was thus the primary means of distributing basic goods to urban residents, from food, milk, and water to pots and pans. Slaves peddled their wares throughout urban and suburban neighborhoods, selling to the domestic servants of wealthy proprietors and middling families who promptly attended them at the door. Vendors also reached a wide range of slave and free customers who bought goods off the street and in public squares. Although slave vendors had to return most or all of their earnings to their masters, many took advantage of the new arrangement that allowed them to sell by themselves, working on Sundays, holidays, and at night to sell products they had made, bought, or sometimes stolen. Those who became successful vendors were able to work full-time with permission from their master and save a portion of their earnings to purchase their freedom or the freedom of loved ones. With permission from their masters, some urban slaves were able to use "wages" earned on the street to rent rooms and live in houses separate from the master's home (Graham 1988; Reis 1993). Slaves who participated in street commerce interacted with the free population not only while vending but also in the living quarters of the urban poor. Slave and free vendors shared many of the conditions of street commerce, and their negotiation and contestation of vending practices often involved the shared history of free and slave labor.

In addition to door-to-door selling, vending took place in public squares, street corners, and the port zone of central Rio. Besides door selling, enslaved African men and women carried out larger street market activities, often under the supervision of Portuguese dealers and policing authorities. In large market areas such as the portuary Mercado da Candelária, Portuguese dealers handled most commercial transactions, but in smaller markets African-born and African-descended sellers predominated. In particular, women of West African origin, as the American nineteenth-century traveler Daniel Kidder noted, were known to have "great commercial wisdom" (C. M. Soares 1996: 60). Urban slave owners valued the commercial savvy of West African women for *ganho* labor, announcing in newspaper ads the specific desire to purchase "strong and corpulent" women "of the coast" to sell goods such as vegetables and fruits on the street (C. M. Soares 1996: 61). Similarly, West African women in the Antilles, Jamaica, and Haiti carried out street commerce. As a diasporic practice, commercial knowledge was acquired in West Africa and then applied to new market relations in the Americas through the enslavement of women (Dias 1995).

African-born women who were vegetable sellers and *ganhadoras*, commonly known as *quitandeiras* (greengrocers), tended to be of the Mina nation.[4] In many West African societies, women were the pillars of commercial activity. The Portuguese term *quitandeira* had come to define the women involved in market practices in Central and Western Bantu-speaking Africa, where Portuguese traders noticed that only women carried out the street commercialization of food. This term then applied to African female greengrocers in Brazil, whose exercise of strong commercial skills brought them some autonomy in urban market relations and slave society. Certain street corners, plazas, and beach areas were notoriously occupied by Mina *quitandeiras*, where slave and free/d Mina women worked together. While providing residents with basic foodstuffs, slave and free *quitandeiras* often entered into conflicts with the police over the appropriate usage of urban space. The police regularly harassed *quitandeiras* and forced them to vacate street corners, pay municipal fines, and suffer incarceration. *Quitandeiras* often responded by collectively resisting street arrest, defending their right to freely market their products on the street, even if enslaved and working for a master (Gomes and Soares 2002). Interpreting police arrest as state intrusion in private matters, masters tended not to defend the arrest, detention, or incarceration of their slave *quitandeiras,* as that also implied having to pay incurred fines and/or bail.

Many *quitandeiras* found protection and a sense of belonging by settling near churches and religious brotherhoods that served Rio's Black, racially mixed, and enslaved peoples. In the second half of the nineteenth century, however, the spaces that African women and men created for themselves to sell on the city's streets came under attack as the decline of slavery gave way to new notions of public order. In 1860, the writer Joaquim Manoel de Macedo (1820–1882), describing the commercial area surrounding the church of Nossa Senhora do Rosário (which also housed an Afro-Brazilian brotherhood), indignantly noted the "decaying, pestilent, and unhygienic" state of the church, which he described as "in ruins." He added that "the streets that surround [the church] completed the sad picture" he was illustrating. To the left, the Largo da Sé was occupied by crowds of African female *quitandeiras* "who sold vegetables and offered daily spectacles of inappropriate behavior, insulting outcries, and gales of laughter, which offended passers-by who were not habituated to such dialects of indecency and immorality." It was unsurprising, then, that Macedo, a medical doctor who articulated elite respectability in several of his writings, would claim that the time of the *quitandeiras* was over and that police and municipal officials had to put an end to such "primitive behavior" (Macedo 1991: 489). And indeed, urban authorities would adopt this behavior as concern over public order increased with the decline of slavery in the latter half of the 1800s.

The Transition from Slavery to Freedom

As historians of Brazilian slavery have noted, the dynamics of urban slave society virtually turned the imperial capital into a "black city" (*cidade negra*). During the transition to free labor, the urban administration directed its efforts toward cleansing the city of aspects perceived as undesirable (Chalhoub 1990, 1996; Farias et al. 2006). Assertive and resilient *quitandeiras* remained a municipal concern, as the gradual turn to free labor in the second half of the nineteenth century increasingly put immigrant participants in street commerce under the gaze of police surveillance and the mantra of public order. Street selling in the port city was now influenced by the Atlantic political economy of free labor, which stimulated European migration to Brazil and in particular increased the Southern European presence in street commerce. Owing to the *ganho* system's capacity to manage slave and free labor simultaneously through analogous licensing requirements, it became the system by which urban authorities regulated the rising numbers of freed and free people participating in street commerce.

The shared history of enslaved and free labor is especially clear in the *ganho* system's role in the later nineteenth-century regulation of enslaved and free *ganhadores,* and thus enslaved and free street vendors. Licensing records illustrate that *ganhadores* were primarily enslaved before 1860, but eventually the system began licensing freed and free workers of a variety of (African and non-African) ethnic backgrounds. Non-slave *ganhadores* became ubiquitous in licensing records after 1860, as the formal end of the transatlantic slave trade between Africa and Brazil in 1850 resulted in the growth of freed and free persons in Rio. In this shifting urban environment, *ganhadores* who were street vendors continued to distribute much of the food and basic household goods that provisioned urban residents. Laboring in conditions similar to those of enslaved *ganhadores,* street vendors who were free *ganhadores* also worked for guarantor-employers who profited from their earnings. Owners of dry-and-wet goods stores, coffee shops, bakeries, and taverns increasingly employed free *ganhadores* in the second half of the century to sell goods such as vegetables, coffee, bread, and tobacco on the street.[5]

The Free Womb Law, passed in 1871, freed all children born of slave mothers, increasing the free population in Rio from 185,000 in 1870 to 220,088 in 1872, while the slave population decreased from 50,092 to 48,939 (Alencastro 1988). As stated earlier, a significant number of Europeans returned to work in the streets as vendors, but in contrast to the colonial era, they now had to apply for vending licenses like other free and slave *ganhadores*. Many owners of taverns, snack bars (*botequins*), warehouses, and cigar and cigarette factories solicited licenses to have immigrants sell on the street.[6] License requests reflected the patron-client relations that shaped the Portuguese, Spanish, and Italian street-selling community, as street commerce was an extension of fixed commercial establishments owned by many immigrants. This allowed goods to be distributed throughout the city in a form of community outreach that connected shopkeepers in central Rio to residents in surrounding neighborhoods.

Because a formal procedure subjected both free and enslaved *ganhadores* to tutelage and patronage, relations of dependency continued to shape the practice of urban vending and the limited freedoms of former slaves and immigrants. With slave abolitionism on the rise in the second half of the nineteenth century, street commerce came to incorporate individuals of diverse ethnic backgrounds, such as enslaved and free Africans, free racially mixed and white Brazilians, European immigrants, indigenous Americans, and Syrio-Lebanese and Chinese workers. The licensing of slave *ganhadores* required the presence of (and payment from) the master. Free *ganhadores* likewise were not free to purchase a license on their own: the licensing process also required that a *fiador* (guarantor), who usually was not a slave owner, bear witness to their dependability and capability. Thus, enslaved and free *ganhadores* of African and non-African ancestry who participated in street commerce contended with the same urban slave system of *ganho*. Free or non-slave status was not a condition that allowed peddlers to liberally sell on the street; instead, they found themselves confined by the urban slave society and *ganho* system that structurally and experientially positioned them between slavery and freedom.

Whereas many former slaves were sponsored by their ex-masters, immigrant peddlers entered into networks of patronage with other immigrant men and women, often of the same national origin. Licensing records show that free *ganhadores* and guarantors were mostly male, and that work was mostly organized along ethnic lines. Multiethnic relationships did form, however. For example, the Portuguese owner of a delicatessen selling cheese, cold meats, and tobacco in central Rio licensed five Portuguese and three Spanish men to work *ao ganho* selling or transporting foodstuffs with a cart also registered with the municipality.[7] Several guarantors who employed immigrants also employed African-descended free *ganhadores*. As the African versus European ancestry of a *ganhador* was strongly conditioned by slave culture, the licensing process reflected the different attitudes employers had toward immigrant and African-descendants. For example, *fiadores* emphasized that a particular worker of African ancestry was "very loyal" (*muito fiel*), trustworthy, and reliable, reminiscent of newspaper language advertising the sale of slaves.[8]

Not only did immigrants from Italy, Spain, Portugal, Asia, other parts of the Americas, and the waning Ottoman Empire change the cultural and ethnic landscape of street commerce, but their growing presence pushed authorities to reinforce the norms of the *ganho* system and reconceptualize regulatory practices. *Ganho* laws targeted street commercial activity and vendor licensing, while urban policing focused more and more on regulating individual street behaviors, such as vagrancy and public disorder. As a result, the number of arrested and detained African, Brazilian, and immigrant vendor *ganhadores* held on charges of vagrancy, public disorder, and theft rose after 1860.[9] During this transitional era of free labor ideology, the practice of street commerce was also reformulated by other policies meant to rationalize, modernize, and sanitize vending practices. For instance, at the turn of the century the state patented a number of "inventions," new vending technologies aimed at improving physical working conditions for peddlers and guaranteeing hygienic standards and selling practices compatible with the "modern" city.[10] Some examples were vending carts with refrigeration, butcher shops on wheels, and backpacked armoires for the sale of knickknacks. However, enforced distribution of such inventions was impractical and thus not pursued, leaving practices on the ground practically unchanged from the slave period.

Police regulation of street commercial activity relied heavily on monitoring licensed street selling and fining and detaining unlicensed vendors. Many vendors were licensed, but arrest records demonstrate that many remained unlicensed.[11] Free unlicensed street sellers preferred autonomous working conditions over the obligations of patronage that came with licensing, considering them too suggestive of master-slave relations. Immigrant and African resistance to obtaining licenses reflected the free *ganhadores'* wish to disassociate themselves from traditional markers of patronage and slave dependency, as demonstrated in 1857 by a *ganhadores* strike in the city of Salvador da Bahia (Reis 1997). In the Bahian capital, a group of free African *ganhadores,* mostly former slaves, organized a nonviolent protest against the state that lasted for about a week, practically paralyzing commerce and the distribution of goods in the city. They were resisting a new municipal edict that forced them to comply with higher licensing fees as well as to wear and display a metal plaque, which in their view was a mark of slavery that violated their free status.

The growth of Rio's urban population following the passing of the Free Womb Law of 1871 led urban authorities to enforce stricter surveillance of unlicensed street vending. In 1879, municipal officials observed that they had licensed only thirty-nine *ganhadores* the previous year. On the one hand, they concluded that this reflected the significant decrease in the number of slaves working on the streets, who traditionally had been the ones to hold licenses. On the other hand, officials claimed, license requests in 1878 were few mainly because immigrants had "invaded" the city and "deliberately neglected to obtain licenses," preferring to remain anonymous in the eyes of urban authorities.[12] As a response to vendors' resistance, policing augmented, and in the winter months of 1879 the municipality licensed approximately one thousand free *ganhadores*.[13]

Though many newly arrived immigrants were perhaps unaware of licensing norms, the motives for the 1857 strike in Salvador da Bahia, described earlier, provide a precedent to suggest that many immigrant vendors, like former slaves, preferred to remain unlicensed. Working as an unlicensed vendor, free of formal ties of patronage to guarantors, employers, and the state, not only circumvented license registration fees but also allowed for a degree of individual freedom. License registration entailed a municipal record with the vendor's address and other personal data, such as age and national origin, as well as the guarantor's name and residence. New immigrants selling on the street relied on temporary arrangements that required time and social networking if they were to evolve into formal guarantor-based relationships. In many cases a formal relationship with a guarantor ensured a steady supply of goods, but the vendor's earnings were then limited by the expected returns to the guarantor/supplier—who, if registered with the municipality, had more leverage to enforce these returns. Unlicensed vendors could operate more autonomously between different suppliers.

Whereas in the first half of the nineteenth century most *ganhadores* were enslaved and African-born, the license requests of 1879 illustrate that free Brazilians of African and mixed ancestry entered the street urban economy in higher numbers as slavery declined. While Brazilian-, Portuguese-, and African-born *ganhadores* were still the majority, the number of Italians and Spaniards had increased considerably by 1879. Many former slaves continued to work as *ganhadores*, following licensing procedures that immigrants preferred to ignore. Because of the *ganho's* system connection to slavery, licenses were colloquially known as "black licenses," even when sought by free, non-African workers like Southern European immigrants (Gorberg and Fridman 2003). In having to solicit "black licenses" and follow municipal procedures that tied immigrants to patron-client relations with guarantors, foreign-born immigrants were incorporated into the local legal practices of an urban slave society that structured some forms of free and slave labor, such as street selling, under one system—the *ganho* system.

Still, it was certainly free African-descended people whose experience as *ganhadores* most resembled the culture of slavery. In the license requests of 1879, Africans outnumbered Italian and Spanish immigrants, but not Portuguese. African-born vendors were the oldest age group of free *ganhadores*, and many had been working for decades, initially as slaves, on the city's streets. Several older African-born men were reported to be soliciting a license in 1879 to continue peddling safely and avoid further police arrest or detention. African ancestry, as reflected by skin color, put Black vendors in a vulnerable position, as they were often detained for being suspect fugitive slaves or vagrants. Of the Africans who solicited licenses, 20 percent were ex-slaves who continued to work for their ex-masters. African street commerce continued to be predominantly Mina, but other African nations were also noted in 1879, such as Cabinda, Congo, Moçambique, Benguela, Angola, Mangue, and Cassangê.[14] Toward the end of the nineteenth century—in a climate of imminent abolition of slavery—authorities less regularly noted African nations in official documents. After the abolition of slavery in 1888 and the founding of the First Republic in 1889, all African vendors were then of Brazilian nationality in official documentation.

A free African-born *ganhador* with a registered license who shared the same last name as his or her guarantor was most likely the guarantor's slave in the past. Several African men continued to live in the same house as their ex-masters, but most lived in separate housing under the urban practice whereby masters allowed slaves who were not domestic servants to live on their own. Once freed, however, former slaves still generally depended on ex-masters for work and access to licenses. Even so, African-descended people developed networks that facilitated licensing procedures for them. For example, it was common for free Africans to request licenses in a group that included individuals who lived in the same household or neighborhood and were sponsored by the same guarantor.[15] Particularly many African vendors lived in the city's central, vibrant Santana parish, popularly known as "little Africa" (Farias, Soares, and Gomes 2005). With the gradual turn to free labor, however, more and more Italian *ganhadores* came to settle in that parish, seeking to enter existing commercial networks that had developed in urban slave society.

The abolition of slavery transformed the world of street commerce as immigrants entered and shaped certain lines of commerce. For example, newspaper sellers tended to be Italian; vendors of fish Italian and Chinese; vendors of milk and fruit Portuguese; and vendors of phosphorous matches Syrio-Lebanese (Chalhoub 1986; Edmundo 1957). The abolition of slavery also ended constraints on the street sale of certain products, such as lottery tickets. During the slave period, specifically after the ordinance of 1841, vendors had not been allowed to sell lottery tickets on the street because authorities believed it would only encourage slaves to gamble.[16] Only after 1889, under republican rule and one year after the abolition of slavery, were licenses granted for the street sale of lottery tickets. Arrest and detention records show that lottery-ticket sellers were routinely inspected, and it was mainly Portuguese and Italian men who engaged in the illegal street peddling of lottery tickets before 1889. After 1889, Brazilians, and in particular African-descended men born in the city of Rio, entered this line of commerce once the abolition of slavery had ended previous restrictions toward lottery ticket vending.[17]

During the slave period, African female vendors were predominant in the sale of vegetables, cooked food, and sweets, as seen in the practices of *quitandeiras* discussed earlier. But as slavery gradually ended, immigrant men entered lines of commerce that had been managed by women, such as vegetable selling. Female peddlers were challenged to compete with the rising number of male immigrants. In line with the growing notion that women's work belonged in the private sphere, most women entered domestic service, as work opportunities were lacking elsewhere (Cunha 2008). One figure who nevertheless endured this transitional era

was the Afro-Brazilian female vendor of sweets and food, who by the early twentieth century had become popularly known to urban residents as the *bahiana*. The end of slavery had stimulated high levels of migration of African-descended men and women from the state of Bahia to the city of Rio. To get by as newly arrived migrants in a post-slave urban economy, women from Bahia sold foodstuffs with the skills and knowledge that many had acquired in urban slavery as *ganhadoras*, specializing in the sale of popular Afro-Brazilian foods and sweets. Thus emerged the esteemed figure of the *bahiana*. Bahianas like the popular Tia Ciata of Rio were celebrated in music and urban folklore and became respected figures among a wide, cross-class range of customers who often protected them from harassing police authorities (Moura 1983).

In the early twentieth century, the persistence of traditional street selling practices provided urban authorities with justification for the eradication or marginalization of street commerce (Benchimol 1990). In Rio, street vending and street vendors became a particular target of the urban renewal policies inaugurated by the regime of Mayor Francisco Pereira Passos (1902–1906). Although the political establishment deemed street commerce backward because of its inherited practices from the slave period, the city had also inherited customary laws of buying and selling—such as the vending of fresh fruit, vegetables, and popular prepared foods—that authorities found difficult to eliminate. Municipal officials could not disregard the strength of local vending practices, which in the early twentieth century occupied an ambiguous yet robust position in formal and informal urban market relations. Urban vending was therefore a modern practice that incorporated elements of forced dislocation, diasporic practices, socioeconomic marginalization, racial segmentation, and resistance in the era of the transition to free labor.

Conclusion

Today in Rio, street vending endures as an important institution of the urban street economy of survival and subsistence. While some street-selling practices have acquired characteristics that reflect current forces of the global economy, such as the peddling of perfume, pirated DVDs, and electronics, other practices remain virtually unchanged from previous periods, such as the selling of homemade sweets, baked goods, and household utensils like brooms. In the early twentieth century, policies of urban renewal and the official notion that street vending practices were "backward" facilitated the marginalization of street commerce. However, customary practices triumphed over desires to eliminate or restrict street commerce, for urban residents continued to buy goods from peddlers. Vending regulation with origins in the *ganho* system adjusted to customary practice and formalized informal arrangements, allowing many twentieth-century vendors to market goods under conditions of licensing. Street commerce continues to be shaped by the uneven relationship between the state and vendors. Nevertheless, through their selling practices, vendors continually claim their right to urban citizenship, their right to exercise free labor, and their right to usage of public urban space.

The ambiguous status of street commerce in Rio's economy, which today includes formal/licensed and informal/unlicensed forms of vending, developed from both the urban colonial slave experience and the subsequent transition to free labor. While the dynamics of street selling in the Atlantic port city shared characteristics with urban slave societies elsewhere in the Americas, the system of *ganho* was a particular institution of Brazilian urban slave society that regulated both enslaved and free participants in street commerce, hence playing a significant role in the transition to free labor. The system of *ganho* was not only an urban institution by which the state regulated urban slave labor outside the master's household: as abolitionism gradually advanced, municipal authorities also used the *ganho* system to accommodate the coexistence of slave and free labor during this transitional period. As growing numbers of foreign-born immigrants, former slaves, and freeborn Brazilians participated in street commerce alongside a decreasing yet visible number of slaves, all were organized by the system of *ganho*, which confined those of free status to a structure that primarily aimed to regulate urban slave labor.

The system of *ganho* formally ended with the final abolition slavery, and the subsequent licensing and regulation of vendors reflected the end of state protection of slave-driven private profits. Thus, by the mid 1880s *ganhadores* no longer needed the presence of a guarantor (often an ex-master) to acquire a formal vending license, and registration with the police sufficed. Although patron-client and "private" relations informally continued to shape connections between vendors and their suppliers, the disappearance of formal patronage in post-abolition licensing procedures also illustrated the emergence of the individual citizen as a legal entity.

Patricia Acerbi is an assistant professor of history at The Sage Colleges. Her research has been awarded by the Fulbright Program, the National Endowment for the Humanities, and several university-level grants. Her article ""A Long Poem of Walking': Flâneurs, Vendors, and Chronicles of Post-abolition Rio de Janeiro" appeared in the *Journal of Urban History*, which was awarded the Arnold Hirsch Article Prize. She is currently working on the manuscript of her book *Street Occupations: Urban Vending in Rio de Janeiro, 1850–1925*.

Notes

1. Posturas da Câmara Municipal do Rio de Janeiro (Rio de Janeiro: Typ. Imp. e Nac., 1830).
2. *Código de Posturas da Ilustríssima Câmara Municipal* (Rio de Janeiro: Emp.Typ. Douz de Dezembro, 1854); *Código de Posturas da* ICM (Rio de Janeiro: Typ. F. de Paula Brito, 1860); *Código de Posturas da ICM* (Rio de Janeiro: Typ. F. de Paula Brito, 1870).
3. Arquivo Geral da Cidade do Rio de Janeiro (AGCRJ), 44-1-30, Ganhadores livres 1880–1887; *Boletim da Intendência Municipal* (Rio de Janeiro: Tipografia da Gazeta de Notícias, 1906); Arquivo Público do Estado do Rio de Janeiro (APERJ), Livro da Casa da Detenção S/N Homens, 1905/1906, 11 October 1905–21 February 1906.
4. The term "Mina" is a Portuguese ethnic designation of enslaved Africans (men and women) brought to the Americas from the African region of the Gold Coast. *Mina* is Portuguese for "mine," and ships departing from the Costa da Mina (Gold Coast) carried enslaved individuals of the designated Mina ethnicity. For readings on the origins and meanings of "Mina" see Hall (2005) and Law (2005).
5. AGCRJ, 44-1-27, 44-1-28, 44-1-29, Ganhadores livres 1879.
6. AGCRJ, 58-4-28, Comércio de fumo 1831-1903; AGCRJ, 58-4-42, Comércio de café 1848–1887.
7. AGCRJ, 44-1-27, Ganhadores livres 1879.
8. AGCRJ, 44-1-28, Ganhadores livres 1879.
9. APERJ, Livros da Casa da Detenção, 1860–1922.
10. Arquivo Nacional, Rio de Janeiro, Fundo Privilégios Industriais.
11. APERJ, Livros da Casa da Detenção, 1860–1922; AGCRJ, 6-1-59, Escravos ao ganho.
12. AGCRJ, 6-1-59, Escravos ao ganho.
13. AGCRJ, 44-1-2-7; 44-1-28; 44-1-29; Ganhadores livres.
14. The Portuguese-constructed "nation" noting African origin/ethnicity was connected to the port or region of departure of slave ships crossing the Atlantic.
15. AGCRJ, 44-1-27, Licenças de ganhadores livres 1879.
16. AGCRJ, 46-2-3, Loterias e bilhetes de loterias 1841–1856.
17. APERJ, Livros da Casa da Detenção, 1860–1922.

Bibliography

Alencastro, Luis Felipe de. 1988. "Proletários e escravos: imigrantes portugueses e cativos africanos no Rio de Janeiro, 1850–1872." *Novos Estudos* 21: 30–56.

Algranti, Lela Mezan. 1988. *O feitor ausente: estudo sobre a escravidão urbana no Rio de Janeiro*. Petrópolis: Editora Vozes.
Badaró Mattos, Marcelo. 2004. "Trabalhadores escravizados e livres na cidade do Rio de Janeiro na segunda metade do século XIX." *Revista do Rio de Janeiro* 12: 229–251.
Benchimol, Jaime Larry. 1990. *Pereira Passos: um Haussmann tropical: a renovação urbana da cidade do Rio de Janeiro no início do século XX*. Rio de Janeiro: Biblioteca Carioca.
Blackburn, Robin. 1997. *The Making of New World Slavery: From the Baroque to the Modern, 1492–1800*. New York: Verso.
Bretas, Marcos Luiz. 1996. "What the Eyes Can't See: Stories from Rio de Janeiro's Prisons." In *The Birth of the Penitentiary System in Latin America: Essays on Criminology, Prison Reform, and Social Control, 1830–1940*, ed. Carlos Aguirre and Ricardo Salvatore. Austin: University of Texas Press.
Chalhoub, Sidney. 1986. *Trabalho, lar e botequim: o cotidiano dos trabalhadores no Rio de Janeiro da Belle Époque*. São Paulo: Brasiliense.
———. 1990. *Visões da liberdade: uma história das últimas décadas da escravidão na corte*. São Paulo: Companhia das Letras.
———. 1996. *Cidade febril: cortiços e epidemias na corte imperial*. São Paulo: Companhia das Letras.
Cunha, Olivia Maria Gomes da. 2008. "Learning to Serve: Intimacy, Morality, and Violence." *Hispanic American Historical Review* 88 (3): 455–491.
Debret, Jean-Baptiste. 1989. *Viagem pitoresca e histórica ao Brasil*. Rio de Janeiro: Editora Itatiaia.
Dias, Maria Odila Silva. 1995. *Power and Everyday Life: The Lives of Working Women in Nineteenth-Century Brazil*. New Brunswick, NJ: Rutgers University Press.
Edmundo, Luiz. 1957. *O Rio de Janeiro do meu tempo*. 2nd ed.. Rio de Janeiro: Conquista.
Farias, Juliana Barreto, Carlos Eugênio Líbano Soares, and Flávio dos Santos Gomes. 2005. *No labirinto das nações: africanos e identidades no Rio de Janeiro, século XIX*. Rio de Janeiro: Arquivo Nacional.
Farias, Juliana Barreto, Carlos Eugênio Líbano Soares, Carlos Eduardo Araújo Moreria, and Flávio dos Santos Gomes. 2006. *Cidades negras: africanos, crioulos e espaços urbanos no Brasil escravista do século XIX*. São Paulo: Alameda.
Ferrez, Gilberto. 1989. *O Rio Antigo do fotógrafo Marc Ferrez: paisagens e tipos urbanos do Rio de Janeiro, 1865–1918*. Rio de Janeiro: Editora Ex Libris.
Gilroy, Paul. 1993. *The Black Atlantic: Modernity and Double Consciousness*. Cambridge, MA: Harvard University Press.
Gomes, Flávio dos Santos, and Antônio Luigi Negro. 2006. "Além de senzalas e fábricas: uma história social do trabalho." *Tempo Social* 18 (1): 217–240.
Gomes, Flávio dos Santos, and Carlos Eugênio Líbano Soares. 2002. "'Dizem as quitandeiras…': Ocupações e identidades étnicas em uma cidade escravista: Rio de Janeiro, século XIX." *Acervo: Revista do Arquivo Nacional, Rio de Janeiro* 15 (2): 3–16.
Gorberg, Samuel, and Sergio A. Fridman. 2003. *Mercados no Rio de Janeiro, 1834–1962*. Rio de Janeiro: S. Gorberg.

Graham, Sandra Lauderdale. 1988. *House and Street: The Domestic World of Servants and Masters in Nineteenth-century Rio de Janeiro.* New York: Cambridge University Press.

Hall, Gwendolyn Midlo. 2005. *Slavery and African Ethnicities in the Americas: Restoring the Links.* Chapel Hill: University of North Carolina Press.

Holloway, Thomas. 1993. *Policing Rio de Janeiro: Repression and Resistance in a 19th-Century City.* Stanford, CA: Stanford University Press.

Karasch, Mary C. 1987. *Slave Life in Rio de Janeiro, 1808–1850.* Princeton, NJ: Princeton University Press.

Kessel, Carlos, and Karen Worcman. 2003. *Um balcão na capital: memórias do comércio na cidade do Rio de Janeiro.* Rio de Janeiro: Senac RJ.

Law, Robin. 2005. "Ethnicities of Enslaved Africans in the Diaspora: On the Meaning of Mina." *History of Africa* 32: 247–267.

Macedo, Joaquim Manoel de. (1862) 1991. *Um passeio pela cidade do Rio de Janeiro.* Rio de Janeiro: Livraria Garnier.

Moura, Roberto. 1983. *Tia Ciata e a pequena África no Rio de Janeiro.* Rio de Janeiro: Funarte.

Reis, João José. 1993. *Slave Rebellion in Brazil: The Muslim Uprising of 1835 in Bahia.* Baltimore, MD: Johns Hopkins University Press.

———. 1997. "'The Revolution of the Ganhadores': Urban Labor, Ethnicity, and the African Strike of 1857 in Bahia, Brazil." *Journal of Latin American Studies* 29 (2): 355–393.

Schultz, Kirsten. 2001. *Tropical Versailles: Empire, Monarchy, and the Portuguese Royal Court in Rio de Janeiro, 1808–1821.* New York: Routledge.

Silva, Marilene Rosa Nogueira da. 1988. *Negro na rua: a nova face da escravidão.* São Paulo: Hucitec.

Soares, Cecília Moreira. 1996. "As Ganhadeiras: mulher e resistência em Salvador no século XIX." *Afro-Ásia* 17: 57–71.

Soares, Luis Carlos. 1988. "Os escravos de ganho no Rio de Janeiro século XIX." *Revista Brasileira de História* 8 (16): 107–142.

Index

African American entrepreneurialism, 121, 219–30
African diaspora, 234
archiving, 191, 208–9
authenticity, 105, 111, 152
    social construction, 105, 111

Bahiana, 245
Bayat, Asaf, 7, 60, 63, 91–92, 167
Berlin, 81–82, 86–89, 92–95
Blomley, Nicholas, 46, 199–201
Bourdieu, Pierre, 89, 166–67
Bromley, Ray, 4, 7, 82, 193
Brooklyn, 21, 26–28, 52, 118, 120, 221
Business Improvement Districts (BID), 8, 44, 52–53, 147

Calcutta, 201–3
citizenship, 10, 22, 49, 54ff., 89, 108ff., 167, 203, 246
    cultural, 108ff., 110
    cultural citizens, 111
    entrepreneurial, 203
    social, 108
    traditional, 108
    urban, 54ff., 246
creative resistance, 59, 61, 68, 72–74

deregulation, 8, 83
Dhaka (Bangladesh), 164–190

discourse, 44–45, 47, 50–53
discrimination, 12, 83, 85, 90, 95, 125, 224

encroachment, 172, 197–210
    quiet, 7, 63, 89, 91–92
entrepreneurial urban governance, 24, 32–35
entrepreneurialism, 118, 120, 121, 122, 124, 129
    African American entrepreneurialism, 118ff., 219–30
    Black entrepreneurialism, 120–122
European City, 9, 81, 82, 93, 94

family, 19–21, 27–32
    flexible family, 19–21, 29–32, 32–35, 35–38
First Amendment vendors, 119, 130n8
food trucks, 38

Galtung, Johan, 166
ganhadores, 236
Garvey, Marcus, 219, 224–225, 230
gender, 5–6, 19–21, 22–25, 83, 95, 106–108, 146
    and globalization, 22–25
    and labor, 20, 22–23, 29–32
    and space, 24–25

Global North, 2, 5ff., 19, 29, 82–92, 211
Global South, 2, 6, 20, 75, 82–92, 164, 167, 183, 210ff.
globalization, 19–21, 22–23, 35–38, 83–84, 94, 105
governance, 19, 59, 24, 150, 184, 223
    contested, 173
    entrepreneurial, 24
    urban, 22, 32–37, 59

Harrison, Hubert, 224, 230
hawkers, 2, 168–84, 191–212, 221
Historical center of Berlin, 81–87
human security, 165, 184
Humboldtforum, 93

immigrants, 5–6, 31–37, 44–52, 96, 101–108, 119–122, 120–128, 139, 223, 230, 240, 243
    African, 120–28, 230
    Black, 122
    Caribbean, 223
    Chinese, 112n3
    European, 234, 240, 243
    Latino, 101–108
    Spanish, 243
    undocumented, 139
informal economy, 3–4, 19–25, 27–29, 30, 63, 70, 74, 82, 103, 113, 151, 168, 191, 192–93, 196, 201, 209–11, 234
    and family, 29–32
    and gender, 23, 29–32
    immigrants, 103
    Los Angeles, 103, 105
informality, 3, 23, 27–28, 63, 82–85, 193, 208
    informal arrangements, 173–74, 179–80, 181–83, 187n13
    informal sector, 167–68, 186n6
    metropolitan, 82, 85, 95
integration, 86, 89–91, 94, 96

Judicialization, 191, 209, 211, 213

labor, 3–4, 19–38, 74, 83, 89–93, 103–4, 108, 118, 120, 125, 129, 140, 143, 147, 151, 154, 168, 169, 192, 195, 201, 203, 211, 224, 233–46
    and gender, 27–32
    and globalization, 19–21, 35–38
    informalized
Latin America, 59–75, 104–11, 140–5
Latino/a, 19–38, 101–11, 130n3, 139–59
Lefèbvre, Henri, 45–47, 140–41
legalizing, street vending, 150–53
Los Angeles, 101–11, 119, 139–59

Malcolm X, 227–228
Mexico City, 59, 60, 61, 63, 65, 66, 69, 70, 73
mobility, 20, 36, 60, 121, 125, 128, 139–59
    urban, 139–59
movement, hawkers, 203

National Hawker Federation, 194
neoliberal, 4–7, 19–23, 29–37, 44–45, 59–75, 83–84, 94–95, 129, 220
neoliberalism, 19–22, 25, 30, 59–65, 70
New York, 19–38, 43–56, 117–29, 139, 144, 219–231
nostalgia
    memory, 102, 104–5, 108, 111
    process, 104
    productive, 105–7, 111

pedestrianism, 191, 193, 199, 200, 201, 203, 205, 206, 209, 211, 213
people of color, 5–6, 85, 88, 89, 119, 220, 234
    communities, 95
    men, 25, 82, 89
    vendors, 90, 92, 95
    women, 85, 89
place, 60, 61, 64, 65, 66, 68, 69, 70, 73, 74
    production, 102, 106
    See sense of place, concept, 104
Planwerk Innenstadt, 93
police, 1, 5, 20, 21, 28, 32, 49, 51, 67, 73, 81, 86, 88, 90–91, 103, 107, 110, 118, 139, 143–54, 165–84, 195, 199, 203–12, 221–30, 235–46

precarious work, 83, 90, 95
public space, 1, 5–7, 20, 24–25, 91, 104, 107, 110–11, 166–67, 171, 173
    and gendering work, 23–25, 27–29
    and labor, 27, 37–28
    as stratified workplace, 25, 32–35
    in the European City, 94–95

quiet encroachment, 89, 91–92
quitandeira, 238

racialization, 8–9, 81, 82, 85, 89, 94, 95
racism, 85, 90
    structural, 90
regulation, 3, 5, 20, 23–24, 34, 43, 46, 51, 82–83,86–88, 90, 92, 94–96, 119, 140–42, 147–159, 164, 192–97, 199–202
    administrative, 81–82, 86–88, 90, 92, 94–95
    commerce, 234–46
    local, 83, 92
    municipal, 34, 36, 222, 236
    spatial, 55, 150–53
    vending, 43, 51, 246
research methodology, 26, 45, 61, 89, 103, 120, 142, 165, 185n2, 208
resistance, 20–22, 37, 59–75, 86, 92, 110, 147, 151, 220, 222, 228, 230, 242
reunification, 88–89, 92–93
    of Germany, 81, 92–93
Right to the City, 45–46
Rio de Janeiro, 233–47
Roy, Ananya, 82, 84

Scott, James, 172
self-publishing, 118, 131, 133, 134
sense of place, 60, 64, 75
    concept, 104
    memory, 104, 106
space
    concept, 103
    place-less, 105
street artisans, 60, 61, 66, 67, 68, 69, 70, 71, 72, 73, 74, 75

street food, 164, 168, 169, 186n8
street food vending
    formal regulation of, 168, 181, 185n5
    public discourses on, 165, 172, 173–74, 183, 186n10
street food vendors, 164–190
    agency of, 164, 175, 184
    evictions of, 165, 171–72, 173–74, 174–83, 183–84
    exploitation of, 181–83, 184
    livelihoods of, 167–171
    mobility patterns of, 169, 177–181, 182
    social networks of, 168, 174, 179–80, 181–82
    tolerance of, 165, 174, 177, 181
street literature, 117, 118, 119, 122, 123, 124, 126, 127, 128, 129, 130n2–5, 130n7, 130n9, 131n12, 132, 134
street speaking, 220, 221
street vending
    areas, 81
    of books, 118ff.
    as deviant practice, 88, 90, 92
    of food, 130f1, 228
    food vending, 82, 87, 88, 92, 96
    in Harlem, 118ff., 221, 224, 225–229
    and immigrants, 119, 120, 122, 125, 128, 129, 127, 130n10
    in low-income US neighborhoods, 118ff., 220
    and neoliberalism, 129, 220
    in New York City, 118ff.
    and political activism, 119f., 221, 223–229
    of printed matter, 118 ff., 219, 228, 229
    practices, 82, 89, 91
    and prison, 118, 130n5
    and resistance, 220
    and slavery, 121
    of souvenirs, 82, 87–82
    vending regulations, 119, 223
    and women, 120

street vendors
    entrepreneurship, 105–6
Street Vendor Project, 45, 49–51, 56
system of ganho, 234

urban citizenship, *see* citizenship
urban Neoliberalism, *see* neoliberalism
urban poor, 46, 51, 164, 167, 172, 238

vendors
    African Americans, 47, 119, 125–129
    art vendors, 48
    book vendors, 48, 118–123
    East Asian, 48
    food vendors, 19–35, 47, 49–51, 53, 55, 82–89, 101–104, 146–148, 156, 164–190
    general merchandise, 48
    Hispanic/Latino, 19–38, 47–48, 101–11, 130n3, 139–59
    legal categories, 47–48
    locations, 47–48
    political strategies, 44–45, 47, 50–52
    products, 47–48
    South Asian, 47–48
    unlicensed vendors, 48, 242
    West African, 48, 124–28
violence
    cultural, 165, 166, 172, 183–84
    direct, 165, 166, 171–72, 173–74, 183
    structural, 165, 166, 171, 173, 181–83
vulnerability
    adapting to violence, 167, 181–83, 184
    coping with violence, 167, 177–181, 184
    exposure to violence, 167, 171–74, 177–78
    sensitivity to violence, 167, 171–74, 177–78
    social, 165–167, 169